THE EAGLE MUTINY

THE EAGLE MUTINY

Richard Linnett and Roberto Loiederman

NAVAL INSTITUTE PRESS
Annapolis, Maryland

Naval Institute Press
291 Wood Road
Annapolis, MD 21402

Library of Congress Cataloging-in-Publication Data

Linnett, Richard, 1957–

The Eagle mutiny / Richard Linnett and Roberto Loiederman.

p. cm.

Includes bibliographical references.

ISBN 1-55750-522-5 (alk. paper)

1. Vietnamese Conflict, 1961–1975—United States. 2. Vietnamese Conflict, 1961–1975—Transportation. 3. Mutiny—United States. 4. Columbia Eagle (Ship) I. Loiederman, Roberto, 1940– II. Title.

DS558.L568 2001

959.704'345—dc21

00-052685

Printed in the United States of America on acid-free paper ♾

08 07 06 05 04 03 02 01 9 8 7 6 5 4 3 2

First printing

To Rafi, Zeke, and Max, for the inspiration.

And to Betty and Veronique, for their support.

CONTENTS

PREFACE

> Whoever, being of the crew of a vessel of the United States, on the high seas, unlawfully and with force usurps the command of such vessel from the master or other lawful officer in command thereof, or deprives him of authority and command on board, or prevents him in the free and lawful exercise thereof is guilty of a revolt and mutiny.
>
> *Legal definition of mutiny, from 18 U.S.C. section 2193, quoted in Glatkowski's appeal*

The classic example is, of course, the mutiny on the *Bounty.* If one searches the annals of American history, since 1842 there has been one, and only one, *Bounty*-like mutiny.

On 14 March 1970 an American tramp steamer commissioned by the Military Sea Transportation Service to carry napalm to Thailand for the war in Vietnam was seized at gunpoint by two young crew members. This book is about that revolt and mutiny.

It is based entirely on documents and interviews. All quoted passages are taken from interviews done by the authors or others; from court transcripts or testimony taken by the Coast Guard, the Federal Bureau of Investigation, and other U.S. government agencies; from written accounts provided to us by participants and eyewitnesses; from published accounts; from unpublished accounts given to us by journalists; or from government documents released via the Freedom of Information Act. Some of the passages in this book involving conversation have been rendered as dialogue. All of these excerpts come from participants' and witnesses' testimony or from interviews. Since we cannot, of course, know for certain what exactly was said in a given situation, the authors have taken some minor license in the wording of some conversations, which are based on a conglomeration of different individuals' recollections. These dialogue passages are italicized, without quotation marks.

Some of the procedures and routines aboard ship are based on the recollections and experiences of Roberto Loiederman, one of the authors, who worked, in the late 1960s, on three ships identical in every respect to the one on which the mutiny took place. We have changed some people's names, at the request of those involved.

The authors would like to acknowledge special thanks to three people without whom this book would not have been possible: Alvin Glatkowski, who was so generous with his recollections; Jean Bair, whose helpfulness gave us a reason to keep pursuing the mystery; and Paul Nagle, whose efforts made this book happen.

Thanks also to Donald Swann, Herrick Morgan, Luke Ciamboli, Roger Enoch Hammett Jr., Marco Smigliani, and Robert Stevenson of the *Columbia Eagle;* Clyde McKay's sisters, Kerry Burrell and Lois Basiger; Clint Johnson of the *Lane Victory;* Don Webb and Norman Idleberg of Naval Intelligence Service and Ralph Wedertz of the Coast Guard; Mark Gatlin and Eric Mills at Naval Institute Press; George Tricker, Dave Goldberg, Jerry Brown, and Dan Duncan of the Seafarers International Union; Rachel Kaufman, Dan Strone, and Matt Bialer at William Morris Agency; Linda Kloss and Larry Taylor of the Federal Bureau of Investigation; Graydon S. Staring and the law firm Lillick McHose & Charles in San Francisco; and T. D. Allman, Andrew Antippas, Richard Arant, Tony Avirgan, Chip Beck, John Berbrich, Barbara Beyer, Barry Binsky, Robert Blackburn, Wilfred Deac, Michael Hannon, Martha Honey, Henry Kamm, Norm Kass, Walter King, Jan Kirby, Robert Linnett Sr., Mario Loiederman, Mary London, Flo Longenecker, C. Scott Moss, Margaret Munson, Bud Nathans, Tim Page, Frank Pestana, Lloyd (Mike) Rives, John Safford, Richard Satzman, Andy Schlessinger, Don Shannon, Will Soper, Richard Speglia, Richard Stambul, Dan Tedrick, Bob Wyman, and Perry Deane Young. In Cambodia, we also greatly appreciated the assistance received from Sok Sin, Kathleen Hayes, Chris Decherd, Matt Reed, Hurley Scroggins, Khourn Meng Kry, Dok Sokhay, Lt. Col. Kevin Fossett, and Col. Michael Norton.

THE EAGLE MUTINY

INTRODUCTION

Cambodia, 14 March 2000

On the thirtieth anniversary of the event which is the subject of this book, the authors were in Cambodia. We went there to see the places where our story took place and, more important, to try to get eyewitness information about what happened to Clyde McKay, the leader of the mutiny, who escaped from confinement—along with U.S. Army deserter Larry Humphrey—in late 1970 and disappeared in the Cambodian countryside.

Expecting to interview former members of the Khmer Rouge, we sought and received help and advice from local journalists as well as U.S. embassy officials. Col. Michael Norton, U.S. military attaché, warned us about traveling into remote areas. A Vietnam veteran with a shaved head and an unwavering look, he advised us that what we found would depend on the risks we were willing to take and how deep we were willing to go. Norton asked us, "Are you looking for information . . . or truth?"

Map in hand, we headed off toward Sangke Kaong, a remote village mentioned a number of times in Central Intelligence Agency (CIA) and Defense Intelligence Agency (DIA) documents, the place where McKay and Humphrey had last been seen. With any luck, we might get both truth *and* information about the men's eventual fate. There were all sorts of rumors. One book, *The Road to the Killing Fields* by Wilfred Deac, speculated that McKay and Humphrey were living as farmers in a northeastern province of Cambodia.

Leaving Phnom Penh, we took a well-paved road north and east toward Kampong Cham, an unprepossessing province seat, where we boarded a ferry to cross the Mekong. From there the road was pockmarked and potholed, dusty and difficult, our four-wheel drive having to swerve constantly to avoid road hazards.

We had read and reread the documents containing eyewitness reports about two Caucasians who were in this area in 1970 and 1971. We tried to imagine what Clyde McKay would have been thinking and feeling as he struggled to survive in that dangerous situation. In his short life he had already gone through a great deal: French Foreign Legion, Spanish jail, getting lost in the Sahara, living in Europe as a man without a country. He was an adventurer, a soldier-of-fortune who knew how to maneuver in strange situations. But what had happened to him here? And, in fact, was it really McKay and Humphrey who were here in these villages, or someone else?

We traveled along dirt roads that wound their way among the rubber plantations. It was hard to imagine the peaceful villages we passed as the epicenter for a theater of war, hotbeds of activity for Viet Cong guerrillas and the Khmer Rouge. Yet that is what they were a generation ago.

When we finally arrived at Sangke Kaong, it felt no different from any other village: dogs, chickens, bullocks, electricity provided by a generator only during certain times of the day. No telephone system. No running water. According to the documents, McKay may have been here.

We asked people, looking for someone, anyone, who might have lived here thirty years ago. Before we entered each stilted house, we removed our shoes, went in, sat on rush mats arranged on handsome wooden floors, and asked our questions. For us it was a moment of great anticipation: we were nearing the end of a long search.

1 DEAD AHEAD

Gulf of Thailand, 14 March 1970, approximately 10 P.M.

A flare rose into a dark moonless night in the Gulf of Thailand, and the deckhand on the bow of the SS *Rappahannock,* an old merchant ship steaming toward Sattahip with a cargo of warheads and napalm, spotted it. The *Rappahannock* was about one hundred miles off the coast of Vietnam and the night skies were occasionally lit by brilliant, fiery bursts of bombs and gunfire in the distance. This flare, however, was different. It was very close, dropping somewhere just outside the shipping channel dead ahead. The seaman on lookout called the bridge and told the mate on watch what he had seen.

The mate was in the wheelhouse with an AB (able seaman) who was on the wheel. After hanging up the phone, the mate stepped outside to the wing of the bridge and fixed his gaze on the darkness. Within minutes, he saw what appeared to be a tracer soar through the sky and land a point on the port bow. The AB on lookout called the wheelhouse again, confirming that he too had seen the second flare. The mate then called the mess hall and asked the ordinary on standby to inform the captain about the flares and ask him what they should do. It might be a vessel in distress. Should they proceed in the direction of the two flares to investigate? Or should they continue on course?

The ordinary did not have to go far to find Captain Lignos, who was in the crew mess hall at the time, playing poker with the men. Lignos did not pay much attention to the unwritten code that separated ships' officers from the unlicensed crew. A fifty-two-year-old Greek national, much smaller than most of his men, and with an accent so thick that his crew barely understood him, Lignos mingled with the seamen. He was wearing Bermuda shorts and a T-shirt when the man on standby told him about the flares.

Lignos was worried that the flares might be a trap. The South China Sea was plagued by pirates who posed as fishermen in distress. They tricked merchant ships into stopping to help and then boarded them. If a ship did not stop, the pirates quietly attached their bumboats like parasites to the vessel's hull and scaled the side with a Jacob's ladder or rope. Once they got on board, the pirates pulled out guns, took crews hostage, and ransacked lockers and the captain's safe. Just as quietly as they came, the pirates disappeared, slipping over the side, evaporating into the inky expanse of water. Merchant crews, which were civilian, had no way of defending themselves. Ship's Articles prohibited weapons on board merchant ships. Only captains were allowed to be armed.

As Lignos reached the bridge, a third flare pierced the darkness, this time much closer. Tucked into Lignos's belt was a snub-nose .38 caliber pistol. He peered out at the sea with binoculars and saw, bobbing on ground swells, a pair of lifeboats filled with men. One of the boats had an outboard engine and it was pulling the other, slowly putt-putting through the rough sea, not making much headway. In the pitch blackness, it was hard to tell how many men there were. But there appeared to be about two dozen. Most were light-skinned, but some were dark. Captain Lignos ordered the engine room to cut the ship's speed to half-ahead, and directed the AB on the wheel to approach the boats.

The *Rappahannock* pulled gently alongside the two boats and cut its speed to "stop engines." Lignos went down to the main deck and peered down at the dark sea. The ship was not fully laden and rose high above the boats, which made it difficult to see the castaways. With his heavy accent, the captain yelled down: "What nationality are you?" A chorus of voices shouted up an immediate reply: "American!" The captain shouted back: "Where is your ship?" And again, the voices from below: "We don't know!" The captain peered down at the boats. He was suspicious, and he shouted again, testing them: "Who is your leader?" He expected them to reply,

Richard Nixon, that is, if they were really American. There was some hesitation down below, and then a single voice shouted back: "I am!"

The captain laughed. He ordered a ladder to be lowered. "Only *you* come up!" he shouted to the man who had called himself the leader. Up the ladder clambered a bald, fair-skinned, lanky seaman. The captain aimed his gun at the man's belly. "What's your name?" The man, obviously American, identified himself as Robert W. Stevenson, second mate on the SS *Columbia Eagle*, a U.S. vessel bound for Sattahip, Thailand, with a load of munitions. He was the senior officer among the men in the lifeboats. He told Lignos that there were twenty-three other crew members with him and all were U.S. citizens. They had been adrift in the sea for approximately seven hours. Lignos tucked the gun back under his belt and asked Stevenson what had happened to the *Eagle.* Stevenson wasn't sure. An abandon ship alarm had sounded on the vessel at about 1:30 that afternoon. When they heard the alarm, some of the men realized it was not a routine drill. They had had one just the day before, and it was Saturday; boat drills did not usually occur on a weekend because the crew would be paid overtime. And so the men were now wondering about the fate of the vessel.

Stevenson told Lignos that when the alarm rang, they all went to their lifeboat stations and Herbert Gunn, the mate on watch, stood on the wing of the bridge shouting instructions. Stevenson said he asked Gunn if the alarm was real and Gunn replied that it was a bomb scare and would probably amount to nothing, but he instructed Stevenson to shepherd the men into lifeboats. Stevenson obeyed. By Stevenson's count, fifteen men remained on board the ship, including the *Eagle*'s captain, the chief engineer, and the chief mate. But no one saw these officers. There was only Gunn standing on the wing. From the lifeboats, it was hard to see who was in the wheelhouse, but there appeared to be movement inside, based on the silhouetted shapes of several men.

Stevenson said that Gunn disappeared for a few minutes inside the wheelhouse, and when he came out again, there was a sense of urgency in his voice. Gunn yelled that there was a live bomb on board. He pointed north and shouted that the nearest land was 109 miles in that direction. He then ordered the boats to cast off and pull away from the ship. Again, Stevenson obeyed. He moved the motorized boat from the port to the starboard side of the ship, and then tied up to the other lifeboat, which was not powered. Stevenson's lifeboat towed the other boat about a mile from the *Eagle* and stopped, waiting for nearly an hour. The men saw a large puff of black smoke blow from the ship's stack and the screw began turning.

"The ship was dead in the water," said Stevenson. "And then suddenly, it was moving at full speed. And we were being left behind. We watched the *Eagle* pass into the horizon. Never did I see the ocean so big."

Gulf of Thailand, 8 April 1970

A U.S. Army helicopter hovered over the Coast Guard cutter *Chase* in the Gulf of Thailand on a hot, hazy afternoon. Inside the chopper were two Naval Intelligence Service (NIS) investigators: Special Investigator Don Webb and his boss, Lt. Cdr. Norman Idleberg. Webb was not well. He had been laid up for a week in Saigon with a strain of colitis caused by intestinal parasites, and he had left the hospital against his doctor's wishes. He and Idleberg were about to join another team from the U.S. Coast Guard, which was also involved in the inquiry into what was being called "The *Columbia Eagle* Mutiny." The chopper was attempting to land on the cutter, and the NIS men overheard the co-pilot ask the pilot, "Have you ever landed one of these on a ship?" The pilot replied, "No, I thought *you* had."

"So we got two army guys at the wheel of this Huey," said Webb, "and neither one of them had landed on ship. And I thought to myself, 'Christ, we're going to be lucky to get out of this thing alive.'"

Webb was usually unflappable in the face of danger. His colleagues called him Jack, as in Jack Webb, the pokerfaced cop from the television show *Dragnet,* because he was hard-nosed, spoke with an intimidating gravelly voice, and grilled suspects mercilessly. Webb was big and solid, over six feet tall, 250 pounds, with dishwater blond hair and a Southern drawl that softened the rocks in his throat like honey in black coffee. At thirty-four years of age, he was already old in a war zone where soldiers were in their teens and early twenties, and officers—like Idleberg—were just starting to push thirty.

Webb was not military; he was a civilian investigator. There were plenty of special agents like him in Vietnam. Many of them were ex-cops, ex-FBI agents, or military veterans like Webb, a former marine. He worked out of the Saigon office of Naval Intelligence, and was responsible for investigating criminal activity among Navy and Marine Corps personnel. The office had jurisdiction in Vietnam, Thailand, Cambodia, Laos, and the Philippines, with twelve satellite offices in Vietnam alone. Civilian investigators like Webb manned these offices. In fact, the NIS was about 90 percent civilian. Most of these investigators were family men in their late thirties and forties. They had left comfortable homes in the States, and for a little extra hazardous duty pay they had suddenly found themselves winging on choppers over war zones, dropping in-country, into the boonies, investigating murders.

Webb's boss, Norman Idleberg, was a career military man. Idleberg was trim and good-looking with dark hair and blue eyes. He was from Colorado, an odd place for a Navy man to come from. He would tell people that he joined the Navy because "I knew that I wouldn't get dirty. I'd get to sleep on a bed every night on a ship."

Idleberg went to officers school and was commissioned an ensign. His first posting was in Pearl Harbor. In 1969 he was chosen to be head of the intelligence office in Vietnam, quickly becoming a counterintelligence expert. He farmed out most investigations to his civilian corps and then analyzed the intelligence when it came back. However, if an assignment had counterintelligence implications, Idleberg would go out into the field, almost always with Webb. They were a good cop–bad cop team. Idleberg was quiet and diligent, and Webb was aggressive. Being the more physical of the pair, Webb was the one who asked all the questions and intimidated suspects.

"Don is my protector," Idleberg would often say.

The Huey chopper, carrying the two investigators, landed on the cutter *Chase* without incident. Webb's stomach tumbled mercilessly in the descent, but otherwise he and Idleberg came out of it intact and were ready for the next leg of their trip, boarding the mutiny ship.

Lt. Cdr. Jimmie J. Davis and the court reporter, Chief Yeoman Ralph Wedertz from the U.S. Coast Guard merchant marine detail, were waiting for them on the deck of the cutter. Davis was heavyset and gregarious, a dogged investigator with a reputation for overzealousness. Wedertz was young, optimistic, and adventurous; at five foot seven, 140 pounds, he had the type of wiry physique that could get him into tight places and easily out again. Although technically the court reporter, Wedertz was, in fact, the advance man, the guy who was asked to go ahead of the others and stake out a situation. And in this investigation, he had been asked to do just that.

Weeks earlier, while the *Columbia Eagle* was still being held by the

Cambodians, Wedertz had been charged with the mission of going into Cambodia and secretly taking photos of the vessel. Wedertz had flown into Phnom Penh with Davis, and then, in order to provide himself with a cover, he had picked up a bar-girl and had gone with her to Sihanoukville, Cambodia's deep-water port on the Gulf of Thailand. "We drove out this long road to the water," said Wedertz, "and she guided me to where we could get a view of the ship. She knew about it because it had caused all this publicity in Phnom Penh." The girl proved very resourceful. She suggested they go into the water together to get even closer to the ship. "And so we went out into the water," Wedertz recalled, "and we were fooling around and stuff and pretending to do kissy-face and I had this camera and I would turn every so often and take pictures of the ship from the water-level."

Now, aboard the *Chase,* Wedertz was much closer to the *Eagle* than he had been when splashing in the waters off the coast. And he would get even closer, as the two teams of investigators climbed into a small motorized craft and headed toward the vessel, which sat motionless and forlorn on a flat sea. The sun was blazing and relentlessly hot.

"The ship looked weird," Webb recalled. "First of all, it was stopped. And anytime you see a huge vessel stopped in the middle of the sea, well, that to me is ominous. I didn't know whether it was because it looked that way, or because of what we were expecting, or the trepidation we had about going aboard with these guys on board, but it didn't look too good."

As the skiff got even closer, the investigators noticed that the *Eagle* was rusty and pitted. The ship's idle booms hung over the deck of the vessel like barren winter trees shorn of leaves, and the lines that hung between them resembled choking vines. The large cargo containers on the after-deck seemed like giant, unused toy blocks. The investigators knew that these contained phosphorus igniters and fuses for the napalm. As a precautionary measure, these were customarily separated from the weapons, which were in the ship's holds. A lone figure stood on the deck, leaning against a rail, and another on the wing of the bridge; backlit against the brilliant sun, they seemed like ominous phantoms. The old tramp steamer also had whitish patches on the midships bulkhead and on the stack. As the skiff glided into the shadow of the *Eagle*'s massive steel hull, the white blotches came into focus. They were huge peace signs, crudely scrawled with wide brushes and dripping white paint. She looked like a ghost ship.

Webb and Idleberg were uneasy. They would be sailing in this shabby steamer some 1,200 miles for nearly five days, with 1,750 tons of bombs in its guts and an unpredictable crew. Webb carried a handgun. "We climbed up and boarded, scared as hell because we didn't know what we were going to encounter," said Idleberg.

The lone figure at the rail of the *Columbia Eagle* was Lt. Cdr. Philip R. Spiker, of the Coast Guard, the officer in charge of the investigation. A quiet, tall, thin man who hid behind dark aviator sunglasses and wore his hair cut extremely short, with just a little brush of hair above his forehead, Spiker had been posted in Asia for many years and was known within the embassy as a "bamboo American." He enjoyed living in Asia, having spent most of his military career there. He had a Vietnamese girlfriend, and unlike many other Americans who had local girlfriends in Vietnam, Spiker was serious about this relationship.

Spiker had been in constant motion since the day the mutiny had come to light, three and a half weeks earlier. He had traveled back and forth from Saigon to Bangkok to Phnom Penh, and together with officials from the NIS and COMUSMACTHAI (Commander U.S. Military Assistance Command Thailand) he coordinated the mutiny investigation. When it was announced that the Cambodian government would release the ship, Spiker traveled to the Ream naval base, next to Sihanoukville, and tried to board the *Eagle.* At first the Cambodians would not allow him on the ship. After the *Eagle* was under way, they had a change of heart and stopped the vessel to allow Spiker aboard.

The entire investigation team now was assembled on the *Eagle.* Although from different organizations, the NIS and Coast Guard men shared similar cultures. They were all investigators, law enforcement officers, and military men and, with the exception of Webb, they were all seafaring men. According to Wedertz, 90 percent of the criminal investigations conducted by the Coast Guard office in Saigon concerned merchant crews.

This job, however, was different. It was the first—and only—mutiny investigation for any of them. The *Columbia Eagle* was a private, commercial vessel that had been carrying a cargo of napalm and other munitions for the U.S. Air Force when it was seized by mutinous members of the crew. Under threat of destroying the ship, the mutineers had forced the captain, Donald Swann, to order an emergency alarm. Twenty-four men abandoned the ship and were later picked up by another U.S. tramp steamer and taken to Sattahip, Thailand. Webb and Idleberg were in Bangkok on a different investigation when the castaways arrived.

"The government held the castaways in a hotel in Sattahip," Webb recalled. "Not under arrest but being watched very closely."

The castaways, however, were of no help; they had known next to nothing about what had happened to them and to their ship. The key to the story lay with the crew members who had remained aboard while the ship was held incommunicado in Cambodia. They were all eyewitnesses to the event, and some of them were alleged accomplices. The investigators' task was to reconstruct the sequence of events that led to the incident, determine who was involved, and separate the alleged accomplices from the rest of the crew. They sat down and interviewed each of the thirteen remaining crew members, one by one, as the ship sailed to Subic Bay in the Philippines, accompanied by the *Chase.* Webb and Davis asked most of the questions.

"I remember Webb," said Wedertz, "he was of the police mentality, you know. Idleberg was more background, he didn't say a heck of a lot. Webb was the aggressive one of the two. Jimmie [Davis] loved to ask questions and Phil [Spiker] loved to let him. People would sort of come and go. It wasn't like a formal board of inquiry."

"I think we tried to keep the crew segregated as much as we could," recalled Idleberg, "because what we didn't want to happen was to have somebody's testimony sullied by somebody else's impressions. You know, you interview a guy and then he goes and tells the next guy, 'Hey, don't tell them about this because. . . .' It probably wasn't easy to manage because while we were doing the interviews we had no idea where the rest of the crew members were. They were probably doing their chores to keep the ship running, so they probably didn't have too much opportunity to communicate with each other. I know that we were concerned about information being spread around. Among a group like that you don't want to be a tattletale."

The journey to the Philippines took four and a half days. During the trip, the situation was extremely tense. The thirteen crew members on board were suspicious of one another, accusing each other of having taken part in the incident. "The crew was mistrustful of each other," recalled Webb. He and Idleberg slept on cots out on deck because it was too hot inside the house. "One night I heard this plaintive cry and it was Norm. And he was calling my name, so I rolled up and saw this guy shaking Norm's arm."

An AB had grabbed Idleberg's arm and was shaking it, and Idleberg was scared. From Webb's perspective, the seaman was attacking his commander. He reached for his revolver and shoved it in the man's ear. "Boy, you better back off there," Webb warned, "or you're going to get yourself killed."

The AB backed off and told the investigators that he wanted protection: another crew member had threatened to kill him. "This was how these guys were around each other," said Webb. "They didn't seem to trust each other."

After conducting their interviews, the four investigators put together an important manuscript, a sprawling text over five hundred pages long, in which they very carefully and meticulously documented the oral history of the only modern American mutiny. The document was formally titled, "The Revolt and Mutiny on Board the SS Columbia Eagle."

The report focused mainly on the two known mutineers, Clyde McKay and Alvin Glatkowski, who were in Phnom Penh, having been granted asylum by Prince Norodom Sihanouk of Cambodia. In newspaper interviews the pair described themselves as revolutionary guerrillas, self-styled apostles of Che Guevara and Ho Chi Minh, members of the Students for a Democratic Society, and the vanguard of a clandestine network of seamen who were planning more mutinous actions on U.S. munitions ships.

Other published accounts portrayed the pair as pot-smoking, pill-popping hippies who took over the tramp steamer as a marijuana-induced lark. The French newspaper *Le Monde* alleged that the mutineers were actually covert U.S. agents, working with the Central Intelligence Agency. Background checks from the FBI and the Defense Intelligence Agency—reports that the investigators had in their possession—painted a different picture. In these, McKay and Glatkowski appeared to be a very complex pair, not easy to pin down.

"I think, looking back at it now," said Idleberg, "when we did all of this, I looked around the ship, and saw the things that were done to it and to the men, and I often wondered if all of it was the work of only those two people. Maybe that's what motivated us to ask additional questions."

The first deposition took place in the captain's modest stateroom, located just below the bridge and consisting of a bedroom and office, both of which had doors that led aft to a thwartships passageway. The portholes in the office had green curtains and looked forward toward the bow. There were a few pieces of fixed furniture: a rectangular dining table, which had a stiff, green, Naugahyde settee on one side and two swivel chairs on the other.

There were moveable pieces as well: a desk, a file cabinet, two chairs. On the desk there was a typewriter.

The first deponent was the fifty-one-year-old master of the *Eagle,* Capt. Donald O'Bannon Swann. A tall man with thinning hair, gray temples, and a round and full face, he sat in his chair uneasily, staring at the reel-to-reel Wollencraft tape recorder on the table in front of him as Idleberg clicked on the machine. Spiker stood next to the desk, wearing his sunglasses even though they were indoors. Wedertz busily scribbled on a stenographer's pad, and Davis and Webb sat on either side of the captain. Swann was instructed to swear an oath, then gave his name, his home address, place of birth, his Z-card number, and his social security number. Then he launched into his version of events.

> The first indication I had of trouble was when I was coming to my room and I heard the chief officer calling, "Captain, Captain." And as I entered the room, Mr. Morgan, chief officer, and Clyde McKay and Alvin Glatkowski were in there and the mate [Morgan] told me, he says, "These men have a gun on me." McKay uncovered his pistol which he had up to that time covered up with a kind of a black file folder. He pointed it at me and directed me to close the door and go sit in the corner and told the chief mate to sit down and Alvin Glatkowski, he had a gun on the mate and McKay put a pistol on me.
>
> When I asked what was the meaning of this, what was going on, McKay said, "First off, this cargo is not going to reach its destination. . . . We have the means of blowing this ship up in a very few minutes. If you don't cooperate and take us to Cambodia, that's what we'll do. Now, if you want to save part of your crew, you can get them off in the lifeboats and we'll take the ship up to Cambodia with a skeleton crew."
>
> I tried to stall and haggle with him and talk to him but he mentioned that he and Glatkowski were both nervous and they didn't want to kill anybody, but that they would. He also stated that "You and I both know since I've gone this far, to draw a gun on you, I can't get into it deeper than I am now. So let's get this thing over with or somebody's going to come in that door and I'll have to shoot him."

2 THE SOLDIER OF FORTUNE

Clyde William McKay Jr. was born on 22 May 1944 in California's fertile San Joaquin Valley, at a military hospital near the post where his father—a career army man—was serving at the time. From the moment Clyde Jr. was born, his family called him Billy. His early years were spent moving from one military camp to another, from Long Beach to Roswell, New Mexico, then to New York, Germany, and South Carolina. In between these postings, McKay's mother Jean would take the growing family back to Hemet, the small town where she had been born and raised, and where she had the physical and emotional support of her family. Jean brought up her children in a house a block away from where her parents lived.

Hemet, California—thirty miles west of Palm Springs, across the San Jacinto Mountains—was, in the 1940s, a rural hub where most residents owned or worked the nearby groves of apricot, peach, pear, olive, walnut, and citrus. It was a small town with neighborly American values: throwing cake sales to raise money for local teams, leaving your front door unlocked, helping one another through daily crises.

Clyde McKay Jr.—Billy to his family, Clyde to his friends—grew up as an outsider. Despising organized activities, never feeling comfortable with other army kids, he preferred to read, which sparked his imagination. Jean saw this early. She bought him a set of the *Book of Knowledge*, which became his constant companion. Often, she would see him reading late into the night.

During the years McKay was in junior high and high school, there were run-ins between him and his parents. Jean felt that her oldest child had inherited his ornery, argumentative side from her husband's family and his curious, spiritual side from hers. It may be that McKay, who now had five younger siblings and a father who was away much of the time, felt that he did not want to bear the burden of being the man of the house.

While in high school, McKay never dated or went out in search of a social life. It just did not interest him. He had his pals, people who cared for him, but being with people was not a priority for him. He did not pay attention to his clothes or his appearance; he would rather read or think than be with others. According to his sister Lois, "Billy never wanted or needed social reinforcement. He never thought he was missing out on a social life."

"Billy had a strong sense of right and wrong," said McKay's sister Kerry. "He was quiet, studious, thoughtful about everything. At the same time he could be sarcastic and cynical, with a good sense of humor."

According to his friend John Safford, McKay was brilliant but easily bored by details and by the hard work that preceded the payoff: he always skipped the preparation to get right to the heart of the matter, whether he was ready for it or not. "This was Clyde's tragic flaw," Safford said. "He had to accomplish everything immediately and then move to something else. He acted on the spur of the moment."

It was this overwhelming impatience, this hunger for life and adventure, that drove Clyde McKay from the time he was a teenager.

Oddly, what changed his life began as a bowel obstruction, then escalated—because of inadequate diagnosis and treatment—into gangrene and multiple surgeries. He lost forty pounds and nearly died while doctors fought to reconnect his intestines. McKay shuttled between extended bed-stays at home and emergency operations at the military hospital. As a result, he lost a year of school and his interest in formal education was never rekindled. He never finished high school. Always moving to the beat of his own drummer, he took odd jobs, including working as a county fireman, which usually meant, according to McKay, "helping old ladies cross the street"—certainly not the life of adventure that he had fantasized for himself.

By the time he was eighteen, McKay had gained his weight back. He was six foot one, weighed 170 pounds, and had brown eyes and hair; he was strikingly handsome. Feeling that it was time to leave home, he decided to join the merchant marine. Typically, he did it in a determined way. He bought a broken bicycle for five dollars and then worked all day to fix it. Taking food and water in a small backpack, he rode all night in the chilly air, up and down hills, seventy miles from Hemet to San Diego. He arrived a little after dawn and made contact with his Aunt Ruth, who knew someone who could get him seaman's papers.

McKay received his merchant marine document (Z-card) on 23 October 1963 and immediately signed up with the Seafarers International Union (SIU). Early in 1964, when he was nineteen, he shipped out for the first time. After that, there would be long stretches when Jean would not hear from her son at all, punctuated by occasional calls from a seaman's mission somewhere telling her that he had been in for a meal or a bed, and requesting that they "say a prayer for him." She would always answer, "What do you think I've been doing every day!" And then more extended periods, months at a time, without any word from him or about him.

In 1965 McKay was working as a wiper on the SS *Monkato Victory* when he jumped ship in Bangkok. Several weeks later, Jean received a call from the Hemet post office: there was a package from her son. Thinking that it was a belated Mother's Day present, she rushed to pick up a big cardboard box that had ten dollars postage due. She paid the money and took the box home, only to find dirty clothes. The owners of the *Monkato Victory* had sent McKay's filthy work clothes to the address he had listed as his home. Jean sifted through the pants and shirts, full of dried grease and paint, and then burned it all. Seeing his dirty work clothes in flames touched the core of the pain Jean felt about the life her son was living; she cried and cried as his work clothes smoldered.

The next time McKay was back in Hemet, he told friends that while in Thailand he had lived in a whorehouse, and that he and a young lady took a river trip in a small boat and inadvertently wandered onto an island where strange-looking residents were surprised to see him. Suddenly, McKay noticed the stunted limbs and missing noses; he realized that it was a leper colony. He and the girl scrambled to get back to their boat while the lepers laughed. McKay said that he was happy to have given them what was probably the first laugh they had had in a long time.

In early 1966, when he was twenty-one, McKay was in Djibouti, in Africa, working on the SS *Yaka*. On 25 February, the day the *Yaka* was to sail for the Indian subcontinent, McKay sat in a bar and knocked down several drinks. He became aware of a table of rough-looking men, of various colors and nationalities, who punched one another playfully and sat with whores on their laps. They shouted and laughed, obviously very drunk. Among themselves—and with the whores—they spoke broken, accented French. Not understanding a word of it but interested, McKay wandered near them. They waved for him to join them and bought drinks for the sharp-looking young man with the striking eyes. A couple of the men spoke English and they told McKay that they were soldiers in the French Foreign Legion.

Clyde McKay would later tape the story of this and subsequent adventures. In that recounting he said that he jumped ship and within days had signed on as a recruit in the Foreign Legion. As a teenager, he had been declared physically unfit for serving in the U.S. military because of his illnesses, but the Legion took him with no questions.

An army brat, McKay felt he knew what military life would be like. But nothing prepared him for the rigors and humiliation of Legion training. He hated everything about it: getting up before dawn to clean his rifle; double-timing up and down the burning-hot, hard-packed, scrubby landscape with fifty pounds of gear on his back and a rifle in his hands; doing guard duty at three in the morning. He hated being told what to do and when to do it, and being yelled at when it was not exactly right.

Most of all, he felt dehumanized by the brutality of it, his essential humanity being crushed under the Legion's need to mold a recruit who would willingly give up his life. During his off-hours he would join the others and they would drink. And drink. And when drinking, the men would talk about their exploits. When the conversation was about weapons and killing, it did not bother McKay; he assumed it was standard bragging, with the additional twist that these men had actually taken part in over-the-border raids into Somalia. Talk about their sexual escapades did not bother him either, nor the ever-present whores at the periphery of the camp.

No, what bothered him was the difficulty of the training, the viciousness of the drill instructors, and the heavy-duty boozing: drinking to get drunk, night after night and all day on Sunday. He felt that if he remained in the Legion any longer, he would turn into an alcoholic, like many Legionnaires.

After nearly four months of training, McKay was more than ready to get out. But how? He had signed a contract. If he tried to escape, where would he escape to? He could try to catch a job on a U.S. ship, but the Legion might grab him before the ship left port and he would be thrown into the brig. Going overland was out of the question. He would have to cross into Somalia or Ethiopia, and he did not have a passport. When he had signed on the ss *Yaka,* he was not required to have one. There did not seem to be any options at all.

Then one day, an escape route miraculously presented itself. He was told by a sergeant that he and all the other recent recruits were going to be sent to France for further training. McKay was delighted. It would get him out of this colonial outpost and into Europe. There he would figure out a way to get out of the Legion. In Europe he would free himself of this nightmare.

A few days after his arrival in Marseilles, he told the sergeant in charge of his training that he felt very ill, his old high school malady was acting up. He was sent to the infirmary. In his halting, limited French McKay talked to the doctor about his bowel obstructions, his gangrene, his surgeries, his nearly dying when he was sixteen. McKay, feeling that the doctor was unconvinced, pulled out all the money he had in his pocket, virtually all he had earned as a Legion trainee, and stuffed it into the doctor's hands. In a mixture of French and English he pleaded, "What do I have to do to get out of this?" The doctor pocketed the money and within a few days McKay was discharged from the Legion "for medical reasons."

So now he was free. But he was in Europe and he had no money and no passport. He went to the U.S. consulate and asked if they could help him. The vice-consul sent a wire to McKay's parents informing them that their son was destitute and needed two hundred dollars.

McKay also told the vice-consul that he had no papers. The vice-consul gave McKay the forms to fill out to replace a lost passport. McKay explained that he had not *lost* his passport; he had never *had* one. The vice-consul was surprised. How had he gotten into France without a passport? He explained that he was a U.S. seaman who had jumped ship in Djibouti, joined the Legion, spent four months in training, and was finally sent to Marseilles on a troop transport. Since he came into France as a member of the French military, there had been no passport check. The vice-consul told McKay to come back in a week.

Back in Hemet, Jean McKay was—as usual—worried about her son;

she had not heard from him in more than six months. Then on 29 June 1966, she received a telegram from the U.S. State Department:

> ACCORDING AMERICAN CONSULATE GENERAL MARSEILLE FRANCE YOUR SON CLYDE MCKAY JR DESTITUTE THERE REQUESTS YOU WIRE UNDERSIGNED $200 MADE PAYABLE TO DEPARTMENT OF STATE PROMPT REPLY REQUESTED.

Within a few hours, Jean McKay borrowed and scraped together the money and sent it to the State Department. The next day she received confirmation from the U.S. government that the money had been received and that it would get into McKay's hands.

A few days after the initial telegram, Jean received an official letter from the U.S. passport office in Washington, which not only wanted a recent photo of McKay, they also wanted to know if he had any scars or other "distinguishing characteristics." Jean searched through the photo drawer and found one she had taken the last time McKay had been home. She sent it, along with a note saying that he had several long scars on his stomach.

When McKay went back to the U.S. consulate in Marseilles several days later, the money was there but the passport was not. The vice-consul told McKay that his mother had sent the needed information, but there was a delay.

A few days later, Jean's heart skipped a beat when she saw a letter from France. She recognized her son's handwriting. It was addressed to her husband, but she quickly opened it anyway.

> Dear Dad,
>
> I'm well and fine now thanks to the 200. I was in the Foreign Legion for the last few months and spent every dime that I had bribing a doctor to get out. I wanted to write sooner but I just couldn't tolerate the thought of mother knowing that I was in that god-forsaken army. I can't explain it.
>
> Please write and let me know how things are at home (if you haven't disowned me yet) c/o the U.S. Consulate here in Marseille. I'll be here for another week. I'm homesick but I can't afford to take a vacation. Its back to the sea for now. I'll be home for Christmas without fail. Say hello to everyone for me. If anyone is taking French in school they better not speak a word of it to me when I return. Your Son, Clyde Jr.

Jean sat down, clutching the letter. The French Foreign Legion! As if she did not have enough to worry about. As if she did not have enough reason for her hair to turn gray. Still, Jean noted that her son had sent the letter to his father, not to her. It touched Jean that her son wanted to keep her from knowing just how wild his adventures were.

In Marseilles, when McKay went back to the U.S. consulate to check on the status of his passport, the vice-consul told him it was still delayed and to come back in a week's time. Another week? Marseilles was much too expensive. His money would soon run out. Passport or no passport, he would need to go somewhere else. So he went southwest and sneaked across the border into Spain.

In Barcelona, McKay took stock: it was July 1966 and he was in a country ruled with an iron fist by Franco, a fascist dictator. He had no papers and he had nearly run out of the money his family had sent him. He went to the U.S. consulate to have them request money from his family. While there, he asked about his passport. The vice-consul, Norman Del Gigante, told McKay that the State Department said that there was still some delay.

In mid-July 1966, Jean McKay received another telegram:

> AMERICAN CONSULATE BARCELONA REQUEST YOU BE INFORMED THAT SON CLYDE TOTALLY DESTITUTE REQUEST YOU URGENTLY WIRE FIFTY DOLLARS THROUGH MORGAN GUARANTEE TRUST, NEW YORK TO BANCO CONDAL BARCELONA.

Jean read it again, to make sure she got it right. He was destitute again, this time in Spain, not France. She asked her relatives for help, then sent off the fifty dollars on 18 July 1966.

The next day, when McKay picked up the money at the U.S. consulate in Barcelona, he asked about his passport. The vice-consul said there was still no news. McKay was unable to stay at a hotel because they would have asked him for documents. He could not work at a regular job, of course, so he lived on the street, hustling tourists. They would offer him a meal or a few bucks in exchange for bullfight posters or knickknacks or some clue about where to find a whore or anything else.

Then one day the other shoe dropped. He was approached by two policemen who asked him for documents. He fumbled through his pockets, finally confessing that he had no passport. In English, they asked him to come to the police station. He was fingerprinted, transferred to a different police station, and then transferred again to a very large prison. During his first week in prison, McKay thought he had been charged with not having the proper papers.

"But after a week, I found out that I was charged with a, what did they call it, a *delito contra el salud público,* a misdemeanor against the public health," McKay said in the tape recording he later made. The problem, he explained, was that he just happened to be "at the scene where some marijuana had been sold," so he too was arrested for selling.

On 3 August, Jean McKay received a telegram from the State Department:

> AMERICAN CONSULATE BARCELONA REPORTS YOUR SON CLYDE MCKAY JAILED ON NARCOTICS CHARGES BARCELONA YOUR SON REQUEST $300 COVER BAIL AND EXPENSES SUCH FUNDS CAN BE SENT YOUR SON CARE AMERICAN CONSULATE BARCELONA INFORM UNDERSIGNED ACTION TAKEN.

Again Jean started to raise money but her husband stopped her. Clyde Sr. feared that Spanish authorities were playing a trick on them. He and Jean had already sent $250, and to what end? Their son was in even worse trouble than before they sent any money. A skeptical Clyde Sr. sent a telegram to the State Department:

> RELUCTANT TO SEND MONEY UNTIL THE FOLLOWING INFORMATION IS RECEIVED: DATE OF ARREST AND SPECIFIC CHARGES, NATURE OF ARREST, MISDEMEANOR OR FELONY? PENALTY UPON CONVICTION. HOW IS DEFENSE COUNSEL OBTAINED AND COST. HIS PHYSICAL CONDITION AND LETTER FROM CLYDE. HIS CHANCES OF ACQUITTAL. REQUEST YOUR RECOMMENDATION UPON COMPLETION OF YOUR INVESTIGATION.

Within a few days the McKays received a telegram from the State Department:

> ATTEMPTING SELL MARIJUANA IMPRISONED BARCELONA PHYSICAL CONDITION GOOD HE HAS NOT YET ENGAGED LAWYER IMPOSSIBLE DETERMINE CHANCES ACQUITTAL UNTIL LAWYER RETAINED TRIAL POSSIBLY IN OCTOBER CAN BE RELEASED PENDING TRIAL UPON PAYMENT BAIL YOUR SON REQUESTED $300 SENT CARE AMERICAN CONSULATE BARCELONA.

Family members—including Jean's mother, Lois McCloy—pitched in and the next day Jean sent three hundred dollars to the American consulate in Barcelona. Clyde Sr. felt that the family was sending good money after bad.

Meanwhile, McKay remained in the Barcelona prison. Day after day, week after week. He imagined that, sooner or later, someone would discover that it had all been a big mistake. He kept thinking that a judge would let him out any day. McKay said, "Every moment a voice inside me was saying, 'Tomorrow I'm going to go free. It's ridiculous. I've been in too long. This can't be happening.'"

The situation in jail was intolerable. Absolutely degenerate. Filthy. Terrible food, basically bread and water. In the water would be some rancid oil and a few beans. The smell nauseated him. It was called soup, but McKay threw it out all the time.

McKay's daily routine in prison was monotonous. In the morning, wake up for count and stand at attention. Clean the cell. Breakfast of bread and coffee. Then time to go outside in the crowded yard. Stay there till noon. Go in for "lunch." Nobody bothered to go downstairs to get the food because it was so bad.

"After lunch," said McKay, "we'd go right back out to the yard, the patio, where we'd sit all the time. Everything was very dirty and the wind would be blowing dust around. . . . Most of the Spanish in there were illiterate and very immature and they'd run around screaming and play their games. It was like being in a mad-house, to be in this yard all day, and I was there during the winter-time. We were still out in the yard and I didn't even have a coat. I traded my coat for a pack of cigarettes one time."

As McKay talked with the foreigners in prison, he realized that in this topsy-turvy world, the people who stayed inside were those who were either not guilty or whose cases were complicated. Those who had clearly committed the crime they were accused of could go to trial quickly. All the rest had to wait.

One man who made an impression on him was an African who was in prison accused of stealing a Rembrandt painting, "The Man with the Golden Hat." The African told McKay that he was not guilty of the theft; the painting was still hanging in a museum. His innocence, quite literally, was on public display. Still, he was doomed to years in prison before his case would come up for trial.

Another prisoner was an American who had been teaching in the Canary Islands. He was on his way to France, where he lived, and went to Barcelona for a little touring. Unfortunately, he was stopped at the entry point. While teaching in the Canaries, he had expelled a girl, and her father had lodged a complaint against him. It would be a long time before the Spanish authorities would straighten *that* matter out. When McKay met him, the teacher had been in jail for four months.

Each day McKay would go out to the yard and look up. There were two high walls surrounding the prison and the distance between the walls was about twelve feet. At the top of each wall there were sharp spikes and broken glass. Guards patrolled day and night from the top of the walls. No one had ever escaped.

The vice-consul would visit every six weeks or so, and during one of those visits, two months after the three hundred dollars was sent by McKay's parents, the vice-consul admitted that he had no idea where the money was. On top of that, McKay's passport had not arrived yet. McKay was outraged. No money, no passport. When would this nightmare end?

Not soon enough. During his next visit to McKay in Barcelona jail, the vice-consul dropped a bombshell. He told the young prisoner there would be no passport for him. The U.S. government decided that McKay's service in the French Foreign Legion put his citizenship in question. He was in danger of being stripped of his nationality.

McKay was astounded. The idea of losing his citizenship scared him. How would he earn a living? How would he travel? How would he see his family and old friends? Did this mean he would have to become a French citizen now? He could barely speak the language. It was ridiculous.

Back in Hemet, Jean McKay received the same devastating news in a letter from the U.S. passport office:

> The [U.S.] Consulate General at Marseilles informed the [State] Department last July that your son had served in the French Foreign Legion earlier this year. Under Section 349(a)(3) of the Immigration and Nationality Act a citizen who enters and serves in the armed forces of a foreign state is subject to loss of United States nationality. Service in the French Foreign Legion is considered service in the armed forces of a foreign state within the meaning of Section 349(a)(3). . . .

> The decision as to whether your son lost, or did not lose citizenship will be made by the [State] Department after an evaluation of all the circumstances of his case. I can assure you that the Department is most reluctant to make a holding that anyone has expatriated himself. However, if it is apparent that your son has voluntarily performed an expatriating act the Department will have to fulfill its responsibility to enforce the provisions of the Immigration and Nationality Act by approving the certificate of loss. Such action will be taken only if it is absolutely clear that that there is no other alternative.

Jean read it again and again. She was worried and confused. When she showed this letter to her husband, he nodded in resignation. He was apparently backing away from all this; it was too much for him. Clyde Sr.—recently retired from the army—had never given much guidance or direction to Jean or the kids. Jean felt that what she needed most was someone who would take control and deal with her son's dilemma.

Not knowing where else to turn, Jean shared the story of Billy's plight with several people at church, including Franklin Cave, a church elder and widower, a retired Marine Corps lieutenant colonel. Colonel Cave had always liked Jean, and he understood the gravity of the situation. Helping Jean gave him an opportunity to do what he knew how to do well: write letters to government officials, make calls, try to cut through bureaucracies. Cave treated the matter like a military campaign. And in the process he ingratiated himself with Jean McKay, whom he had always found to be attractive, kind, and charming.

Jean, for her part, was grateful beyond words to Colonel Cave for his involvement. It was obvious that Clyde Sr. was neither capable nor emotionally disposed to help his son through this crisis. Jean met with Colonel Cave and they planned what to do. Or rather, it was the authoritarian and well-organized Cave who told Jean what they should do. Soon, they were getting together nearly every day.

Cave wrote letters to George Murphy, California's U.S. senator, as well as to their congressman, Representative John Tunney. Tunney's office was very accommodating, and Colonel Cave's repeated letters and phone calls produced results. Jean McKay and Colonel Cave found out through Tunney's office that the congressman was going to be at March Air Force Base nearby, so they made an appointment to see him. They sat with him for a half-hour explaining the situation and Tunney promised to do whatever he could. Tunney kept his word. In early October, he wrote to the McKays, saying that he was continuing to "keep in contact with the Department of State regarding your son."

By late October Jean still had no indication that the three hundred dollars she had sent two months earlier was being used in her son's behalf. At Jean's urging, Lois McCloy, Jean's mother, sent a letter to the U.S. consulate in Barcelona asking what had happened to the money.

The American consul in Barcelona, St. John Bargas, wrote Lois McCloy that "this office has been in touch with Clyde on various occasions. He appears in good health, and the letters he has been receiving from home have boosted his morale. Clyde hopes to engage a lawyer with the money which he expects to receive from home."

Jean, Colonel Cave, and Clyde Sr. read this letter and were furious. They had sent the money in August, ten weeks ago! For Clyde Sr. it confirmed that he had been right all along; he knew that the money would end up in the hands of some larcenous Spanish official.

Colonel Cave felt that what was required was more pressure. He drafted a letter, signed by Jean and Clyde Sr., which was sent to Secretary of State Dean Rusk: "On August 24, 1966, after considerable trouble borrowing [the money], we wired the requested $300 to the American Consulate, Barcelona, Spain. . . . Our son's grandmother . . . received a letter today . . . stating that NO MONEY HAD EVER BEEN RECEIVED!" Demanding an "immediate investigation," they added that they were "desperate for information and relief for our son." Copies of this letter were sent to the offices of Senator Murphy and Congressman Tunney.

The next communication that Jean McKay received from the U.S. government was a stark, three-page letter summing up her son's actions, including his having jumped a ship in Thailand the year before, and the times he used U.S. consulates to send home wires saying he was destitute and needed money. The list of McKay's past actions was clearly the State Department's way of telling McKay's parents that their son had gotten himself into trouble and they should not threaten or demand. The Department suggested that the McKays trace the remittance of the three hundred dollars. As a final slap in the face, the State Department official added that he was "sorry to have to inform you that a preliminary finding has been reached to the effect that your son expatriated himself by joining the French Foreign Legion."

Jean McKay was emotionally exhausted by all this, but Colonel Cave thought it would be best to continue to send aggressive messages to the government. In a letter to the U.S. consulate in Barcelona, the McKays asked that their son's citizenship "be immediately restored to him." Cave also wrote a letter to the State Department pointing out that Clyde McKay Jr. was not a criminal, "but adventurous," and imploring that everything be done to get him a speedy and fair trial, and to make sure that he not lose his citizenship.

But still McKay languished in jail, month after month. Around Christmas of 1966, finally, the consulate located the three hundred dollars and sent a letter to McKay's parents informing them that the money had been in the central bank all along. McKay used the money to buy things for himself in prison and to pay fees to an attorney recommended by the U.S. consul.

On 20 February 1967, McKay wrote his mother:

> . . . I'm in hot water from all directions for *nonsense.* I think I'm on a losing streak. Things will be better tomorrow! I hope. . . .
>
> I miss everyone. I'll be home for next Christmas, *for sure.*
>
> Don't worry about me. I'm alright. I like the contrast. Before I came here it was always good food, good food, good food. I didn't even know what bad food tasted like. I'm in a cell with 2 Swiss that are here for stealing gasoline so I'm learning German now.
>
> I'll write again as soon as possible. Until then
> your son
> Clyde Jr.

Finally, after eight and half months, Spanish authorities advised McKay that he would have his trial that very day. He was rushed out of prison with his few belongings and driven to court, where he saw his lawyer for the first time since Christmas. As McKay understood it, his attorney's argument to the judge was this: if he had been guilty of selling marijuana, as charged, then he would most certainly have had adequate funds to pay the bail and run away from Spain. Since he did not pay this bail because he did not have the money, it was evident that he was innocent of the charge. McKay later said, "On this ridiculous defense, I was acquitted."

He walked out a free man on 6 March 1967. He had no money left after paying his lawyer, so the first night he drifted down to the Barcelona waterfront and went aboard a Dutch ship. The seamen told him to help himself to food and then sack out in the recreation room.

The next day McKay went to the U.S. consulate to ask about his citizenship. The vice-consul told him that it was not the Americans who were delaying the process, but the French. The French government had not yet provided the U.S. State Department with proper documentation about McKay's service in the Foreign Legion.

McKay could not imagine why the French government was diddling him like this. Of course, he only had the U.S. State Department's word that it was the French who were delaying the process. Maybe it was not the French who were screwing him. Maybe it was the United States' fault. Maybe it was his own country that was doing this to him.

Either way, McKay was still a man without a country. Desperate, he picked up an official-looking sheet off the counter and asked the vice-consul to stamp it. The vice-consul shrugged and obliged. McKay figured that few Spaniards would know enough English to question him if he said that this document showed that he had legal papers. Back on the streets, McKay survived as he had before, by helping tourists get whatever they wanted. His life was as precarious as it had been before he went to jail. He had no passport or entry stamp into Spain and, to make matters worse, he now had a jail record. Since he could not sleep at a hotel, no matter how cheap, he was sleeping wherever he could. And he had to watch out for the *guardia civil.* They would swoop down on street hustlers periodically, and the first thing they would do is ask for papers.

A few days after getting out of jail, McKay made contact with a Swedish sailor and told him about his problems. He wrote his grandmother:

> . . . I managed to find a Swedish passport which more or less fits me. The name on the passport is Leif Erickson. I can use this for Spain but I don't know if I can travel with it or not. If the police ask me on the street for identification and I have none, I must go to prison for 30 days more.
>
> The council tells me that they expect to hear something regarding my citizenship within the next month. If you can send me the fare back, please send it. I can't use it now, but perhaps I will be able to by the time it gets here. If I can get the council to issue me my Seamans documents I can take a ship back and get paid for it.
>
> I'd like to write more but I have little time. I must go and sell some Bullfight posters to some tourists to make some pesetas ($). I send another letter soon.
>
> Your grandson, Clyde W. McKay Jr.

For a few days at least, McKay was able to get a room for less than a dollar a day. He had been on a losing streak, but now, surely, things were going to start looking up for him. He was past the worst.

One night about a week later, in Barcelona, McKay met a German tourist who had a sports car. Well on his way to drunkenness, the German suggested that they drive out to the only beach spot in the area, Casteldefels, about ten miles away. The German drove fast on the expressway. Suddenly, out of nowhere, a slow-moving motorcycle came up in front. The German slammed on the brakes but it was too late. The motorcycle and its driver went flying . . . and then just disappeared.

Shaken, the German slowed down and asked McKay if he thought they should stop. McKay told him that he had just spent eight and a half months in prison with no evidence against him.

"I told the German guy that he could do what he wanted," said McKay, "but I wasn't going to stay there."

So the German continued driving. In the morning, however, he had second thoughts. He went to a Barcelona police station and confessed that he had been in an accident. And he mentioned that there had been an American with him.

A few days later, in Hemet, Jean McKay received a wire:

> AMERICAN CONSULATE GENERAL BARCELONA SPAIN REPORTS CLYDE HELD BY POLICE AS OCCUPANT OF AUTOMOBILE WHICH STRUCK AND KILLED POLICE SERGEANT NEAR CASTELDEFELS APRIL 21 MCKAY NOT DRIVING BUT FLED WITH DRIVER AFTER INCIDENT EXACT CHARGES WILL BE KNOWN AFTER HEARING APRIL 24.

Jean sat down. Would there ever be an end to these disasters? She called Colonel Cave and read him the latest news. He helped Jean draft a letter:

> Dear Congressman Tunney:
>
> Would you please help a most distraught mother by obtaining the facts on the above dismaying events? Cannot the French government be urged in our president's forceful way to reach a decision re Clyde's citizenship status? What do we do if they determine he is a French citizen with regards to the current trouble he is in? I feel that if I could just get my son back home he would not be in trouble.

The U.S. vice-consul in Barcelona—none too happy to see him back in jail—told McKay that his crime was "complicity in manslaughter." Because it was a *guardia civil* who had been killed, the first legal battle was slated to be with a military court. When McKay told other prisoners that he would be judged by a military tribunal, they crossed themselves and walked away. Somehow McKay got hold of a newspaper account of the incident and it said that he and the German had murdered the man, shot him with a gun. It looked bad.

The prospect of an indefinite stay in a foreign jail was unendurable—the degradation, the humiliation, the demeaning routines, every day the same futility, the knowledge that there was nothing to look forward to except another day in hell. He would rather kill himself than go on like this.

McKay stopped having any contact with Spanish prisoners, whom he saw as disgusting hoodlum-illiterates, vicious children who were determined to make life as miserable as possible for one another. He would look at them and imagine he was executing them in a hundred ingenious ways. Getting back at them for all the humiliation and indignities they had heaped on him.

On those rare times when he could take a step back from these thoughts, McKay would realize that there was a word to describe his condition: madness. He was going through a breakdown. He had to do something to break this downward spiral. So he went on a fast.

Day after day he ate nothing, hoping that the crazy thoughts would go away. He fasted and sat, sat and fasted. He made no eye contact with Spanish prisoners, giving them no opening to approach him. As he grew weaker and weaker, his crazy thoughts did not go away. In fact, they became more intense. He would close his eyes and suddenly he would feel that he was somewhere else. Anywhere else. Back in Hemet. Or at sea. Or in a port somewhere. He felt an increasing distance between himself and reality.

McKay was sinking closer to starvation when a fellow prisoner interfered. It was the man accused of stealing the Rembrandt painting, the man McKay called "the African." The African took McKay under his wing and made sure the young man ate some good food. Something substantial to give him strength and energy.

"There was this person who had luxuries in there, this Negro I told you about," said McKay in the tape he later recorded. "He was a friend of mine, he had a big cell to himself, which he had had built for him. He had his food brought in, he could buy cognac, wine, anything he wanted. He had everyone working for him. The padres in prison would conduct his telegraph, the sisters superior would make his telephone calls for him, and the guards would mail his letters for him. He had everyone on his payroll."

The African also gave the young man the name of a lawyer—Señor José Roig—who visited McKay and gave him a bright outlook on the case. Roig told him that all he needed was money to buy his freedom. At the same time McKay was visited by the U.S. consul, who had information about his citizenship status. McKay wrote to his grandmother:

> Dear Grandma
>
> . . . My lawyer and the Vice-consul have conferred with the judge. They tell me that it is strictly a matter of money. . . . My lawyer tells me that I could go free immediately for 2 thousand dollars. If you can find *any* money to send my lawyer please send it quickly. A couple of hundred dollars can mean a year less that I'll have to stay in this dreadful place.
>
> I have one piece of extremely good news! The consul has informed me that I have regained my citizenship. When I am free I will have my passport and perhaps my seaman's document. . . .
>
> If you can find any money to send to my lawyer please send it rapidly and I may be able to get out of this mess. . . .
>
> Yours Truly,
> Clyde McKay Jr.

Jean McKay picked up the letter at her mother's and then read it and reread it with Colonel Cave. At least her son had his citizenship back. That was an enormous relief.

But two thousand dollars! That was almost the price of a car, or a year's rent for an apartment. How did they expect her to pay that on their meager army pension? Yes, of course, she would have to ask relatives again, but how often could she keep going back to the same well?

When she talked to Clyde Sr. about it, he seemed to back away. For months it had been Colonel Cave who had done most of the work. And it had been relatives who had put up the money. Jean was angry that her husband was not there for her emotionally during this difficult time. She had to face it: the gap between them was unbridgeable.

Jean told Clyde Sr. that she wanted out of the marriage. It was not just this round of disasters, it was the vast differences between them; the situation had become unbearable for Jean, who said it was time for them to separate. Clyde Sr. packed some things and left.

A few days later, Jean received a letter from her son's lawyer in Spain:

> I am the layerer of your son Clyde McKay and take charge of this matter which is not so easy.
>
> Anyway I hope to be able to get him free soon. It's only a question of time and about the question of explaining by your son.
>
> It's not necessary to be worry about [coming] over because I was already to the American Consulate and they told me it's not necessary.
>
> Sincerely yours,
> José M. Roig

The next letter that Jean received was from the U.S. vice-consul in Barcelona, Norman Del Gigante, who said that McKay's attorney suggested that Jean send one thousand dollars to be used in the court case. The vice-consul wrote that Jean could send the money to the U.S. Department of State, and they would see to it that McKay received it.

So now it had come down to one thousand dollars! Enormous as that sum was, at least it was half of what McKay had said it was going to be. Again, with her family pitching in, Jean scraped together the money and Lois McCloy sent the money order. With Colonel Cave's help, Jean wrote a letter that stipulated to the State Department that—before releasing the money—they "ascertain *positively* that Clyde *will* be released upon payment of this money *before* you forward it."

The U.S. consulate in Barcelona wrote back that they could not release the money to McKay under these conditions. The situation was at an impasse. Days passed. When McKay received word of the latest problem, he was furious.

In Hemet, a few days later, Jean received a telegram that affected her more than anything else that had happened. It came from Tunney's office and it was a copy of a telegram sent from the U.S. consulate in Barcelona to the Department of State, quoting a letter that McKay had sent to the consulate. McKay wrote:

> MY LAWYER INFORMS ME THAT IF HE IS UNABLE TO NEGOTIATE FOR MY RELEASE VERY SOON THIS OPPORTUNITY WILL BE LOST. THIS IS MY ONLY HOPE OF LIBERTY AND IT MAY WELL BE EXTINGUISHED BY THIS INSANE DELAY. I HAVE SPENT ONE LONG YEAR IN THIS PRISON. I CAN-

NOT ENDURE THESE DEPRIVATIONS LONGER. I SINCERELY HOPE THAT THIS PETTY CONFUSION OF TERMINOLOGY CAN BE REMEDIED *BEFORE SUCH TIME AS I WILL FIND IT NECESSARY TO TERMINATE MY EXISTENCE.* ESPERANDO. CLYDE W. MCKAY JR. [emphasis added]

The Consul added his analysis of McKay's letter:

CONSUL VISITED CLYDE TODAY AND ADVISED HIM PATIENCE. CONSUL BELIEVES CLYDE DRAMATIZING TO GET ATTENTION AND RAPID ACTION *BUT POSSIBILITY DESPERATE ACT CANNOT BE RULED OUT* CONGEN [Consul General] CONCERNED OVER CLYDES STATE OF MIND AND REQUESTS DEPARTMENT INFORM PARENTS AND OBTAIN FATHERS AGREEMENT RELEASE MONEY WITHOUT RESTRICTION [emphasis added].

That was all Jean needed to hear. No matter what Clyde Sr. or Colonel Cave said, she wanted the thousand dollars sent immediately, with no strings attached. Within a few days, Lois McCloy received another letter from her grandson:

Dear G'ma,

. . . The consul visited me today. He has received the money. My lawyer wants to set me free on bail and then seek permission from the court for me to leave Spain. . . .

I can't tell you how happy I am to know that it's only a matter of weeks until I will be free and out of this terrible country.

Excuse me if my letters seem a bit disorganized and hard to follow. I must sit here in the yard all day. The Spanish yell, scream, push each other about and frequently bump into me. Under these conditions it's almost impossible to write a letter.

Give my love to everyone at home.

Clyde Jr.

But days turned into weeks. In prison, McKay waited. And waited. He felt that he was back to square one.

A dark depression took over, even worse than what he felt before, because now his hopes had been raised and then crushed. He felt utterly helpless. Hopeless. This place was hell on earth. The Spanish prisoners came at him like so many flies or mosquitoes. He had kept them away from him for more than a year, but it was becoming impossible. They were too vicious. He was too much of a target for them.

"You see," McKay said in his taped commentary, "I'd say that I underwent quite a change mentally from all this. I was trying to fight, I didn't want to accept the, I didn't want to accept the values in prison. I kept to myself usually, and I more or less withdrew into myself. Because I didn't want to accept the values in prison, because I felt that if I did that, if I did that, then the prison would have won."

But finally there was no way to avoid these "values." McKay apparently turned to the African once more, who provided help and protection. Later, when talking about these events, McKay said, "Finally, I smashed through a mental wall that I had carried with me all my life. I fought hard against it. Very hard. But when I finally broke through, there was a release on the other side. My break*down* became a break*through*."

Suddenly, one day—with no advance warning—Señor Roig, the lawyer, and the U.S. vice-consul came to the prison. They had one thousand dollars in hand. They told him it was time to go to court to pay bail. McKay could hardly believe it was finally happening.

When they went to the magistrates, they were told they would need twenty-five hundred dollars. McKay's heart sank. He saw himself going back to jail. The vice-consul and Señor Roig protested. After a negotiation, the magistrates relented, accepting five hundred. The attorney quickly paid the money. McKay was set free on bail on 19 September 1967 and received a U.S. passport.

Within days, McKay's mother got a letter from the U.S. consulate in Barcelona, telling her of the latest events. Jean now knew that her son had been released and that he had a passport. Soon he would be out of Spain. She expected to hear from him within a day or two at most. But, as always with her first-born, it did not work out that way. She waited days, then weeks, but did not hear from him.

After paying bail money, court costs, and his attorney, Clyde McKay had about $120 left. He had his passport, but he could not stop looking over his shoulder. Still feeling weighed down by his "losing streak," he saw freedom as a temporary luxury. He knew he had to get out of Spain as soon as possible. And he could not go to France.

He left Barcelona and headed southwest, toward Andalusia. In Malaga he ran into some people who had a car. They were going to Africa and said that McKay could come along if he paid his share of gasoline costs. McKay went with them, crossing the Straits of Gibraltar into Morocco. At the Moroccan border he made up a story as to why he did not have Spanish entry or exit stamps on his passport. McKay had become good at making up stories to tell authorities.

They traveled to the southern border of Morocco. There, McKay met a different group of travelers, an Alsatian couple and a Dutchman traveling in an old, beat-up Land Rover, a car with dozens of bullet holes along the sides. It was obviously in bad shape mechanically, but the car had a romantic air about it; it seemed the right vehicle in which to cross the desert.

Their plan, as they plotted it out on a map, was to go through Spanish Sahara, then Mauritania, and finally to Senegal; then drive down the coast to Dakar, where McKay expected to catch a ship back to the United States. At least he would save his family any further costs.

They left Morocco via its southern frontier, a desolate outpost, and traveled down the coast of Spanish Sahara. As the landscape became sparser and drier, they got water and food where they could, sleeping on the side of the road, until they reached Aaiún, the capital, a featureless desert town. They filled up their water and gasoline jerrycans. After a couple of nights in cheap hotel rooms, they traveled on, heading toward Mauritania. "I wanted to get away from Spanish Sahara," McKay said. "I wanted to get as far away as I could from any country that had a connection to Spain."

As they rode from Aaiún out into the desert, they stopped at a well. There they saw a Bedouin with a camel. He had a bucket with a long rope. The Alsatians and the Dutchman, apparently thinking that there was something romantic about getting water from a desert well, asked the Bedouin if they could use his bucket to pull up some water. The Bedouin agreed.

McKay was astounded. "They wanted to get rid of the good water we had gotten in Aaiún, pour it out, and exchange it for well water," said McKay. "Questionable well water. I thought they were nuts. But I couldn't stop them." In spite of McKay's protests, they emptied out their containers, pulled up slightly salty, brackish well water, and filled their containers with it.

After this, they traveled on trackless roads toward Mauritania. It turned into a trail that no one had apparently traveled for months. In the broiling desert sun the engine overheated. They kept putting more and more of their (salty) well water into the radiator. As salty and brackish as the water was, they also kept on drinking it. Soon there was precious little of it left. The

Alsatian man said that, if worse came to worse, they could always drink water from the radiator. He had read that people do that in the desert.

What they did not realize was that they had gone in a direction different from the one they had marked on their map. They thought they were in Mauritania but they had not entered that country. They had traveled south instead of southeast, so they were still in Spanish Sahara, about two hundred miles from Aaiún, in the middle of nowhere.

Finally, they came to a dune, an enormous mountain of sand. The Land Rover could not get past it. When they tried to turn back, smoke and sputtering steam billowed from under the hood, then the motor stopped. They opened up the hood and inspected the car. They had blown a head gasket.

By now they had drunk nearly all of the well water or put it into the radiator. Despite what the Alsatian had said, they could not drink the water that was in the radiator now because it had oil in it from the head gasket leak.

"We were in one of the worst parts of the Sahara, a flat area that might have been a lake a million years ago," McKay said. "Salt and sand were everywhere: on the ground, in our clothes, in the radiator, seeping into our skin. And no trees, nothing for shade." The Alsatian woman started to cry. The Dutchman laughed insanely and lit a cigarette. McKay pulled out a Gauloise and lit up. They could hear themselves puffing away. The silence was overwhelming. As the sun moved across the sky, they used the car itself for shade. That evening, as the sun set, they started walking, the four of them. They walked about an hour or so. McKay wanted to go one way, but his companions chose a different way. So McKay walked off by himself. Once he was alone, he felt better. He felt he had an increased chance of survival this way. He walked and walked and walked. There were little white clouds in the sky. There, over there was the Big Dipper. Follow that line and there's Polaris. Due north. Realizing he had been going east, not north, he changed course, now walking in the right direction.

There were no trails. There were tire tracks in certain places, but they could not be followed for any long distance because the vehicles would apparently go in a snake-like pattern in order to avoid the sand dunes. Here, here's a track where a vehicle might have turned. But it was impossible to determine which way it was going or where it had come from. McKay walked all night.

The next day, during the daytime, he could not walk; it was outrageously hot. When the sun was higher up, he looked for a little shade next to a rock. After sipping the last drops of his water, he stayed there all day and watched the sun move across the horizon.

When night fell, he walked again, following the stars northward. He looked up at a sky even starrier than the sky he was used to seeing on ships. He walked. And walked. All night long. His water was gone. His mouth felt dry, his lips parched.

After sunrise, the temperature rose. About an hour after the sun came up, McKay could see heat waves rising. In the horizon it looked as if there was water, just like a mirror, making the mountains look enormous. A couple of hours later it was hot beyond anything he had ever known, even in Djibouti. McKay searched for shade wherever he could. He was a little farther north now, so there were some bramble bushes. He nestled himself down. He did not know how much longer he could survive.

"And the next night I started walking again and tried to go north if I could," McKay said. "And still I couldn't really see anything, but I just kept on going." By the next day it was forty-eight hours since he had last had anything to drink. His mouth was dry and cracked. He needed liquid urgently. He lowered his water container and urinated into it. He forced himself to drink it. "It was hard, it tasted terrible." He nearly vomited, but he knew that if he did, it would only make things worse. He felt that his life was measured in minutes.

"I started having hallucinations," McKay said. "It was terrifically hot and I'd be talking to people who weren't there and they'd walk away and they'd say good-bye, and then I'd question myself: 'Why didn't I ask them for a drink of water?' And then I'd remind myself: they're hallucinations. That's all they are."

Finally, among all the visions, one stood out from the others. In the swirling hot air currents, he saw two other figures. And they were both himself. He was here and he was there, and these two selves carried on a conversation. According to his mother, McKay said that one of these selves told him to build an altar.

Then the other self argued: *Build an altar? Why do that? That's what they did a long time ago, in Biblical times. You just don't do that nowadays. It isn't necessary any more.* But the first voice kept insisting: *Build an altar!*

Pushing himself, he reached out, grabbed a rock and placed it on the sand near him. Then another and another and another. Meanwhile, there was the implacable sun, the heat, his entire body turning dry like the desert, the aftertaste of urine in his mouth. Still, he reached for stones and piled them. Within a few minutes he had built a small pyramid. An altar. Once he had finished, his strength ebbing away, he looked at it. His altar.

And that is when he heard it. The noise. A mechanical whir. He looked around. Through the heat currents, he saw it. It looked like a truck.

He forced himself up. He blinked and focused. A mirage? The truck was not moving, it was just idling. And there was a little Arab teenager, wearing a turban, walking around in front of it. McKay was exhausted, of course, but he ran down and collapsed into the arms of one of the Bedouins.

"They took me to the nearest Spanish police station," said McKay. "The chief of police told me, 'You are a very fortunate man. Extremely fortunate that they found you. That was the only truck going by that area in the last three months. It is very, very rare to get a vehicle through there. It's a miracle that the truck came by, and that they followed your tracks and found you out there. And in the eleventh hour, because you would not have survived another half-day.'"

The police gave McKay something to eat, let him take a shower, and then he went with them in a Land Rover to look for the other three who were still lost. "And we went out into the desert," McKay said. "We came to where we could find tracks in the sand. They found a cigarette one left here. They could look at two sets of tracks and say, 'This was made yesterday, this one was made today.' And they followed the right one. They even found where one of them had lost a wallet, under a bush. They brought the wallet back with money in it."

Within another hour they found the Alsatian couple huddled together near a bramble bush. Having given up hope, they were overwhelmed when they saw the Land Rover headed toward them. A half-hour later they came across the Dutchman, who was walking around in circles, arms akimbo, like a demented cartoon stork. The Spanish policeman and Arab trackers took all four to a hospital in Aaiún. On the way there, the Dutchman spoke deliriously of having eaten a pack of cigarettes. He laughed crazily, carrying on a conversation with himself.

The hospital was as bad as anything McKay had seen in other parts of

Africa or in India. Toilets were clogged with feces. Urine and blood were in the hallways. McKay felt that if he stayed here, he would get deathly ill. He and the Alsatian couple were given beds in the ward, but the Dutchman was sent straight to medical attention.

The next day McKay and the Alsatians went to visit the Dutchman. When they got there, they saw nurses covering his face with a sheet. A doctor explained that the Dutchman's liver had stopped functioning. The Alsatians said angrily that they told the doctors that the Dutchman had eaten cigarettes. Why had nothing been done about it? The doctor shrugged and shook his head.

McKay remained another day, sleeping in the ward, eating the food offered to him, taking showers, trying not to touch anything or anyone. The next day he took a truck out of Spanish Sahara and entered Mauritania. "I was in a country that had no diplomatic relations with the United States," McKay said. "They suspected me of being a spy."

After that it was a series of hit-and-miss trains, trucks, and buses until he reached Senegal. There, McKay sold the few things he had in order to pay for the ferryboat down the coast. He had hoped to catch a job on a ship, but once in Dakar, he decided he did not want to waste any more time. McKay had the U.S. consulate send a wire to his mother.

On a late November 1967 day, Jean McKay waited at the small Riverside airport with Colonel Cave. They had arrived more than an hour early. The tarmac had slick spots from the season's first rain, only a few days before. The San Bernardino Mountains were clear and sharp in the intermittent sunshine. It was cool and pleasant.

Jean edged closer as her son stepped out of the helicopter and onto the tarmac. He had only the flimsy clothes on his back, a fez he wore jauntily, and a carton of cigarettes. As Jean approached her son, she was shocked at his appearance. Her well-built, handsome son had lost so much weight! And the look in his eyes! She hardly recognized him. He was thin and haggard, drawn and aged.

And there was something else. Her son, always so kind and funny and generous, looked somehow empty; it was as if his soul had been emptied out, as if his spirit were broken. He looked like someone who had been stripped bare and beaten down by life.

During the weeks he spent in Hemet after flying in from Senegal, McKay walked every day. He would saunter several miles to visit friends or to enjoy nature. Discomforts did not seem to bother him. He never asked anyone for help or for a ride; he just walked, sometimes spending hours on the road and never complaining.

On occasion, McKay would go to see his father, who was living in a one-room, rundown apartment in a depressing section outside of Hemet called Homeland. During these visits, father and son would drink a few beers and exchange small talk about the son's adventures.

After her son's first few days in Hemet, Jean's view of him changed. She began to see him less as someone whose spirit had been broken and more as a kind of monk. "When Billy came back, he was a different boy from the one that left, definitely. He was different in many ways and he was very, what would you say, introspective, you know, he was very thoughtful. He was not of this world. Worldly things—clothing and cars and making money and stuff—that was not his world. His world was larger than that. It was beyond that."

McKay's sister Lois saw her brother as someone who had been "beaten down, drained." But his sister Kerry had a different opinion. When she saw her brother at that time, she felt that he had "a self-assurance. If he had survived Barcelona and the Sahara, if he could cross international borders almost at will, without papers and wanted by police . . . then he could survive anything. Anything."

Once McKay had gained some weight back and received his duplicate Z-card, he went east, to New York. Having worked as a wiper—the entry level job in the engine department—long enough to be eligible to move up in rating, he took a course run by the Seafarers International Union. For six weeks he attended daily classes at the SIU hall in Brooklyn. On 26 February 1968—two years and one day after he had jumped ship in Djibouti—McKay passed the Coast Guard exam and received the upgrade to oiler/fireman-watertender.

> Dear Mother, I passed my Coast Guard test on Friday and took a fireman's job on the SS Cortez on the same day. The company bought a first class ticket for me and I joined the ship in Portland on Saturday morning. The food is excellent. The living quarters are good. I sail today. Due to arrive in Da Nang, Viet Nam on March 17 [1968]. The ship will probably return to the west coast in mid-April. I made an allotment for 100 dollars every 2 weeks.

Here's my Viet Nam address: c/o Denis Freres, 196 Bach Dang, Da Nang, South Viet Nam.

Say hello to everyone for me. Your son, Clyde Jr.

After the *Cortez,* there was the *Halcyon,* the *Beloit Victory,* and other ships. Between early 1968 and late 1969 Clyde McKay shipped out steadily to Vietnam and the rest of Southeast Asia, the area that seamen called "the Zone" or "the bonus area."

For merchant seamen, the Zone was a surreal, grotesque amusement park. Children surfed the contaminated shore with Styrofoam bomb protectors, and hustlers tried to cadge money by saying "America numbah one, Russia numbah ten." Everything was suffused with the overwhelming smell of frying fish oil, kerosene, urine, cheap perfume, tropical rain, lush vegetation, garbage.

It was hard to tell where the war ended and Vietnam began. Near bombed and crumbling buildings ringed with sandbags, there were makeshift whorehouses made out of corrugated beer cans, and whores of all ages beckoned from gutted alleyways. For most seamen, the Zone had the two foundations of life in port: sex and booze. Many seamen enjoyed going to the Zone. They were especially happy about the bonus pay. Some hoped that the war could go on forever, or else be replaced by another war, in some equally accommodating place.

During the time McKay worked on Vietnam-bound ships, he apparently immersed himself in revolutionary ideas—ideas that were part of the air a counter-cultural person would have breathed in the late 1960s. Drawing together from what he read and what he heard—perhaps even from other seamen—McKay evolved his political thinking. His revolutionary and antiwar attitudes deepened. McKay learned pieces of political rhetoric by heart: Sartre, Marcuse, Fall, Bertrand Russell.

McKay worked during spring 1969 on a vessel that was put under foreign flag in Taiwan. As a result, the entire crew was set to take a flight back to the United States. When McKay learned that they were going to travel on economy class, he protested. He knew that the union contract called for first-class seats in this situation. There was a standoff. McKay refused to board the plane. Finally, airport police had to put McKay on the plane forcibly. A change had taken place in McKay. He had begun to put theory into practice.

In late 1969 and early 1970, McKay got together with John Safford, his childhood pal. Having served in the army, Safford was now in graduate school. Although their life paths were radically different, the two remained close friends. They sat up late into the night, telling stories and exchanging thoughts. According to Safford, when the subject of Vietnam came up, McKay said that "war protesters and draft resisters were people who had the courage of their convictions." McKay quoted parts of Senator William Fulbright's *The Arrogance of Power* "like it were scripture." For example, "In Vietnam we have allowed our fear of communism to make us once again the enemy of nationalist revolution, and in that role we have wrought havoc."

The book McKay carried with him and that he read over and over was *Viva Che!*, a collection of essays about Che Guevara. The book was a celebration of Che's life, published in 1968, a year after his death in the Bolivian jungles. A typical passage, which might have influenced McKay, reads: "The death of Che Guevara places a responsibility on all revolutionaries of the world to redouble their decision to fight on to one final defeat of imperialism. This is not the time to make long speeches dedicated to Che's memory, but a time for practical courageous action." Che was McKay's idol, the person he was using as a role model. McKay told Safford that he thought that Che was right: The United States was doing in Vietnam what it had done elsewhere—manipulating and controlling the ruling class to crush popular opposition. Vietnam was just the current example of America using the most powerful weapons in the world to destroy people who were determined to try to make their lives better.

McKay told Safford that if German civilians during World War II passively abetted the Nazi horror, then what he himself had done was worse. Having worked on ships going to Southeast Asia, he had actively participated in the war effort. He had collaborated with genocide. He had been part of the problem. He was now determined to live a life of revolutionary ideals; anything else would make him the worst thing he could think of: bourgeois.

Since returning to Southern California in late November 1969, McKay shuttled to and from Escondido, where his mother now lived with her new husband, Colonel Cave, to Hemet, where some of his old friends were, to the Los Angeles area, where his father lived.

Right after Thanksgiving, McKay was away for a couple of weeks. His sister Kerry recalled that "Billy hadn't really been planning to ship out, when he got a call from Northern California and he was told to meet someone." Kerry got the impression that her brother rendezvoused with a leftist or revolutionary group that urged him to stop a load of bombs from reaching its destination.

"An antiwar group might have zeroed in on him for some reason," said McKay's mother. "Who knows how that would have taken place? Maybe at a speech or rally, maybe he just sat down and talked to someone, that's how he ended up in prison in Spain, just meeting someone in a bar. That's how he got into the Foreign Legion or in the Sahara. Maybe it was the same way in San Francisco, just meeting someone at a bar."

John Safford spoke with McKay after he came back from Northern California and said that McKay "spent a while listening to antiwar speakers in Berkeley before returning to Southern California. It was easy for him to take them seriously."

After he came back from Berkeley, McKay and his father spent a couple of days together. In Escondido, on 14 December, they went to a gun shop, where McKay paid for a pistol: a blue, 9 millimeter P38 Walther, serial number 230508, five inch barrel. McKay was told by the gun-shop owner that he could not simply take this weapon with him. He would have to come back for it, and he said he would do so in a month. McKay's father asked no questions about it; after all, the elder McKay was a military lifer, used to weapons. As far as he was concerned, his son did not need a special reason to buy a pistol.

Just before New Year's, McKay took a bus down to San Felipe in Mexico's Baja California. His Aunt Ruth, who had a home there, was ill with the flu. It was at this time, in Mexico, that McKay withdrew most of the funds that Ruth had put away for him during the last few years. With this money McKay bought Mexican gold pieces, a money belt, and a gold saint medallion and chain. McKay then used Aunt Ruth's car to drive her to San Diego, where he spent a few days nursing her past her illness.

McKay's appearance had changed during these last few months. He now wore a money belt filled with gold pieces. Around his neck hung a gold medallion. He chain-smoked Gauloise cigarettes and sipped black coffee nonstop. Along the way he had picked up a tattoo on his right upper arm. For a person who had never affected any kind of special appearance,

Clyde McKay now looked more and more like a hardened soldier of fortune.

On 20 January 1970, McKay returned to Escondido, where he picked up the pistol he had ordered a month earlier. He also bought plenty of ammo. McKay then went back to Hemet to see old friends and family before going out to sea. Among those he visited was a middle-aged family friend who asked McKay for a favor.

"[This man] had had polio as a child," said McKay's mother. "Well, he wanted to go to Las Vegas, he wanted to go to one of these houses of ill-repute 'cause he'd done this previously, so he talked Billy into driving him there. And so Billy did, and while this fellow was being taken care of in this house of ill-repute, Billy is sitting in there with the girls and they naturally were hoping for some business and he was just talking with them, he didn't have anything to do except talk to them . . . and wait for him. When he was finished, they drove all the way back."

For McKay the situation must have been as strange as anything he had ever gone through: a night-time ride from Las Vegas to Hemet, driving a crippled man who had just been serviced at a whorehouse, McKay playing chauffeur and angel of mercy. In the darkness, McKay poured out his anguish. He told this man that he felt guilty about having worked on ammo ships. Beneath all this there may have been a deeper, darker guilt that had eaten away at him for more than two years, ever since his ordeal in Europe.

The crippled man agreed with McKay completely. *Yes,* he told the young man, *you are responsible whenever you're taking part in something. You worked on ammo ships, so you are responsible. Yes, you do have to accept that.*

"Evidently, the fact that it was wrong for him to have worked on those ships to Vietnam, this was very much on Billy's mind," said his mother. "Billy had been thinking about this for quite a while."

Just before he left Hemet for good, McKay saw John Safford one last time. "The night before he left," said Safford, "Clyde confessed to me that he felt guilty being part of a crew that was delivering bombs for an immoral purpose. He said that if he had the courage of his convictions, he would find a way to hijack the ship and take the bombs where they would serve a better purpose." When Safford asked McKay to fantasize, McKay said that he could pull it off with "just one or two loyal helpers."

"Of course," said Safford, "at the time I considered his statements somewhere between idle dreams and a lot of hot air."

3 THE BOY SCOUT

There is a bend near the headwaters of the Savannah River where it snarls and almost turns back on itself. It is a sudden twist on an otherwise lazy stretch. The Atlantic Ocean is more than one hundred miles distant from this point and the Savannah quickly straightens and rolls between miles of cotton fields toward the sea. In the lower piedmont the river changes again. It curls like a snake and runs turbulent and muddy through flatlands and gloomy forests of cypress and cedar where the only signs of civilization are old wharves—jutting out of the woods—with strange names like Frying Pan, Cut Finger Cut, Ring Jaw, and Devil's Elbow.

Alvin Leonard Glatkowski Jr. was born in the very crook of the bend in the river, in a city protected from the capricious waters by levees. The town that would be the birthplace of one of the only two American mutineers of the twentieth century was, appropriately, a shipping port. Augusta, Georgia, was a busy inland harbor connecting the cotton fields of the deep south—as well as the red clay quarries of the piedmont—to the rest of the world. Between Augusta and the sea, barges filled with textiles, cottonseed products, and bricks plied the river constantly.

The other industry for which Augusta had a singular reputation was the manufacture of weapons. At Fort Gordon, a U.S. military reservation just west of downtown Augusta, there was an arsenal, the fourth largest builder of warheads in the nation. The Augusta Canal passed the reservation, and there was a small loading dock. Private barges leased by the Military

Sea Transportation Service picked up pallets and crates of munitions that were stacked as deck cargo.

Many barges passed down that canal and through the heart of Augusta, each vessel carrying enough firepower to level the city and her sister city, North Augusta, across the river in South Carolina. The barges continued downriver through swamp and rain forest, past the bayous and marshes before reaching Tybee Sound in the great seaport of Savannah, where they were unloaded and their cargo transferred to steamships that carried the weapons to U.S. military bases in Sattahip, Thailand, and Manila Bay, the Philippines—places that would play prominent parts in the mutiny, twenty years later.

Alvin Leonard Glatkowski Jr. was born to Virginia Glatkowski and Alvin Glatkowski Sr. in St. Mary's Hospital in Augusta on 11 September 1949. According to his father, when his newborn son received a physical before leaving the hospital, the doctor—an army colonel—turned him over on the examination table and the infant peed in the colonel's face. He came into this world a rebel.

Alvin Glatkowski's father, Alvin Sr., had been given that name in honor of the acclaimed American war hero of World War I, Sergeant Alvin York. The legend of the daring Sergeant York was that he had taken a vow to obey the commandment, "Thou shalt not kill." When the U.S. Army served him his draft papers in 1917, York pleaded for exemption as a conscientious objector. His appeal was denied. But it was not York the pacifist who had inspired the name. Rather, it was the Sergeant York who was the reluctant hero, the man who single-handedly captured 132 German fighters and slaughtered 25 in the Battle of Argonne. Alvin Glatkowski, the mutineer, was named after his father, who had been named after a paradox: a peaceful man who aggressively took up arms. Years later, Glatkowski would proudly tell friends that his name did not come from his father so much as from an American war hero, a very complex man who had fought the good fight against imperialistic warmongers. Ironically, from childhood through adolescence, Glatkowski Jr. was called Leonard, his middle name, or Lenny by his family and friends.

The marriage of Virginia and Al Glatkowski Sr. was a rocky one. A restless man, Al Sr. resigned from the army. After Alvin Jr.'s younger brother Tom was born, Al Sr. moved the family to southern California, where he picked up piece work. They hit hard times. Alvin Sr. eventually walked out on the family.

Alvin Glatkowski—Leonard—was three years old. Tom was less than one. They never saw their father again. Despite her many burdens, Virginia was single, attractive, and young. It was not long before another man came into her life: Sam Hardy, a Navy third-class machinist's mate stationed in Long Beach.

Hardy was a big man, six foot seven with powerful arms and hands. He was from a family that lived a harsh, isolated life in Nocatee, Florida, a sparsely populated region. At the age of nineteen, Sam Hardy struck out on his own. He hitchhiked to Fort Myers on the coast and signed up with the Navy. He was posted in the engine department as a wiper. Sam rose steadily up the ranks, from oiler to fireman to third-class machinist's mate. Relocated to Long Beach, California, he met Virginia.

Leonard was six years old and his brother Tom was four when Sam Hardy married their mother. In Long Beach, the family was relatively happy. Soon they would move along with Sam's moods and fortunes up the coast. Sam was aggressively working his way up the Navy ladder. Already, he had secured the necessary hours and recommendations that would place him into the position of first-class machinist's mate.

Hardy pushed hard for his promotion and got it. As a result, the Navy transferred him to Oakland, a brief stopover but a significant one. Ann Hardy, Lenny's half-sister, was born there. Her arrival signaled a major change. From then on, Hardy began to divide his family into two distinct entities: Virginia's Leonard and Tom, and *his* kids. Ann was the first member of Hardy's family. There would be more.

As Sam and Virginia had children of their own, Hardy began to show more and more anger toward Leonard and Tom, children of a complete stranger. The fact that his wife had the children by another man irritated Hardy, especially as Leonard and Tom became adolescents and got into mischief. He tried to correct the problem with violence. It seemed to be the only way he knew.

From Oakland, Hardy was transferred to San Diego. Then they moved back to Long Beach. The Hardys moved up and down California as frequently as a coastwise merchant ship. The family never settled long enough in one place for anyone to feel at home. Along the way another child, Robert, came along. Finally came the news Hardy was waiting for: he was offered a chief machinist's mate position in Norfolk, Virginia. Hardy shuttled his family across the continent when Virginia was pregnant with yet another child, Carol. She was born in Norfolk, during the final leg of the Hardy odyssey.

Ann, Leonard's half-sister, would remember the name of the street for the rest of her life. Neoma Drive was a narrow suburban lane through a flat grid of modest homes. Their house was number 228: two stories, with yellow asbestos shingles. Neoma Drive was a dead-end off busy Tidewater Drive. The naval base was a few blocks away and the harbor was just beyond that.

"Lenny was a big achiever when he was growing up," Ann recalled. "He was in the Boy Scouts. He was always winning awards and he was very industrious. He had a paper route. He mowed lawns. He sold donuts. Anything to make money. And he was always there. When my mother went out, he was there. He was the baby-sitter. I would cry and he would hold me and say it's okay . . . or he'd say let's go do this and let's go do that. He had rabbits. We had the only house in Norfolk with a roof lined with pigeons."

The house was close to Northside Junior High, which Leonard and Tom attended. When they arrived in Norfolk in 1963, Leonard was in the ninth grade and Tom was two years behind. Neoma Drive was a family neighborhood, a good place for them to grow up. And, most important, Sam Hardy was hardly around. After he became a chief machinist's mate, he seldom came home. He was gone on a ship sometimes up to nine months at a stretch. During his absence the family lived happily but frugally.

"My mother did without a lot, for us kids," recalled Ann. "She scrimped and saved and many times she fed us a pot of beans and corn bread. We weren't a well off family. We were what you'd call a lower middle class family."

Leonard was the leader, the big brother, and at times, the surrogate father. He cleaned the yard, fixed things around the house, watched the children, and sometimes shopped for groceries. Sam's children were in awe of their older half-brother. They were especially fascinated with his hobbies. Leonard raised pigeons and rabbits in a shed he and Tom built in the backyard. He had a coin collection, stamps, and model airplanes. He was an avid swimmer and loved to dive off the high board at the public pool. In most of these activities Tom was his sidekick.

"Once they were going down to this place in Norfolk near where we lived, it was called Mason's Creek," Ann recalled. "It's right outside the Navy station. Leonard and [Tom] were catching rats and selling them to the Old Dominion University. To the biology department. We had rats in the garage because they were breeding them. Leonard and [Tom] had more things going on all the time."

One of the "things they had going on" was the Boy Scouts. Leonard and Tom both joined Troop 44, sponsored by a local Presbyterian church, in June 1964. Leonard excelled at scouting. In August 1965 he received the Star Scout rating after winning five merit badges. He completed first class, second class, and star rank in quick succession. Scoutmaster John A. Shepherd considered Leonard a model scout. "He loved to go camping and he was good at it. We used him as an instructor in things like making a fire with flint and steel and in classes on edible roots, berries and nuts."

Sam spoiled his own children. He made sure that Ann, Robert, and Carol had what they wanted while Leonard and Tom had to fend for themselves. As a result, the boys were industrious. They worked after school, doing odd jobs. They earned enough money to buy their own school clothes, which Sam refused to purchase. And they had to buy their own school lunch.

Their independence seemed to enrage him. The more successful Leonard and Tom were, the more resentful Sam became. In depriving the boys, he apparently hoped to prove their dependence on him. Leonard and Tom shattered the illusion. They did not earn enough to pay for the roof over their heads but in every other respect the boys were nearly self-sufficient, and this cut more deeply than simple boyish pranks. It undermined Sam's authority.

Each time Sam Hardy returned from sea, the happy household and Leonard's authority as the oldest child were shattered. He singled out Leonard as a rival for the leadership of the family. Leonard was close to his mother, and the children loved him. Sam was uncomfortable with this, and he made a point of breaking it up. Sam Hardy never touched his own children. It was "Virginia's boys" and their mother who were victimized.

"[Tom] or Leonard would mow the grass and the grass wasn't cut the right way, according to my father," recalled Ann. "Or my dad would walk up into a room and there would be dirty clothes on the floor. Anything he could find, he would look for stuff. I remember one time he took a shovel and hit Leonard with the hard end of it in the head because of some yard work Leonard had done that wasn't right. It was very cruel and very brutal."

Ann was only seven when she first witnessed the abuse. It was so intense that her feelings toward her own father began to change. "I felt guilty. I went through a period when I deeply despised and hated my father. At one point, I probably would've killed him. I loved my brothers dearly. They may have been only my half-brothers but they were my brothers."

Ann could not forget one particularly violent encounter. "Our front porch was made of concrete and . . . I'll never forgive [my father] for this. And I'll never forget it. He took Leonard and [Tom] by the hair and pounded their faces into the cement floor. Over and over again. And I remember there was blood, and my mother was trying to pull him off. I mean, my father is a huge man and she's trying to pull him off. And while he's hitting Leonard and [Tom], he's beating *her*. The babies are in the house—me and [Rob] and baby [Carol]—and my father is beating my mother in front of our eyes."

The brutality scarred the children, especially the Hardy kids. It was especially painful for them to witness the savage treatment of their mother. "A lot of times when the fights were going on between my parents, we could retreat to our rooms," said Ann. "We just wanted to get out of the house or so far away from it because it was frightening. Many times I saw my mother's face bruised and battered, you know, black eyes."

"My father threatened to kill my mother," said Ann. "I heard him actually threaten to kill her." The violence toward Virginia, according to Ann, usually began after she would try to stop Sam from beating Leonard and Tom. Sam would turn on her so viciously that Ann would run outside the house and down the suburban streets screaming for help. "The neighbors didn't pay any attention to what was going on. They didn't seem to care. Thank God people care about that kind of stuff nowadays—spousal abuse —that's what it was."

After the mutiny, when reporters descended on Norfolk asking questions, the neighbors on Neoma Drive and others in Norfolk who knew him were astounded to learn that the mutineer/hijacker was none other than their own Leonard Hardy, the Boy Scout, the boy next door. "He was always friendly and polite. I can't believe he would be mixed up in something like this," Mrs. White, who lived across the street, told reporters. Ann, however, remembered it differently:

> My family had very few friends, because after people realized what was going on in the house they wouldn't come back. They would disappear. And when the neighbors came over or a friend from work, we were scared

to death. We didn't know what was going to happen. We had to be on our best behavior. Dad would act good. He would be a pleasant person to be around and he'd act like the ideal father. After they left, he would beat Leonard brutally because he had eaten too many of the cookies my mother had put out on the table for the visitors. I mean brutally, savagely. And then he would grab the table, which my mother had set up very nicely, and he would upend it, the whole table, breaking the dishes, scattering the food and drinks.

All of us just prayed for him to go back out to sea. The whole house would change the day he left. It would be totally different. Things went back to normal.

Not entirely. Leonard was changing. The friction between him and his stepfather forced him to grow up fast. He lost interest in his hobbies. He neglected his pigeons and rabbits, eventually giving them away or releasing them. "I think about those model planes that Leonard used to make," recalled Ann. "My dad would get in a rage and he'd go in and break them up, and Leonard would have to put them back together. Leonard put all that time and effort into those planes, and my father would just destroy them. Just like he would tear up the ceramics my mother used to make. Something that brought pleasure to you, you weren't allowed to do it, or you weren't allowed to have it in your possession. My father was like a child with a temper tantrum."

Even Leonard's scoutmaster, John Shepherd, saw where the problem lay. "He did real well in scouts until he and his stepfather started having a problem. This was the beginning of his association with other elements."

Melvin Sanders, a classmate from Granby High School, was one of the "other elements." A charismatic troublemaker, Sanders lived only a few blocks away from the Hardys. Leonard drifted into Sanders's orbit and according to Ann, he became one of Sanders's followers. "He kind of looked up to Melvin," said Ann. "I think he was the guy who steered Leonard in the wrong direction, got him out of the Eagle Troop scout stuff. Leonard was very susceptible to influences outside his home life. Anything rebellious."

Leonard and Melvin once took Virginia's car out for a joy ride, according to Ann, and they got caught. Years later, FBI agents investigating the mutiny did a background check on Glatkowski and uncovered several misdemeanor arrests for marijuana possession, being drunk in public, disorderly conduct, and driving without a license. Prior to the mutiny on the *Columbia Eagle,* this was the sum total of Leonard's criminal record. The FBI found that he had no history of serious offenses or violent behavior. Leonard's rap sheet reflected an adolescence that was errant but not truly criminal.

In early 1967, following in the family tradition, Leonard decided to go to sea; not, however, by joining the Navy. He chose the world of commercial shipping, the merchant marine. Leonard wanted to see the world, and this was the only way he could afford to do it. The Vietnam War had opened up enormous opportunities in the merchant marine. The U.S. military was chartering private carriers to haul equipment, goods, and firepower to the war zone on a massive scale. Merchant marine trade schools were doing a brisk business in turning out crews for these ships.

Leonard left Norfolk when he was seventeen years old and headed for the Harry Lundeberg School in Brooklyn, New York. Operated by the Seafarers International Union (SIU), the Lundeberg School taught the skills needed for engine, deck, and steward jobs. The school was a way of joining the union, which was filling its rosters with as many people as it could get, nearly all of them unskilled and inexperienced.

When he signed up at the school, he decided not to use the name "Leonard Hardy," the name he had been known by during his years in Norfolk. No, he would not use that name anymore. He was out of that house. And he would leave that name behind as well. He wanted to distance himself from his family and stake out his own identity. From now on he would go back to the name he was given when he was born: Alvin Glatkowski.

The Lundeberg School was in Red Hook, a tough working-class neighborhood. The heart of the "Hook" was the Erie Basin, a harbor protected by a 2,500-foot breakwater built up largely of ballast dumped from the holds of vessels. Behind this artificial peninsula lay five covered piers and twenty-seven warehouses. The residential blocks of Red Hook were squalid, overcrowded, and hemmed in by railway tracks, freight car sheds, and massive gray loft buildings. On Atlantic Avenue, the main strip, there were shops and coffeehouses with Arabic signs alongside rowdy bars filled with merchant seamen.

This was once the busiest shipping center in the country. Up until the 1930s tens of millions of dollars worth of American lumber, scrap iron, and automobile parts, as well as raw sugar, coffee beans, and rubber from South America, annually cleared through this port on its way to Europe, India, and the Far East. The Depression hit Red Hook hard. Shipping slowed to a crawl and then shifted to the west, to Manhattan and New Jersey. The Lundeberg School opened in 1957, long after the heyday of the Erie Basin. By that time Red Hook had become known for its poverty and crime rather than for its waterfront.

The Hook was like no other place Glatkowski had been before. It was dirty and dangerous. Unlike Norfolk, which was tempered by the disciplined presence of the Navy, and Long Beach, which was all business and no nonsense, the Hook's bars, rooming houses, and whorehouses boiled over with adventure. It was the kind of experience that a spirited young man hungered for.

Glatkowski signed up for a seven-week course in deck department skills. For him and for many young men seeking work on ships, the deck was the most desirable department. The engine room was a filthy, loud, foul-smelling sweatshop, an oven in the summer. There were no horizons to gaze upon in the engine room, just a numbing maze of pipes and catwalks. The steward department was even less attractive. These were the cooks and bakers, messmen and pantrymen, and that lowest of all jobs on a ship: the bedroom steward (BR), the one who makes up the beds of the licensed personnel and cleans their rooms. To Glatkowski, these jobs were as tedious on ship as they were on the beach. No janitor job for him. He wanted to sail on deck, feeling the breeze in his hair and the spray of water. He looked forward to seeing foreign ports as they approached and the endless horizons as they departed. On 17 April 1967, Glatkowski received his U.S. merchant mariner's document, number Z-1244028. He could work at entry-level jobs in all three departments.

In September 1967, after working on a few ships, Glatkowski turned eighteen. He faced a critical decision: he was required to register for the draft. He did not agree with the war in Vietnam. He was convinced that the killing was senseless, and he was determined not to go. Like most young men of his generation who were opposed to the war, he had few choices. Being in the merchant marine would not provide him with a deferment; the military granted deferments to merchant seamen only under very special circumstances. He could try to get some other deferment or even slip away to Canada. Instead, he registered in October 1967, and he was given 1A status. Later, he said that he had successfully petitioned to change his status to 1AO, the letter O indicating that he was a conscientious objector.

During the Vietnam War, a person who wished to register as a conscientious objector (CO) was required to submit a written petition to the army. The CO applicant was then interviewed by a chaplain or priest, a military psychiatrist, and an investigating officer from the military. The CO had to prove to these people that he sincerely objected to taking part in war and this objection had to be based on moral or ethical training and belief, or on religious training and belief. Like his namesake, Alvin York, Glatkowski said that he told the military that he refused to participate in the killing, but for moral reasons rather than religious. Also like his namesake, Glatkowski was an objector, but he remained eligible for military service.

In the late 1960s, Glatkowski continued shipping out regularly, usually on deck as an ordinary, but also in the engine department, as a wiper. He was on India runs, which also went to Karachi, Durban, and the Cape Verde Islands, as well as runs to Africa, Japan, and Korea. His record shows nine voyages from 1967 to 1970.

When Glatkowski was on the beach, he sometimes lived with others in semi-communal homes in Norfolk, not far from where he had grown up. With these companions, he became immersed in antiwar activism. He later described himself, during this period, as an "extremely immature Marxist, leaning more toward being an anarchist than a Communist."

"He lived in downtown Norfolk," Ann recalled, "over near Old Dominion University, which was the hippie community of Norfolk. It was right outside the college there. My mom took us over there a couple of times and his apartment was what you would call really psychedelic. I mean you could tell they were into psychedelic drugs. And the typical little hippie girls sitting on the front porch. There were no beds, no furniture. Just the walls painted real bizarre and a little palette for a bed on the floor."

Although he did not live at home anymore, Glatkowski made a point of visiting his family whenever he returned from the sea, and whenever Sam was not around. "He was always giving us gifts from his trips," said Ann. "I still have an amethyst he brought back for me. He got great joy out of bringing back pieces of rare sandalwood, or fragrant oils. He was always bringing things back. And these people at his house were living off him. He would just give and give and give. This was the type of lifestyle that he led. He would always share things."

In 1968, Glatkowski caught the SS *Hermina*, a Vietnam run. It would be his only trip to Vietnam. What he saw affected him so strongly that, years later, he would look back and write about it in an unfinished, autobiographical screenplay.

> You should have seen those [soldiers]. . . . They're shaking all the time. Scared outta their minds and sick of what they're doing. They don't know who they're killing most of the time. Everything is death. The whole place smells like rotten dead stuff. . . .
>
> I wandered off into the jungle after our ship docked off the coast last time. It looked so beautiful. Reminded me of how I used to go exploring in the Everglades in Florida as a kid. I came into this village and these gunmen came through. Vietnamese, maybe from the North. Maybe South. They could have killed me. I obviously didn't belong there, but we ended up eating something and they left and I left. I don't know why I'm telling you about it except that maybe if I'd have been armed or if I'd obviously looked like a soldier maybe I would have been dead. I must have looked harmless, a harmless idiot in the middle of a crazy war. A war that will go on as long as they make money off it.

Glatkowski wrote that what most disturbed him were the burn victims, whose faces and bodies were scarred. "Now they're using a bomb called napalm. Yeah. Do you know what it does? It sticks to the skin and burns and there's no way to get it off. It mutilates innocent people, children. We carry it over in ships, they load it into planes and when they drop they explode and go everywhere like a jelly. There's no escape."

In October 1968, while sailing on the *Hermina* back to the United States, Glatkowski was warned for failure to perform duties. The trip, obviously, had unsettled him. When the *Hermina* came back from the Zone, it paid off in Long Beach, so Glatkowski remained there, staying with his Aunt Emma in southern California. He got a job on the beach, pumping gas. He went to the SIU hall in Terminal Island once in a while, but the only jobs were to the Zone, so he decided to stop shipping out for a while. After the *Hermina*, he had vowed never to take another Vietnam run.

Glatkowski's decision not to return to the Zone was also influenced by another startling event, the death of his closest childhood friend. Nicknamed

Jettie, he had always dreamed of flying jets. Glatkowski said he was deeply affected not only by the fact that his friend was gunned down while piloting a fighter plane, but also the way in which he found out about it. Glatkowski included this incident in his screenplay. In the scenario, "Alvin" is in Aunt Emma's house and he notices a magazine on a table, a well-known *Life Magazine* edition featuring photos of all Americans who had died that week in Vietnam.

> (Alvin moves into the living room and picks up Life Magazine off the coffee table. There are pictures across the front, of soldiers killed in Vietnam. He stops suddenly in shocked disbelief.) "Oh my god! It can't be. Oh no, no! It's Jettie. There's a fucking picture of my buddy here. He's dead. He's fucking dead. Jesus. I can't believe it. He went to Nam and got himself fuckin' killed." (He sits on the edge of the sofa with the magazine before him, shaking his head, on the verge of tears.) "No, no . . . it shouldn't have been Jettie. My best friend. I can't believe it. . . . It's a goddamn waste . . . the whole war is a waste. . . . We're leveling the whole country and it's not going to do a damn bit of good."

At the gas station, Glatkowski worked with a guy who introduced him to his sister Flo, a dark-haired, dark-eyed beauty who looked like she had at least some Indian forebears. Flo had grown up in Goleta, near Santa Barbara. For her, Glatkowski was part of a world with which she had had little contact: hippies, revolution, and seamen. She was attracted and fascinated. They spent days and nights together.

Glatkowski wanted to spend his birthday with his mother, so he went east, arriving in Norfolk on 11 September 1969, his twentieth birthday. At this time, according to his mother, Glatkowski said that he intended to upgrade himself and get a rating, or maybe even try to get into the Merchant Marine Academy. He told his mother about Flo, and one night he called her. During the call, according to Glatkowski's mother, Flo's father got on the line and asked to speak to Virginia. He said that his daughter was pregnant, and he insisted that Glatkowski return to Long Beach to marry Flo. Glatkowski complied.

One week after his arrival in Norfolk, one week after his birthday, Glatkowski and Flo were married in Long Beach. Flo had been hesitant—she knew that her parents and Glatkowski despised one another—but she did it for the sake of the baby. Their shotgun wedding was strange and unsettling. To Flo, that day showed both sides of Glatkowski's complex personality. Soon after waking he had taken care of her during a bout of morning sickness, patiently pressing a damp cloth on her forehead as she knelt over the toilet, throwing up. Then that night, after the wedding, when Flo's father and uncle grudgingly told Glatkowski that—for Flo's sake—they could get him a "good position" at McDonnell-Douglas, Glatkowski erupted with the kind of violent diatribe he had often hurled at her and her parents: *A revolution is coming! And when it comes, I'm going to be out in the streets with a rifle and if you're inside your nice, safe houses, I'll be shooting at you!*

Before the night was over, Flo's father said that it was high time for a divorce. It was not just Glatkowski's talk about revolution and overturning society that bothered Flo. It was also his indecision. His "wishy-washiness." She saw him as a follower who was ready to go along with anything new and exciting. One day he would talk about joining the army. The next, he wanted to go back east. The next, he would talk about going back to school. He would make a life-changing decision one moment, then a few days later come up with something completely different about what he wanted to do with his life.

For his part, Glatkowski was sick of living at Flo's parents' house. Glatkowski and Flo rented an apartment that he called "decadently bourgeois": nice furniture, wall-to-wall carpets, pool, courtyard. They were there for a month when Glatkowski—restless and angry for reasons he could not define, frustrated at working at a gas station—caught a vacation run to Alaska. It was three weeks as an ordinary on the SS *Lompoc,* a baby supertanker. During those cold days on deck he injured his hand, but he made good money. He liked coming back and throwing a few hundred-dollar bills in the air to show Flo that he could make money without help from her family. What was bad about coming home was that Flo had moved out of the apartment and back into her parents' house.

Glatkowski, resigned to living on the beach again, looked for a job and took the first one he found. He began working for two dollars an hour as a handyman at a retirement home. In early 1970 he was back at his hated in-laws' house and working at a crummy job.

This was not the life Glatkowski had dreamed of for himself. In fact, this was hell. The arguments with his in-laws were not merely bickering, they were screaming, insulting fights, teetering on the verge of violence.

Flo, who played the role of peacemaker, began to think about committing suicide. One night, as she heard Glatkowski and her parents screaming, she swallowed a mouthful of pills, not even sure what they were. She gagged, threw up, and survived.

But Glatkowski did not know if he could survive any more in this situation. As he watched his teenage wife's belly get bigger and bigger, his patience for this living arrangement—for this life that had chosen him—had gone way beyond its breaking point.

4 TERMINAL ISLAND

Long Beach, California, February 1970

As Clyde McKay went from the glaring southern California light into the dark SIU hall at Terminal Island, his eyes adjusted. He looked around. There were about fifty or sixty men in the hall. They were bullshitting, playing cribbage, milling about, smoking, waiting for the next call.

McKay looked at the large shipping board. SEAFARERS INTERNATIONAL UNION was bannered horizontally across the top. Down the left side, vertically, were names of ships that were crewing: *Connecticut, Seatrain Savannah, Mayaguez, Monterey, St. Louis, Calmar, Ponce, Seamar, Marymar.* Below each ship's name was a destination; some said CW (for coastwise) and some said IC (for intercoastal). Across the top of the shipping board were the job categories, divided into the three departments: deck, engine, and steward. Wherever jobs were available, a number was written in the box formed by the cross-hatch. There were some jobs available, in all departments, and almost all were for ships going to the Zone. Even the ships that were listed as coastwise, those going to Seattle or Portland or San Francisco, everyone knew that from there they were headed to Southeast Asia.

McKay went up to the agent/dispatcher. Jerry Brown, age twenty-eight, was slim, and of average height, wore glasses, and spoke with a Cajun accent. McKay told Brown that he was a B-book fireman and asked how things were going. Brown told McKay that he could have his pick of ships. There was always a need for a fireman. McKay moved away from the board.

The men in the hall were mostly white, some blacks sitting by themselves, a few Asians. A half-dozen Filipinos—most likely cooks—and two or three Hawaiians. McKay had mixed feelings about his fellow seamen. His politics had taught him that they were the proletariat, the salt of the earth. He also knew that, for the most part, they had no sympathy for unions or for the antiwar movement. Some had families and lived more or less normal lives when on the beach, but many were rootless men whose isolated lives on ship extended to isolated lives ashore.

Though their work took them to exotic ports, most of these men lived insular lives and never really traveled far from the world in which they felt comfortable. Whatever the continent or country, in war or peace, they simply went from one redlight district to another. They all had numbing similarity; only the women's language and skin color varied.

At every table in the union hall, there were the familiar phrases, like the punctuation marks of every conversation.

A sailor without a knife is like a whore without a cunt.

He's just a boll weevil—loo-oo-kin' for a home, don't wanna do no work.

In the old days we had wooden ships and iron men, now it's the other way around.

First your money, then your honey, then you lose your shoes.

Lookin' for sea-pussy, playing drop the soap in the shower.

Somebody Jonah'd the ship, didn't pay his whore.

My old lady was screwing some Jody and spending the allotment checks.

Norwegian steam . . . Dutch courage . . . Ragheads . . . Squareheads . . .

Someone mentioned the NMU, the National Maritime Union, the rival seafaring union. Predictably, someone else said softly, so as not to be overheard: *NMU . . . that stands for Niggers, Mexicans and other Undesirables, don't it?* Everyone at the table laughed and nodded, as if they had never heard it before.

In 1970, as it had been since its founding, the SIU was still largely segregated; almost all men of color were in the steward department. The SIU's racial make-up meant that it would be rare for a white man to serve a black or brown man, while the opposite was quite common. Even the work language reflected the SIU's racial segregation. For example, in the SIU, the winch drum on which wire rope was rolled was called a "niggerhead," as in: "take a few turns around the niggerhead."

There were other divides besides the racial one. In the hall, the older guys usually sat separately from the younger guys. Just like on every ship. At sea, the middle-aged men hung out in the messroom, drank booze on the sly, played cards, and talked about the price of sex. As if living in a parallel universe, the young guys hung out on the fantail, smoked marijuana, listened to music, and laughed at the men who hung out midships.

McKay felt that the older seamen looked at him and at all the other young seamen with suspicion, if not outright loathing. He was not wrong. The middle-aged seamen, who had served during World War II, had run great risks and taken losses in a just war to save the world. Then, after the war, they had struggled for many years to build up their union standing, had put up with years of hardship to get their "A" book, and had suffered through the lean years when a seaman had to have a full book. They had been on the beach, sometimes waiting for months before being able to catch a ship, usually only as a vacation replacement.

Then came the Vietnam War. The war not only created an enormous number of jobs for regular seamen, it created a surge of new seamen: young men who had dropped out of dead-end jobs and wanted some adventure. From 1965 through 1970, anyone could easily get a Z-card—all such cards began with "Z" followed by a string of numbers—and then could just as easily get a job on a ship. It was common for someone to get a Z-card, pass a physical (at a cost of thirty-five dollars), go to one of the maritime unions, and catch a ship, all in one day. And if one caught a pier-head-jump—a ship already pulling out to sea—it was actually possible to get a Z-card in the morning and be working on a ship in the Pacific Ocean that night.

The unions not only needed bodies to man these ships, they also needed men with ratings (AB, fireman, oiler), and there were not enough of these rated men to go around. That is why the unions were permitted to send men with only three months' experience as wipers, or six months as ordinary, to a union-sponsored six-week course that would help them pass the Coast Guard test and get them a rating. The result was a slew of inexperienced and sometimes incompetent ABs, firemen, and oilers.

In short, this was a time when virtually anybody who had dreamed of shipping out could do so. Anybody could live out the universal fantasy: sail the wide ocean, see a war, go to whorehouses, climb up a mast, steer a huge ship.

Anyone with a Z-card could make some quick bucks, because on most of the Military Sea Transportion Service (MSTS)–chartered ships there was plenty of overtime, especially for the deck department. You could save anywhere from one to two thousand dollars per month (a goodly sum in the 1960s), provided you did not blow it all on whores, booze, or poker. Or get plastered and robbed your first night in port. Which happened, on occasion.

Seamen, young or old, including McKay, were ornery about the right to throw their money around. It was a comment of respect toward another seaman: *He loves to spend his money.* They got paid off in one-hundred dollar bills, and it almost seemed like Monopoly bills. McKay had heard seamen say it many times, and he felt it too: If I want to throw my payoff into the drink, it's my goddamn right to do so. And if a seaman did blow his whole payoff, it was no big deal. There was always another ship.

By early 1970, however, the situation was changing. There was a feeling that this period—during which seamen could ship out any time they wanted—would soon come to an end. When it did end, merchant ships would again become the province of real seamen, men with full books and a lifetime commitment to the sea.

McKay listened to Jerry Brown, the dispatcher, who sounded as if he were personally giving out the jobs. It was a familiar rhythm: *I got the St. Louis going up to Oakland, then to the Zone with bonus cargo. Double your base pay while the vessel's within fifty miles of the Zone, plus ten percent bonus till you offload. I need a fireman . . . an oiler . . . an AB. . . . I got some steward jobs too. I want full books first. Then B-books. You C-card men, hang in there, I might have something for you-all. If you wanna go to work today, come on up here.*

With his slim build and reading glasses, Brown was the opposite of the standard image of a union goon. As patrolman-dispatcher, he was the man who went out to meet incoming SIU ships, pay off the men, and handle any beefs that might have come up during the trip. He also dealt with the job calls every hour, working from lists phoned in by the shipping companies. He would make sure that full-book men got priority over B-books, B-books over C-cards; if two men with the same union rating threw in on a job, he made sure that the older card got out first.

In his gentlemanly southern way, Brown generally tried to make sure that known troublemakers did not get shipped out and that anyone who was falling-down drunk got reasonably dried out before getting on a ship. But there was only so much winnowing that a dispatcher could do. His main obligation was to the union, who was paying his salary and whose contracts with the shipping companies obligated them to send each ship enough warm bodies with the minimum qualifications.

McKay, looking around for someplace to sit, saw two young guys who were playing chess, a game he liked but had not had much time to play recently. He approached the table. One of the seamen was Bruce Gray. The other was Alvin Glatkowski. Gray later told the FBI that he had met Glatkowski at the union hall a few days earlier and the two of them were playing chess when McKay approached them.

Glatkowski, however, remembers meeting McKay differently. Finding a wallet on the floor while he was in the union hall on his own, he saw the photo on the Z-card inside and located its owner, McKay, who was playing chess with Gray. The three men struck up a quick acquaintance, the kind of camaraderie that came readily to young seamen, who tended to gravitate toward one another in SIU hiring halls. Like most young seamen, they talked about jobs, ships going to the Zone, and the extra wages paid on vessels that carried bonus cargo.

At the next job call, on the hour, McKay, Glatkowski, and Gray walked up to the dispatcher's lectern. When the call ended, the three drifted sideways to the bulletin board. They saw a black-bordered news article thumbtacked to the board: "U.S. Government-Chartered Munitions Ship Sinks in Heavy Seas." They came closer and read that the *Badger State,* an NMU ship, had gone down two months earlier with a load of napalm. Most of the crew had died. McKay said, *You think it was sabotage?*

Glatkowski said that he looked around self-consciously. Had any of the seamen around them heard what McKay said? It did not seem so.

McKay pressed on; he asked if Glatkowski thought that the *Badger State* could have been blown up. *You know, by men working on it?* To Glatkowski, this comment was so completely off the wall—especially with other seamen milling around them—that he did not know how to respond. He suggested that they not talk about it here.

McKay, Glatkowski, and Gray walked to Joe Biff's, a nearby bar. Almost immediately after they came in, a song came on the jukebox: "I'm just an Okie from Muskogee." This was not just any song. It was a twangy, country-

and-western homage to salt-of-the-earth patriots, those who went to Vietnam and despised what was going on at the degenerate coasts where hippie-yippie types were driving all that was good and decent in America into the sea.

McKay noticed two guys shooting pool and made sarcastic comments aimed at them: Hey, we got us a couple of Okies from Muskogee over here. True Americans. From the Heartland. McKay, Glatkowski, and Gray all laughed when the two pool shooters disgustedly walked out.

Glatkowski and McKay did not go back to the union hall that day. Instead, they talked about themselves. They exchanged anecdotes and sea stories. Both were veterans of Fantail Clubs, that part of the crew found on every Vietnam ship, and most other U.S. vessels, that hung out back aft and got high. They talked about their adventures, and to Glatkowski's astonishment, McKay said that, among other things, he had been in the French Foreign Legion; jumped two ships; spent more than a year in Barcelona prison; and wandered in the Sahara, where he nearly died.

McKay's demeanor was self-deprecating. He spoke slowly, carefully choosing his words. He seemed to downplay everything, making the truth of it unquestionable. It was almost beyond belief that a twenty-five-year-old had done so much, had had so many adventures.

Glatkowski had his own stories to tell: demonstrations and marches, Marxism, anarchy, Black Panthers. They shared a resentment for the way America had "oppressed freedom movements at home and abroad." An immediate bond formed between them, a feeling of shared future.

The next day Glatkowski and McKay met again at the union hall, then spent much of the day hanging out at Joe Biff's. Glatkowski talked about his trip to Vietnam on the *Hermina;* he described how he had wandered into a relocation center outside of Cam Ranh, and how—when he walked out of there at night—he had almost been shot at by U.S. troops. They talked about napalm and about what they called "Nixon's illegal bombing" of Viet Cong sanctuaries. They found that they saw eye to eye on many issues.

That night McKay, Glatkowski, and Gray hitchhiked to Gray's apartment. There, Glatkowski and McKay talked some more. They realized that Gray either would not or could not be part of these kinds of discussions. With loud music on, they could talk without Gray's being aware of what they were saying.

Glatkowski was impressed by how articulate and well-read McKay was, as well as passionate and idealistic. McKay quoted from William Fulbright's *The Arrogance of Power:* "We should support nationalism rather than fight Communism"; from *Viva Che!:* "The time has come for each to take his place in the fight"; from Bernard Fall's *Street Without Joy:* "A guerrilla war mounted from outside a nation is a crude act of international vandalism." He said that America was the enemy of popular revolution and that the Vietnam War was the most recent testing ground for America's imperialist blood lust.

McKay said that he felt guilty about having worked on ammo ships to Vietnam. If German civilians during World War II were responsible because they refused to see and hear the horror that was going on around them, then the two of them were worse, much worse. They had taken part, had actively helped out, in an immoral enterprise. Glatkowski agreed. But the question was, what could they do about it?

The next day vicious Santa Ana conditions prevailed along the coast. One-hundred-mile-per-hour winds spread fires into the dry timber, sailboat masts cracked like matchsticks in the high gusts, and ships' mooring lines chafed with the heavy tides.

Glatkowski and McKay met at an all-you-can-eat lunch place in San Pedro, overlooking the water. If they really wanted to stop a cargo of ammo from reaching the Zone, what could they do? At first, they joked around. Wouldn't it be cool to put acid in a ship's drinking water?

Little by little, McKay became more serious. He wondered if there really was a way to stop a load of bombs from getting there. Supposing such a thing could occur, would Glatkowski be willing to take part? Glatkowski thought about it. Well, maybe, but only if they could get more people involved. But what if it was just the two of them?

McKay then said, *Okay, let's say we could get more people involved, would you be willing to do it?* Again, Glatkowski thought about it. *Maybe,* he said finally, *maybe . . . but only if it could be done without hurting anyone.* McKay did not let go of the idea. *Okay, let's suppose that's possible . . . let's suppose the cargo could be stopped or destroyed without hurting anyone.*

Glatkowski wondered how somebody could do that. McKay shrugged. It's not that he had thought it all out, he was just talking. Speculating. Everything was framed hypothetically. *Let's imagine. Let's suppose.*

During the next few days, Glatkowski and McKay met at the hall regularly, went to lunch, hung out at Joe Biff's, then had dinner somewhere in Long Beach or San Pedro. Inevitably, the subject would come back to sabotage and stopping a load of ammo.

Glatkowski had met other seamen who thought about these things. But they were just bullshitters, guys who would grab the next ammo ship, work all the overtime they could, chase pussy in the Zone, then talk against the war all the way back. Bullshitters. Glatkowski felt that McKay was different; he seemed ready to do more than just talk.

McKay's repeating refrain was that "something" had to be done. Drastic action. That it was up to them. McKay said that if he could, he would blow up one of those fucking ships. Glatkowski's heart skipped a beat: destroy a ship?

Glatkowski wondered aloud how that could be done. McKay said that he had a pistol, a Walther P38 semi-automatic. He said he had bought it in Escondido over Christmas. And ammo. He suggested that Glatkowski should get one for himself. Glatkowski said that he could not buy a gun; he was under twenty-one. McKay offered to buy it for him. Glatkowski said he did not have the money. McKay shrugged. They would pick up a gun during the trip.

Glatkowski felt that, with each conversation, his defenses were being torn down. Not only that, but the stakes were being ratcheted up. First, it was the idea. Then, imagining it happening. Now they were seeing themselves doing it.

Glatkowski finally told Flo that he had quit his handyman job so that he could ship out again. He told her that he was sick and tired of that job. Two bucks an hour and no hope of moving up. He would make good money on a ship, money they would need for the baby.

Flo felt, in her heart, that his going away would be a relief. Over these last couple of weeks Glatkowski had not only had screaming bouts with her parents, he had argued with her as well, about every little thing. Hours at a time, they would hardly talk to one another. It had gotten so bad that the previous week she had escaped from the tension for a few days—she had gone to visit family in Goleta, where she had grown up.

But now she was back and she was packing his two suitcases for him. She did it while hardly saying a word. Glatkowski thought she was angry because he might not be back in time for the birth of the baby. As always, Glatkowski took an optimistic view, promising to be back in two months.

SIU Hall, Terminal Island, Tuesday, 17 February 1970

Jerry Brown, the dispatcher, opened up the glass window to the job board and wrote some new ships' names and erased the names of those that had left port. He chalked numbers inside the cross-hatched squares, showing which jobs were available. McKay surveyed the board: some new ships, some old ones. The *Columbia Eagle* caught his eye. It had come down from the Bay Area, from Port Chicago, and it was still missing crew members, including a fireman. Brown wrote "S.E.Asia" under its name and scribbled "bonus" on the same line, next to the ship's name. Bonus cargo. Ammo. Napalm, probably.

While Glatkowski and Gray waited for the next call, drinking bad coffee from a vending machine and smoking cigarettes, McKay went to speak privately with the dispatcher. Brown later said that McKay came up and told him that he would take the fireman's job on the *Eagle*. Brown jumped at the suggestion, telling McKay that he did not need to wait for the next call. Before giving Brown his registration card, McKay said that he had two friends who also wanted to be on that ship and pointed to Glatkowski and Gray.

Brown said that he had two jobs left on the *Columbia Eagle*, both in the steward department. Pantryman and BR. McKay thought a moment. *Is that all there is?* Brown nodded. McKay said okay, they would take the jobs. All three. He gave Brown his registration card.

McKay went back to the table where Glatkowski and Gray were sitting and told them they could get jobs on the *Columbia Eagle.* But there weren't any engine or deck jobs left. Glatkowski would have to work in the steward department. Glatkowski and Gray compared cards. Gray had the older one. Gray said he wanted the pantryman job; Glatkowski would have to settle for BR. Glatkowski told McKay that he had never sailed as BR and that he did not know the first thing about it. McKay scoffed at this. It's just doing sanitary for the licensed guys. Glatkowski knew that, but he felt it was a boot-licking job. McKay told Glatkowski to keep his eye on the larger picture. They would be together, on the same ship.

Near them, at the lectern, Brown waited.

McKay pleaded with Glatkowski to throw in his card. If the younger man refused to do so, McKay said he would pull his own card back. Glatkowski still hesitated. Nothing might come of their sabotage ideas. Up to now, it had all been castles in the air. A whole lot of "what ifs." But he sensed that McKay was not a bullshitter. If Glatkowski agreed to take this job on the *Columbia Eagle,* it could mean the end of the life he had been living.

The question was: Was the life he had been living worth keeping? What if he did not take this job? What if he stayed on the beach? He could get a job doing what he did before—working as a two-dollar-an-hour handyman. Or pumping gas. Living in a small apartment, Sunday visits with the in-laws.

Fuck that.

Or . . . he could give in to Flo's parents and get a "good" job, a nice apartment, become a proper bourgeois.

Fuck that too.

Or . . . he could go on shipping out. But could he? He had a B-book and no rating. If shipping got any worse—and it looked like it was going to—he might be able to pick up entry-level jobs on ships going to the Zone. Other than that, there would not be any work for him at sea either.

A dead end no matter where he looked. Except in one direction: Clyde McKay, who was urging him to throw in on this ship. If Glatkowski chose to go on the *Columbia Eagle,* he and McKay would be planning a way to throw a wrench into the war machinery. He would be doing something big, something meaningful, much more meaningful than anything he had ever dreamed of.

The *Columbia Eagle* at anchor, Subic Bay, 13 April 1970.
U.S. Navy

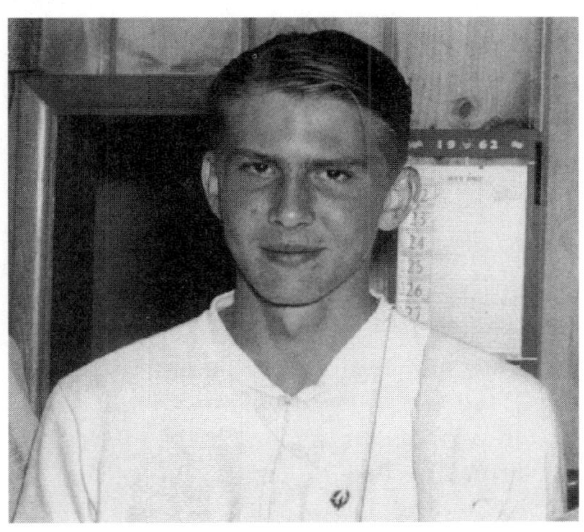

Clyde McKay, age eighteen, just before signing on his first merchant ship.
Courtesy of Jean Bair

Special Investigator Don Webb and Lt. Cdr. Norman Idleberg, two members of the Naval Intelligence Service investigative team, on the *Columbia Eagle* displaying the American ensign with a peace sign painted on it by the mutineers.
Courtesy of Norman Idleberg

The mutiny investigation team ties up alongside the *Columbia Eagle. Left to right (men without hats):* Special Investigator Don Webb, USCG Lt. Cdr. Philip Spiker, and USN Lt. Cdr. Norman Idleberg.
Courtesy of Norman Idleberg

Ordinary seaman Billy Campbell lowers a line from the *Columbia Eagle* to the boat carrying the mutiny investigators.
Courtesy of Norman Idleberg

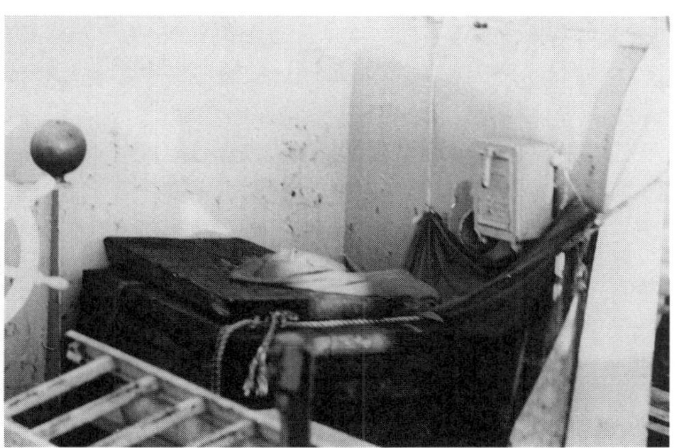

The remains of the "hippie tent," where the mutineers slept, on the poop deck of the *Columbia Eagle*.
Courtesy of Norman Idleberg

Herbert Gunn, third mate.
Courtesy of Roger Hammett

Marco Smigliani, able seaman.
Courtesy of Roger Hammett

Walter Drabina, chief engineer.
Courtesy of Roger Hammett

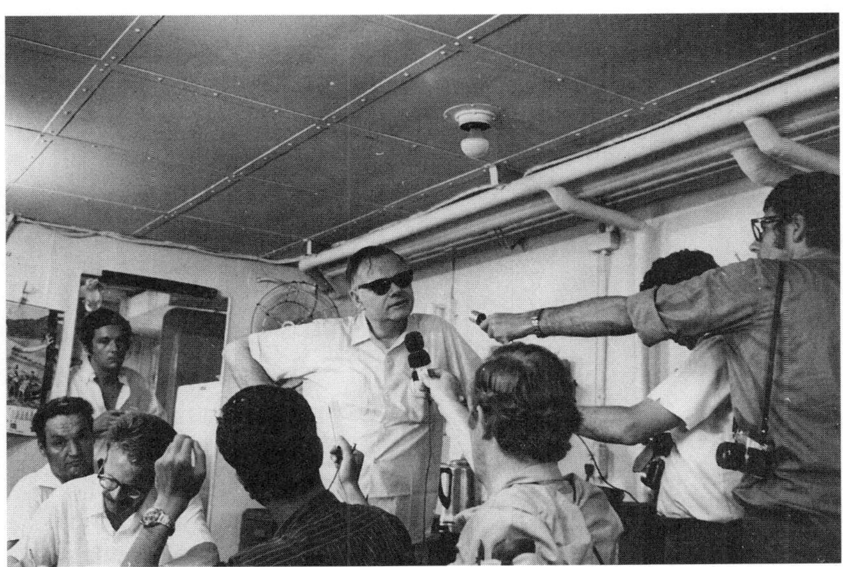

Capt. Donald Swann talks to newsmen about the *Columbia Eagle* mutiny, 8 April 1970.
United Press International

Clyde McKay *(left)* and Alvin Glatkowski *(right)* are interviewed by Fred Emery of the *London Times* at the Chrui Changwar naval base, 2 July 1970.
Associated Press

Prison ship at the Chrui Changwar naval base, where Clyde McKay, Alvin Glatkowski, and Larry Humphrey were held.
Courtesy of Andrew Antippas

Clyde McKay and Alvin Glatkowski pose before the Mekong River prison ship, 3 July 1970.
Associated Press

Larry Humphrey in Phnom Penh, 12 September 1970.
Courtesy of Martha Honey

Clyde McKay
in Phnom Penh,
12 September 1970.
Courtesy of Martha Honey

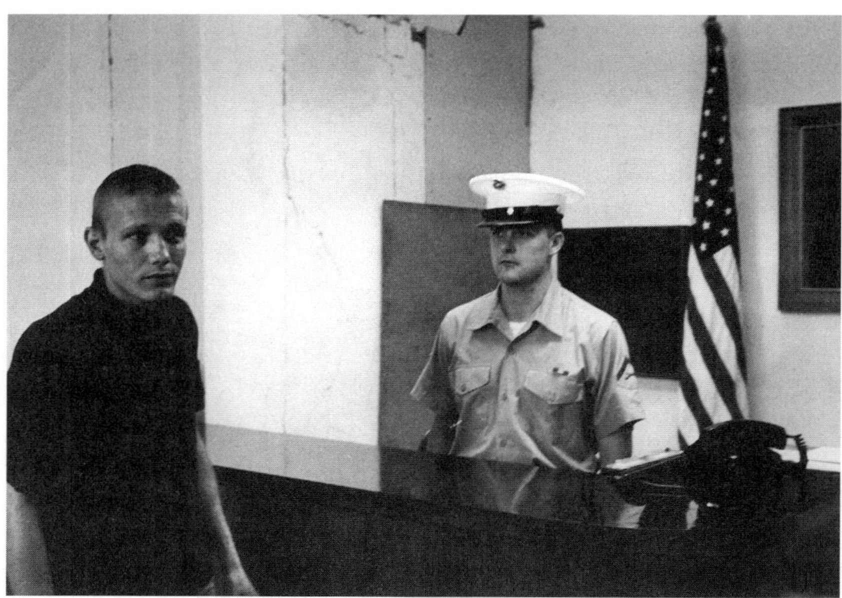

Alvin Glatkowski *(left)* surrenders at the American embassy in Phnom Penh, 15 December 1970.
Associated Press

5 LETTING GO

Long Beach/At Sea

Because Flo did not drive, Glatkowski was taken out to the docks by his mother-in-law, Betty Longenecker. Most of the trip was carried out in silence, both of them trying not to argue. One thing Glatkowski did say, however, was that once he got paid off, maybe he would move with Flo and the baby back to Virginia. They arrived at Long Beach Pier at 6 A.M. Glatkowski thanked his mother-in-law and both were relieved when she pulled away and Glatkowski went toward the ship.

The *Columbia Eagle* was moored at pier 245J. A Maritime Commission Victory-type freight vessel, shaped from stem to stern in a classic V pattern, it was unlike modern container ships, which tend to be blocky and rectangular. The bow of the *Eagle,* with its raised fo'c'sle head, was peaked; at the after end of the ship, a raised poop deck made the stern look slightly peaked as well. The ship's house, where all the men lived and where the bridge and wheelhouse were located, stood slightly aft of the center of the vessel. Forward of the house there were three holds, and aft there were two. Looming above these holds at a working angle, booms webbed with blocks and cables stood ready to load cargo. Looked at from the pier, the ship's gear resembled giant fingers playing cat's cradle.

Built by the U.S. Navy in 1945 at Portland, Oregon, and originally christened the *Pierre Victory,* the vessel was designed to carry supplies and munitions to the European and South Pacific theatres in World War II. After the war, like many other Victory ships, she was decommissioned. In 1968 it was bought by the Columbia Steamship Company of Portland, Oregon, renamed the *Columbia Eagle,* and used for commercial shipping. The *Eagle* weighed 7,606.42 gross tons. Its registered length was 440 feet, breadth 62 feet, and 35 feet in depth. Although reasonably well-maintained, the *Eagle* had taken scores of trips during its long career. Although a functional vessel, it was old and tired and looked its age, with rust eating away at the hull and superstructure.

On deck, the hatches were open, revealing stacks of wooden crates that had been loaded by stevedores over the last few days. This was the cargo. The ship's manifest listed a variety of warheads packed within these simple boxes, including 90-mm, 20-mm, and 40-mm bomb cartridges, 66-mm rockets, dummy cartridges, rocket mortar, nose rockets, depth charges, propeller assemblies for torpedoes, ammo components, Hawk missiles, small arms, and air defense guided missiles. Carrying approximately 1,750 tons of bombs below, the cargo included a number of crates that were stamped with labels that read "Napalm B batch, number 840 Mfd. 717 lb., American Electric, Inc., La Mirada California." Most of the *Eagle*'s cargo was napalm bombs, the 500-pound (BLU-27) or 750-pound (BLU-32) types.

When Glatkowski boarded the *Eagle,* carpenters were still building cribs to secure the crates. It was delicate work. The smallest mistake or accident could spell disaster. Three days earlier, a fire had broken out in the hold. The sound of fire bells on a vessel carrying thousands of tons of heavy firepower is a deadly serious matter. The men had rushed to their fire stations and rolled out hoses, preparing to avert a catastrophe. The captain called the engine room for water pressure. It turned out to be an electrical fire on one of the forklifts that shifted the ammo crates around the holds. The flames were put out quickly. "No damage to ship or cargo," the ship's logbook reported. The incident, however, had shaken up the men. They were nervous. Seamen tend to be a superstitious lot and some on the *Eagle* considered the fire a bad omen, similar to a red sky in the morning.

At 6:25 the pilot came aboard. A tugboat was made fast to the *Columbia Eagle.* The captain ordered standby engines, a signal to the engine room to be ready to change speed at a moment's notice. Almost immediately, the gangway was raised by a couple of deckhands. Dockside workers threw the loosened mooring lines off the bollards, the huge metallic mushrooms that sprouted every few yards along the pier. Then the *Eagle*'s deckhands reeled in the lines: bow line, stern line, spring line. The men singled up on the lines, leaving one forward and one aft. At 6:48 A.M. longshoremen released the last two mooring lines, and winches rolled them through the water, then through a chock, and finally up into the ship. Deckhands flaked the wet mooring lines on deck. The tug gently pulled and nudged the vessel out of its berth, while on the bridge the pilot gave instructions to the AB on the wheel: Steady as she goes.

The tug released its tie to the ship, which moved on its own out to anchorage. The hook was dropped, and then the paw was placed on the anchor chain, leaving five shots in the water. At the top of the gangway, the chief mate posted the sailing board: "Ship sails 5 PM today February 19th, 1970, for sea. H. E. Morgan, c/o."

The *Eagle* had been moved out to an anchorage in the harbor, away from the port, where it would meet with a barge that carried cargo crates. These crates, containing fuses and detonators, would be put into cribs and then lashed on deck, to keep them away from the munitions in the holds. The fuses were highly volatile and would be the first to ignite under intense heat. The logbook does not specify why this cargo was loaded from a barge at anchorage; it was either a safety consideration or because the *Eagle* had used up its valuable dock time.

After the cargo was loaded, the stevedores used the booms to put the pontoons—enormously heavy box rectangles of steel—on top of the hatches. Once all the pontoons were on, the *Eagle*'s deckhands went from hatch to hatch. The sailors spread themselves around, unfolding a tarp. One side waved the heavy tarp while the other side pulled, gaining inches, first one way, then the other, until the tarp was evenly overlapped on all sides without any bubbles or creases. Then they tucked in the corners, folded it over, and placed it neatly inside the cleats. Jamming the battens between tarp and cleats, they drove in the wedges. The cross-battens were then placed thwartships across the top of the hatch. The deck crew moved aft in this manner until all five hatches were secured.

Securing gear was the next duty. Again, going from hatch to hatch, the bosun, James "Tennessee" Northcutt, placed men at the winches and guy lines: inboard, outboard, schooner. Each man, watching the bosun for signals, had his own part in the group dance. Steam winches hissed and clanged, letting out billows of white smoke, wire was run out, preventers put on, and guy lines maneuvered, until all the booms were secure. By giving way on one guy line and pulling with the other, by inching the wire ropes back and forth, the men moved the booms up or down and left or right, until they finally found the cradle.

On this day, on the *Columbia Eagle*, the routine did not go smoothly. The bosun and the day-man, Norm Pettersen, were seasoned deckhands, and some of the other ABs had been around the block a few times. But there were two ABs who had little or no experience working gear: Marco Smigliani and Roger Hammett. The bosun and the day-man yelled at Hammett. A big, gentle, middle-aged AB who was inexperienced at handling guy lines, Hammett was an easy target. The bosun moved Hammett off a guy line, cursing him for his lack of experience.

Green deckhands were not the only potential danger while securing gear. A loose boom, wire running amok, shackles falling on bone and flesh, or a leg stepping into a coiled line all had been known to cause serious damage. "Fingers and toes" was a standard caution in these situations. Because some of these men were drunk, hungover, or stoned, and a few of them had never worked gear before, there was a palpable sense of relief when the last boom was finally secured. When hatches were battened and booms were in place and guy lines were all finally taut and secure, the ship was ready, at last, for the trip across the ocean.

At 4 P.M. a launch picked up the carpenters and stevedores. On the bridge, the captain and chief mate tested the phone, clock, whistle, steering gear, navigation lights, and general alarm. The ship was a rustbucket, but all had to be in good working order. The bosun and the chief mate started heaving anchor; link by heavy link was reeled aboard while an ordinary stood with a fire hose, using the powerful water stream to knock off muddy chunks dredged up from the sea bottom. In twenty minutes the anchor was aweigh. The tug, which had been standing by, left with the pilot. The *Columbia Eagle* started steaming away from Long Beach, slowly moving up to sea speed, gradually increasing rpms by opening nozzles, until she was running full ahead. Soon after the ship left the coastline, the captain set the course at 252 degrees, slightly south of west, following the rhumb line rather than the Great Circle, avoiding the North Pacific. It was the same with most MSTS–chartered ships: skirt past cold weather and rough seas, even if it meant traveling longer distances and taking more time.

Rough seas can shake cargo lashings loose if the cargo is not secured in a proper manner. This is what most seamen thought had happened on the *Badger State,* notwithstanding McKay's speculation that it was sabotage that had destroyed that ship. Preventing any type of stowage disaster was the chief mate's job. Not satisfied with the way the cargo was lashed, he had the deckhands go down in the hold the first night the *Eagle* was at sea.

Billy Campbell, an ordinary seaman, later said, "After we picked up this stuff [the fuses and detonators] out on anchor, we left Long Beach. There wasn't even security. One of the mates had made a mistake. He had signed the longshoremen's ticket that they were finished with work, so they just quit and walked off the ship." Lashing cargo is not normally part of the deckhands' job and Campbell was angry that he had to do the work that the longshoremen should have done properly. He testified that the sailors had to go "down below and shore up these bombs and put big cables around them and lash them down to keep them from turning over." The job completed, the chief mate wrote in the logbook: "2100 Sailors finished securing cargo in #4."

By midnight that first night out of Long Beach, there was a moderate north-northwesterly sea and swell, and the ship was riding in an easy motion. The lights of southern California formed a faint nimbus on the eastern horizon. Gulls cawed and whirled, hoping to pick up garbage. The *Columbia Eagle* was on her way across the Pacific.

At Sea

Columbia Eagle (CE) Logbook, Friday, 20 February: Lat. 33°-22' N, Long. 123°-41' W. Course 252 Vis. good. Vessel rolling easily in long low NW'ly swell.

Wearing oil-stained jeans, a work shirt, heavy steel-tipped work shoes, and a bandanna, McKay—after breakfast—went to the engine room for his four-hour watch. He entered by way of the fidley, the engine room upper deck, where seamen often hung their clothes to speed-dry them in the heat and wind rising up from the blowers blasting air from below. As he came into the fireroom, McKay, who was the 8–12 fireman, nodded to the engineer on his watch, 3d Asst. Clifton Johnson, then looked at all the relevant information written on the fireroom blackboard.

The first thing McKay did was to check the water gauge. This was the main thing, the water level. If there was not enough water in the boilers, it could be disastrous. If the water level was too low, he pumped water in. If there was too much water, he slowed down the feed pump. Next, McKay looked at the oil pressure gauge; it had to be in the range of 200 PSI. If it was too low or too high, he changed the tips on the burners, long metal rods that were inserted into the boilers. By putting in burners with different-size tips, he could shift the pressure up or down. Next, he checked the steam pressure gauge. A Victory ship at sea normally ran at a steam pressure of about 500 PSI. If the pressure was too low, he added more fire. If it was too high, he lowered it. That way he helped keep the ship running at about fifteen knots or fifteen nautical miles per hour, a nautical mile being equal to 1.15 standard miles.

On a Victory ship, a fireman's job was largely manual and when a ship was changing speeds often—for example, while coming into or leaving port—the engine room would get hectic. While at sea, however, a four-hour watch would often pass with little work. After inserting a clean tip at the end of each burner—something that was done at the beginning of every four-hour watch—a fireman could lazily relax into a kind of meditative state, flicking his gaze every so often toward the gauges. This was fine with McKay, because he was not a good fireman. Dreaming much of the time, moving slowly and clumsily and therefore spilling oil on occasion when changing burners, he was the kind of less-than-competent rated man all too common on Vietnam-bound ships.

After his watch was over, McKay entered the mess hall, accompanied by his watch partner, a Honduran named Jose Caceres, and sat down at the table for the black gang. McKay looked at the menu, which changed from day to day, but with a weekly pattern. If steak and ice cream were on the dinner menu, it had to be Thursday or Sunday. Today was Friday, which meant that there was always a fish option.

On the *Eagle,* as on other American merchant ships, the food was decent and the men could have as much as they wanted: lots of meat and potatoes three times a day and rice twice a day. Fresh fruits and vegetables when leaving the States. Milk. Fresh-baked bread and desserts. A platter of meats and cheeses put out at night—"night lunch."

The mess hall pantry, which the crew had access to any time, was stocked with dry cereal, as well as fiery hot sauces, pickles, and peppers traditionally used to mask the taste of the throwaway cuts of meat that men born into southern poverty knew well—tripe, pigs' feet, lard, ham hocks, fatty bacon. It did not matter to them that, on ships, they had other, better options; many gravitated to the foods they remembered from childhood.

McKay ordered lunch from the crew messman, James Johnson, one of the two black men in the crew. Johnson was six feet tall and in his forties, had a pencil-thin mustache, and wore glasses. Although he was always polite and often smiling, his demeanor was not self-deprecating. He was self-assured and did not take any guff from anyone. McKay, a semi-vegetarian, probably asked for clam chowder, salmon, rice, vegetables, and coffee. Lots of coffee. He was rarely seen in the mess hall or down in the engine room without a cup. Once his food arrived, he would have picked out and thrown away the bacon pieces—breakfast leftovers—inevitably mixed in with the vegetables.

The minimum food rations that the shipping company was required by law to provide were listed in a document that all U.S. ships posted in the mess hall: the Articles of Agreement. Drawn up generations ago, the Articles included, for example, how many hard-tack biscuits and how much salt fish should be given to the crew, food that had no relevance to the varied and lavish rations that current U.S. seamen were served. The Articles also listed the maximum amount of time that men signed on for (anywhere from six months to a year), and the parts of the world where the ship might travel. And there was one final stipulation at the bottom in bold, capital letters: "NO GROG OR DANGEROUS WEAPONS ALLOWED, AND NONE TO BE BROUGHT ABOARD BY THE CREW."

McKay was a fireman, a rated man, but Glatkowski's position was much lower on the food chain. BR was the lowest rated and least glamorous job on the ship. He was responsible for cleaning the rooms and bathrooms of the officers, or, as most seamen preferred to call them, the licensed men. Also, he would change linen when required.

Since his job required him to be in the rooms of the licensed men eight hours each day, Glatkowski managed to see a great deal of their private lives. He had time to inspect their medicine cabinets, desk drawers, and lockers. He could see what each one dumped into the little trash can inside the room. As a result, he knew which ones drank heavily; which officers took uppers for "weight control"; which ones took downers or tranquilizers, or heart or blood pressure medicine; and which officer had a gun in his safe (the captain). Glatkowski made a mental list of everything he saw.

"I had this job as BR, which is a boot-licking job," said Glatkowski, "but the nice thing is I was able to spy on them, see what they were up to, listen in on conversations. I mean I got the inside poop on what was going on."

When he was alone with an officer one-on-one, Glatkowski was polite. This was not an act. He was by nature respectful toward those who had experience and knowledge of the sea. Glatkowski got to know a little about the officers, the men whose rooms he cleaned.

The captain of the *Columbia Eagle* was Donald O'Bannon Swann. At fifty-one, Swann was tall, with a round owlish face, strong cheekbones, and a receding hairline; a pair of reading glasses were usually tucked in his shirt pocket. Born in Baltimore in 1918, Swann was fourteen when his family moved to Superior, Wisconsin. His first job on the Great Lakes came as a result of a change in the shipping rules. Until the summer of 1937, deckhands had to stand watches of six hours on, six hours off. This meant only two watches per ship. The new 1937 regulations stated that watch standers would now do four on and eight off, meaning that a third watch—three more deckhands—would be needed for every vessel. Swann applied for the job the day after the regulation went into effect, and he was hired immediately. Marrying in 1938 at the age of twenty, he continued to work on lake vessels every summer. His first child, a son, was born in 1940.

Having built up enough watch standing time as ordinary on lake ships, in early 1941 Swann received his AB ticket and started working full-time on ocean-going vessels. When the United States became actively involved in the war, he worked on ships running dangerous missions to Murmansk, North Africa, and Italy, delivering men and materiel. In 1943 he was sent to Fort Trumbull in New London, Connecticut, where he earned his third mate's license. It was also in 1943 that his second son was born. By the time the war ended, Swann was working as a second mate. After the war, he continued his rise in the merchant marine, getting his chief mate's and master's licenses. Swann remarried in 1952 and after having worked as a captain for Columbia Steamship Company out of Portland, Oregon, for a couple of years, he settled in that city.

There are all kinds of captains. Some are harsh and cutting, keeping the men in line with a look; some are drunk much of the time, rarely coming out of their rooms, letting the chief mate handle the day-to-day work; some are weak, constantly deferring to port captains, ships' agents, or foreign pilots; some are nervous and paranoid, imagining that the sea has a personal vendetta against them. And some, like Swann, try to get by with the least hassle possible. As far as he was concerned, if the men wanted to bring beer aboard and no harm was done to the operation of the ship, that was okay with him. If men gathered on the fantail during their off hours, that was their business. As long as they stood their watches and did not screw up, he left them alone. Swann's main drive was to avoid conflict or problems at any cost.

On the first day, when Glatkowski was cleaning the captain's stateroom, he told the old man that his wife was "in a family way." The old-fashioned phrasing and the fatherly thought behind it appealed to the captain, who himself was twenty when he was married and twenty-two when his first son was born. The captain was solicitous of Glatkowski, assuring him that if they got word that the baby was born during the trip, Glatkowski could use the ship-to-shore phone to make contact with his wife. Glatkowski was grateful. "Glatkowski seemed like a nice guy and respectful," observed Swann.

After the old man, the next man in the ship's hierarchy was the chief mate, forty-nine-year-old Herrick Morgan, known to his friends as Harry. Morgan was born in Medina, Washington, in 1920. His father worked as chief engineer on a ship that tended lighthouses along the Pacific coast, and his mother was a circus performer. She could walk long distances on her hands, even when she was well along in years. When Morgan was three, his father died and his mother moved to San Francisco, where she met another man who raised him from the age of six. Morgan adored his stepfather; when this man died, Morgan said, "it was like a little piece of me died too."

In 1940 Morgan was attending San Francisco State College and studying art ("spending every penny on tubes of paint") when, "on a lark," he got a Z-card. His first ship was the *President Harrison* and he sailed as ordinary. He continued shipping out, got his AB ticket, then attended a private seamanship school that prepared him for his third mate's license, which he received in 1943. During the war he worked on merchant ships plying the South Pacific theater. After the war he continued shipping out, eventually getting his master's license. By the time he signed on as chief mate on the

Columbia Eagle, Morgan had worked at sea for thirty years, shipping out of San Francisco while living in a house in Sausalito. He was married, with a daughter and a son.

Many seamen never marry, while many others marry and divorce several times. Most of those who are married generally look forward to shipping out; it gets them away from wife and home for a while. Morgan did not fall into any of those categories. He had been married only once and loved being home with his wife. In Morgan's eyes, age had only made her even more lovely. *You put up a penny and I'll put up a hundred bucks,* he would say. *And I bet you that my wife is more beautiful than Elizabeth Taylor.* Then he would pull out a photo of his wife. All would agree to lose their penny bet.

Redheaded and a chain-smoker, Morgan was handsome in a craggy way. He was about six feet tall and had a pugnacious Humphrey Bogart way about him that made him seem bigger than his size. Independent, tough, take-no-shit, hard-drinking, capable at his job, loyal to his friends, and laughing at pomposity, he was the kind of character that was more common along the San Francisco waterfront before that city became gentrified.

The chief mate was a strange mix. In his free time, he painted seascapes and read books by John Steinbeck and Jack London. At the same time, he despised hippies and war protesters, all those "of the Jane Fonda ilk who are selling out our country." Morgan's anger and resentment cast a wide net. It not only included young people, minorities, and financial cabals headed by shadowy Semites, it also included the American government, which he believed was "out to get us." As far as he was concerned, you did not mess with that alphabet soup of faceless spooks that would kill you faster than look at you: the CIA–FBI conspiracy.

Another licensed man that Glatkowski regularly saw was the 12–4 third mate. Everett (Herbert) Gunn was fifty-seven and lived in Lomita, California. A dead ringer for Vince Lombardi, with a full head of mostly white, wavy hair, Gunn was pudgy and short, and wore horn-rimmed glasses. He had received his master's license long before either Swann or Morgan received theirs, yet he was working as third mate, which would normally indicate either a lack of ambition or some blot on his record. In Gunn's case, it was the former. He was fond of saying that a ship's skipper was the "one person on earth who was an absolute monarch . . . but who the hell wants to be a monarch?"

Gunn was born on New Year's Day 1913 on a farm in rural, sparsely populated Lunenburg County, Virginia—one hundred miles southwest of Richmond, the cradle of the Confederacy—and he carried with him the resentments and prejudices of his native land. The third mate was a staunch supporter of George Wallace and racial segregation; he despised the Kennedy family, Earl Warren's "Communist Supreme Court," and Senator Fulbright. Gunn was not shy about writing letters to people in power to let them have a piece of his mind.

Gunn had an ongoing battle with his waistline and took weight-reducing pills—that is, amphetamine—to control his appetite. Glatkowski had the feeling that Gunn's drug use made him sympathetic toward the younger generation. In this, Glatkowski was mistaken. Gunn had no sympathy whatsoever with protesters or antiwar activists.

One licensed man, however, who was sympathetic to the antiwar cause was Jeffrey Wright, the Australian-born, sixty-year-old second assistant engineer. When doing his rounds as BR, Glatkowski chatted with Wright occasionally. He felt comfortable enough to ask the Wright how he felt about working on this kind of ship, and the youthful-looking Wright would respond: "I don't know why we're carrying napalm" and "Why do we have to drop this shit on peasants and farmers?"

Glatkowski also became moderately friendly with Orville Mills, the radio operator. A tall, distinguished-looking gentleman with silver hair and jet-black eyebrows, Mills had a wooden leg, his souvenir from being on a merchant ship that was torpedoed during World War II. Called Sparks, as on every ship, Mills had been sailing as radio operator for forty years and was—at sixty-four—the oldest man on board. "Glatkowski seemed very nice," Mills recalled. "Well-educated and did his work and never bothered. And usually when I'd come to breakfast, he'd come up and mop the place out and by the time I got back up there, why everything was over with."

These were some of the licensed men whose rooms Glatkowski mopped and soogied every day. When Glatkowski was not working, he would be with the rest of the crew.

Glatkowski's fo'c'sle mate was John Browder, the third cook. They would run into each other mostly in the galley or in their fo'c'sle when getting up or changing clothes. "Ski talked about his family," Browder recalled. "You see, his wife was going to have a kid around the 15th of April, and he stated that he would like to be back before she does have it."

At the beginning of the trip, Glatkowski was friendly, and he treated his fellow seamen with courtesy. Luke Ciamboli, the 4–8 oiler, said that Glatkowski had a different side as well. Ciamboli said that Glatkowski would sometimes be confrontational with the rest of the crew, throwing out "individuality, recognition, all those words, not really making any sense."

Or Glatkowski might talk about the demonstrations in which he had participated. "Glatkowski said he had been locked up or something," Mills said. "He said he was carrying placards on some kind of peace movement or something, you know, protest—I imagine Long Beach or something around there. . . . Well, it was like 'Blacks are as good as we are,' or something like that . . . so the Mate and I both started in on him about that stuff. And he said, 'Stop that. I won't argue with the two of you.' And he walked out."

"Glatkowski was shy and talked little," one crew member said, "while McKay was adventurous, the Errol Flynn type."

"I was always astonished at the look in McKay's eyes," said Ciamboli. "He never seemed to blink. His eyes seemed to be staring all the time and he never seemed to blink. Every so often he asked me how things were going down below. I thought that maybe he wanted to study to become an engineer and he took an interest in the engine room. He was always asking me if everything was going all right."

"McKay had those hippie ways," said Clifton Johnson, the third assistant engineer. "He wore a big medallion. He seemed to be quite green on the job. He bumbled around a lot. He would spill oil when changing burners. A good fireman never spills oil. He smoked a French cigarette, Gauloises, had the picture of a helmet on the package. He smoked a lot and drank an awful lot of coffee. He seemed to need a great deal of stimulation. He was over six feet tall, well built, broad shouldered, good arms but appeared clumsy."

James Johnson, crew messman, recalled an odd encounter with McKay in the mess hall. "Clyde McKay said something to me, I can't recall exactly what it was, but it sounded funny and stupid. I told him to go lie down as he was nuts, he was sick, and he replied something to the effect, 'Do you think I'm nuts?' and I said, 'Yeah.' Then he said, 'You will see, you will see.'"

Sometimes McKay did outrageous things. In the mess hall, in front of everyone, he would shove his fingers into Glatkowski's food, scoop up some of it, and taste it. "Mmm, that's delicious," he would say sarcastically. He urged Glatkowski to do the same. Or he would encourage Glatkowski to join him in wearing silly hats and other inappropriate clothing to the mess hall.

"We were provoking them all the time," Glatkowski said, "and provoking one another. We were always raising the ante between ourselves, and we were always raising the ante between the crew and us together. There were times when we would play poker. We'd come in and sit down and McKay would take off his money belt and lay down some gold coins and everybody's eyes would pick up and I'd say, 'Shit, Clyde, give me one of those' and he'd toss a gold coin over to me. And somebody would say, 'Is that real?' Everybody would be dumbfounded."

Most nights there was a poker game in the mess hall after supper. A blue bedspread—what the men called the "jack-off curtain," normally strung on a wire outside a man's bunk in order to provide a certain amount of privacy—was spread out on a table, fresh decks of cards appeared, and the game would begin. As always on these ships, it was for table stakes: dealer's choice, no wild cards. More than 90 percent of the hands would be seven-card stud, sometimes high-low, and a good bit of money changed hands. It was not uncommon for men to win or lose a couple hundred dollars in a night, and occasionally—though very rarely—that much might be bet on a single turn of a card. They played with cash, not chips, and each man put his bills in front of him.

One of the regular players in the game was twenty-one-year-old Marco Smigliani, 12–4 AB. Smigliani was handsome, dark, wiry, and tough; he was always laughing, joking, and gesturing. While on lookout at night on the bow, he would belt out operatic arias at the top of his lungs. Born in Italy and brought to America when he was seven, Smigliani was a naturalized citizen and very patriotic. After getting out of high school, he worked on a ship to Vietnam. While in Da Nang, he became friendly with some soldiers, so they took him on patrol. It got into his blood: the danger, the smell of battle. When he got back to the States, he signed up for the Marines and was sent back to Vietnam.

Smigliani was one of the very few people, on any ship, who knew from their own experience the difference between what it was like to be in Vietnam in the military and what it was like to be there in the merchant marine. As a marine, he had faced death. As a seaman, he faced incurable clap. As a marine it was mud and blood. As a seaman, it was saunas and whores. As a marine it was discipline and the chain of command. As a seaman it was do your job and tell the bosun to go screw himself.

Smigliani said that once, when he was telling a story about a Marine attack on a village, Glatkowski blurted out, *What do you think about these bombs we're carrying? What do you think's going to happen to the people they get dropped on?* Smigliani said he ignored Glatkowski. Then McKay muttered, *Baby-killer.* Smigliani reacted furiously. *I was in the jungles of Vietnam, I never saw any civilians! You want to talk about baby-killers,* Smigliani snapped at McKay, *This napalm we got on board, this is the stuff that kills babies! This fries everybody!*

Later, in the passageway, McKay said it to Smigliani again. *Baby-killer.*

"So he did it again," said Smigliani. "He called me a baby-killer again, and you know, I worked him over pretty good on his belly, you know what I mean? I beat the shit out of him. But as I said, he was a stand-up guy, so he came and apologized to me. After that we became friends. That's why I lent him my record player."

CE Logbook: Lat. 27°-46' Long. 143°-26', Avg. Speed 13.04 Reduced speed by 10 rpm to ease vessel laboring in heavy sea. Vessel pitching heavily to a very high WNW sea & swell. Heavy spray. Partly cloudy, vis. good.

When there were heavy seas and it was cool and windy, the deck was an uncomfortable place to be, so McKay brought the portable record player into the mess hall, along with Smigliani's records: Frank Sinatra, Tony Bennett, Nat King Cole.

Don Sather, the chief electrician, had some records he contributed to the mix: Santana, Rolling Stones, Cream. While sitting in the mess hall, Glatkowski put on a record. Bruce Gray and a few others—including the twenty-year-old wiper, Dan Mornin, a bearded college dropout who had a habit of coming up with extemporaneous rhymes, a skill that endeared him to the other young guys aboard—listened to the music.

Later, when asked by the mutiny investigators how he became such good friends with McKay and Glatkowski, Mornin replied, "Just by sharing the same problems, I guess. We are of the same age and we have many of the same things in common in that, such as . . . look, it's a hard thing to say because, well, you can't talk to the older people on the ship about the same things, so you talk to the people that are the same age as yourself, you know. I don't know if you understand what I mean. But like, if we were to discuss the war in Vietnam or anything like this, you wouldn't be able to discuss it with any older person like you would be able to with somebody [your own age]."

One day, when the younger crew members were listening to music in the mess hall, Ciamboli, the crew's union delegate, came in and eyed the young seamen coldly. He left, then came back in a few minutes, posting a notice. Glatkowski read it and reacted. He went toe-to-toe with Ciamboli while other crewmen looked on. "I had a run-in with Glatkowski once," said Ciamboli. "I put a notice on the bulletin board to hold down the noise in the mess-hall because people were sleeping in the area and he started giving me an argument about it. He said I was overstepping my authority."

"They had a discussion, Ski and Luke," said Roy McCarthy, the middle-aged 12–4 fireman, "and then Ski brought up about his rights. The BR had that crap you get down in Haight-Ashbury and whatnot. You get the same thing from all these guys, about the fact that there should be peace and that sort of thing."

Trying to avoid any more conflict with the older guys, Glatkowski got a piece of tarp from the bosun and constructed a tent on the poop deck. With this, the young guys had a place where they could have a little more privacy. The poop deck, however, was not ideal; they did not get much lee from the tent and winds whipped up around them. Besides, on the poop deck they were partly visible from the bridge. So they started gathering on the fantail instead. Behind the afterhouse, covered by a structural overhead that protected them from weather and kept them hidden from prying eyes, sitting on cots, they could listen to music and pass joints around. Gray and Mornin joined in and formed the core of a group that gathered nearly every night on the fantail.

To a degree, the young guys' talk paralleled that of the older men who hung out midships. Like the older guys, the young guys on the fantail talked about whores and ports (*You'll be the first one down the gangway, holding your dick in one hand and waving a twenty-dollar bill with the other*) and the good times they had in seaman's hangouts like the Mosquito Bar in Bangkok or Toby's in Karachi or The Cages in Bombay. Although McKay or Glatkowski might drop in a comment about "this fucking cargo," the young guys on the fantail usually made jokes about the munitions in the holds. *Hey, if anything happens on this ship, she ain't going down. Uh-uh. She's going straight up!*

The young guys might talk about constellations (*There's Orion's Belt, that's Cassiopeia*), about their tattoos or their work on ship or the guys they worked with, about the food, their girlfriends, or maybe about the luminous plankton that sometimes made the water sparkle, gem-like, in the moonlight. The most pronounced differences between the younger and older men were that the young smoked marijuana and were usually opposed to the war. Young people gathering on the fantail to smoke marijuana and listen to music took place on every merchant vessel going to Vietnam and on most other American ships of that era.

When they were off watch, Glatkowski and McKay would get together constantly. "McKay was always together with Goldilocks, his partner in crime," said Gerhardt Ratter, the 4–8 fireman. "They would always be on the fantail together or in the mess-hall together. They'd be together constantly. Ski and McKay would be by the tent when I'd go up there on the fantail to get some sun. In it, around it, or on the fantail."

When Glatkowski and McKay were alone, they often talked about the war and their complicity in it. "We discussed this stuff for hours and hours on the ship," said Glatkowski. "That it was our moral obligation to stop those bombs. We talked about the Nuremberg Trials, that we should not be good German soldiers who just go along with an illegal war. About doing our part to help the downtrodden people whose lives are being destroyed by American bombs."

They talked about the plight of Vietnamese villagers and children, as well as the responsibility they themselves bore for having carried ammo on previous trips to the Zone. This hit a raw nerve for Glatkowski, who recalled an afternoon in Cam Ranh, on a previous ammo run to Vietnam, where he saw someone scarred by napalm. The sight of seared human flesh was seared in his memory. He could not forget it. McKay shared that same burden of guilt. In his unproduced screenplay, Glatkowski put these words into McKay's mouth: "[The United States is] turning every kid [in Vietnam], male or female over the age of seven into a prostitute. . . . And what do you think it's doing to us? Don't you feel some kind of responsibility for what happens?"

Glatkowski wrote that even though he was sold on the idea of doing something, mutiny and sabotage were still hard for him to swallow. Glatkowski would talk about his wife and their expected child. He was worried about them. He did not want to do something that would hurt them, or bring them trouble and shame. McKay upbraided Glatkowski for his attachment to "bourgeois ideals."

"Clyde always made a point about my 'bourgeois ideals,'" Glatkowski said. "And yes, I admit, I came from that place. I was attached. And I examined what he said to me."

Apparently, McKay was afraid that these "attachments" might end up preventing his partner from going all the way. McKay knew that he had to separate Glatkowski from the world he was connected to; otherwise, he would lose his "loyal helper" at the crucial moment. In Long Beach the discussions between them had been relatively painless: all hypothetical. Now that they were on an ammo ship, however, the talk took on an urgency that was impossible for Glatkowski to wish away. They knew that the cargo was scheduled to be offloaded within a week. There was not much time left. They needed to make a decision and come up with a plan.

6 PITCHING AND ROLLING

At Sea

CE Logbook: Av. Speed 13.958 Partly cloudy, vis. good. Vessel rolling and pitching moderately in NxE'ly sea & mod. NW'ly swell.

Rolling is the action of a vessel port and starboard; pitching is the action forward and aft. When the two are combined, there is an uncertainty of motion, a sense of not knowing which way the ship is going to go next. There are moments when a ship seems to hang in mid-air before deciding which way to plunge. Sometimes, in a heavy sea filled with swells, the vessel's bow will pitch into a trough. When this happens, there is no cushion for the bow's downward movement, and the vessel smashes violently into the water.

When there are storms or heavy winds in the middle of the Pacific, a person gets a feeling of being at the very center of these phenomena. Here, in this vast body of water that connects Asia and America and Australia, is where weather patterns begin, where storms and other weather systems start before heading off to the land masses that surround this ocean. This is where weather begins.

Every day, several times each day, Glatkowski and McKay would find moments to be together, apart from others. With McKay doing most of the talking, they would go over their options again and again. Would they need to take charge of the vessel first? How would they control the bridge? They would need another gun. Where and how will they get it?

Glatkowski was skeptical that they could seize and hold on to a ship and its crew with just two guns. But McKay was certain that they could. They worried about bullets flying around the cargo and setting off an explosion inadvertently. And about controlling the rest of the crew . . . how were they going to do that? They were silent for a few seconds. Perhaps they would need help.

At a time when McKay knew that his watch partner was in the mess hall, he took Bruce Gray to his fo'c'sle. Saying that there was something he wanted to show the pantryman, McKay quickly opened his locker, took out a black plastic folder, unzipped it, and revealed the pistol.

Gray was surprised. "Clyde showed me his pistol and just said, 'Look at this.' I said, 'Why do you carry that for?' He said, 'Well, you have dangerous ports and I like to carry it because I want to be alive.' So I just looked at him kind of oddly, you know."

Apparently, McKay did not spell anything out; he was testing Gray to see what his response would be. To see if he would understand instinctively what was going on. McKay put his pistol away and did not pursue it. At least not then.

"We tried talking to Gray," said Glatkowski. "It just seemed that he wasn't all there, not too bright. He got high but he had no political content at all."

They knew they would have to approach Gray again, this time more explicitly. And that they would have to try to make Dan Mornin aware of what they were doing. But could these two be trusted when the time came?

CE Logbook: Av. Speed 15.875 Partly cloudy, smooth sea, small SSE swell, vessel in easy roll. 1020 Fire & Boat Drill held—6 lengths of hose led out under full pressure—1030 abandon ship signal sounded. No boats swung out due to motion of vessel. Crew mustered at their stations & instructed in their duties. Motor in #2 L/boat given 5 min test run.

At 10:20 A.M., after the morning coffee break, there was the weekly fire and boat (F&B) drill. A well-worn routine, this was an exercise they had all gone through once a week whenever they were at sea. As was normal with F&B

drills, a notice on the board announced it ahead of time. The men, therefore, were ready, wearing life jackets and caps. Once at their fire stations, they rolled out hoses and held them while water pressure was supplied by the engine room. They had to hold on tight so that the force did not jolt them backward. After a minute or so, the pressure was turned off, the water in the hoses was squeezed out, and the hoses were rolled up and put away. A few seconds later the abandon ship signal sounded: seven short whistles followed by the same on the general alarm bell. Almost sleepwalking through the drill, laughing and joking, the men went to their abandon ship stations and waited.

Sometimes a drill involved lowering davits and putting lifeboats into the water. But not this time. This time, the motor in #2 lifeboat was turned on and tested—there was no motor in the #1 boat—but the boats were not lowered. Instead, a mate called out each job rating and then that man answered what his job would be in case of a real emergency. Mate: *Twelve to four ordinary!* Ordinary: *Fend off painter and lower boat.*

The point was to have the action so ingrained that the men would respond automatically during a real emergency. That was the theory, at least. A theory that would be put to the test soon. Before the *Columbia Eagle* would see land again, the lives of most of these men would depend on whether they knew what to do in an emergency and whether the lifeboats were in working order.

The weekly F&B drill was one of the routines around which seamen's lives revolved. Like getting their laundry exchanged once a week or having the slop chest open on such-and-such a day, the F&B drill was a dependable shipboard rhythm, a crucial grounding element in an otherwise isolated and disconnected life.

That night Glatkowski and McKay met in Glatkowski's fo'c'sle. They looked at a map of East Asia, at the sea corridor from Japan south to Vietnam. As far as McKay and Glatkowski knew, the ship was headed to Japan for bunkers. From there, they had heard, it was going south, between Taiwan and the Philippines, would stop in Vietnam, then proceed on to Thailand. McKay suggested that they seize the ship and take it to China.

Glatkowski proposed an alternate plan. What about taking the ship directly to North Vietnam? Right to Haiphong harbor. Let the North Vietnamese know ahead of time what they were doing so that the Viets would not blow them out of the water. McKay did not like that plan. They would never make it. U.S. warships and Coast Guard cutters patrolled the waters near North Vietnam. McKay felt that taking the ship to China was their best chance. They could surrender to the Chinese, hand them the munitions, and ask for political asylum.

Glatkowski suggested another plan. Why not sail the ship to Singapore where they could take on bunkers and travel to the Persian Gulf? They could make contact with Palestinians there, and deliver the bombs to them. McKay dismissed the idea as romantic and not very practical. The Palestinians do not have an air force. They are guerrillas. The napalm would be worthless to them. McKay insisted that China was the best option.

CE Logbook: Av. Speed 15.32 Vessel rolling and pitching moderately to a very high NW'ly swell. Partly cloudy, vis. good.

As the weather warmed, Glatkowski and the other young crew members would go out on deck and watch the whitecaps and swells, but the older seamen would almost never pay attention to their surroundings. If someone caught these older seamen glancing at a spectacular sunset or at the ever-present dolphins and flying fish, they would get embarrassed and say something like: People pay thousands of dollars to take cruises; and here they're paying us!

The nerve center of shipboard life for these "real" seamen was the mess hall. At night, maybe after having had beer or whisky on the sly in their fo'c'sles, they would filter in to play cards or cribbage, or simply hang out. It was mostly the middle-aged seamen who socialized in the mess hall, living in a past revised by memory or in a future that would never be.

In the mess hall, news circulated about a change in the ship's plans. The *Eagle* was not going to Japan for bunkers; instead, it would go to Lokanin Point, Bataan, in the Philippines, an area in Manila Bay with villages, an oil pipeline, and an American military base. And there was another change: the ship was not going to stop in Vietnam on its way to Thailand. Instead, after taking on bunkers in Bataan, it would go directly to the U.S. base in Sattahip, Thailand. As usual, no explanation was given for the change. A port might be backed up with ships waiting for a berth, there might be bad weather conditions, or security might be an issue. A ship carrying hazardous cargo had to take all these matters into account and proceed cautiously, especially when going near a war zone.

For Glatkowski and McKay, the change in the *Eagle*'s schedule meant that they would have to adjust their own plans. Looking at a map of Asia, Glatkowski met McKay on the fantail to go over their options. They had planned to get a gun in the first port. Would they be able to get one in Lokanin Point? They had both been to Olongapo. It was easy to buy a gun there, easy to buy just about anything. It would probably be the same in Bataan.

But the new route meant that when they seized the vessel, they could not take it to China. To take the ship from the South China Sea to China would mean running the gauntlet of U.S. ships patrolling the Vietnamese coast. That was out of the question.

"I came up with the next suggestion," said Glatkowski. "A practical, good suggestion." He proposed that they seize the ship in the middle of the Gulf of Thailand and then redirect the vessel west, to that part of the Malay Peninsula that is largely part of Burma. Thailand shares the peninsula with Burma, the southeastern part of which extends like the tail end of a kite, separating Burma from the gulf. At one place on that peninsula, the width of the Thai part was no more than ten miles. The map showed a village called Prachuap near the Gulf of Thailand, leading west to the Maw-daung Pass. They would have to cross through several miles of mountainous and densely forested Thai countryside to get to Burma. The problem was that Thailand's government was a monarchy aligned with the United States. If they were caught there, they would be turned over to the United States.

But if they could make it to Burma, they would be in a socialist country that was politically neutral. There were Chinese and Soviet embassies in Rangoon. Although the country maintained diplomatic ties to the United States, its sympathies in the war were clearly with North Vietnam. Glatkowski figured that they stood a good chance of obtaining political asylum in Burma. His idea was to beach the ship near the village of Prachuap, get the crew off the vessel, and set fire to the cargo. Then they could trek toward the border, avoiding populated areas, and—on the other side of the frontier—surrender to Burmese authorities. McKay was intrigued.

Unbeknown to them, the plotters were being watched by Billy Campbell, a forty-one-year-old ordinary on the 12–4 watch, who later testified that he had been sneaking around the young seamen ever since the ship left port. Campbell was squat, five foot seven, and—according to Smigliani—"he looked like a guy who got off the ship and hit the first bar and never went anywhere else. Ratty-looking, always bitching and moaning and complaining."

Born in Alabama in 1928, the youngest of fourteen children, Campbell never made it out of the seventh grade. As a teenager, he did a stint in a cotton mill, then joined the Navy. After that it was welding school, the shipyards, and finally working on ships as an ordinary seaman. In between, he married several times. He caught gonorrhea from his second wife, but this did not end the marriage; catching her in bed with another man did. Campbell's third marriage was to a woman who was pregnant when he met her. The marriage ended when he caught her making love to two other women. According to Campbell, who detailed his life in a psychiatric evaluation that was conducted following the mutiny,* his third wife had married him so that her child would have a last name. He found this out from his sister-in-law. The doctor who evaluated him reported that Campbell had "mild cerebral dysfunction" and was in a constant "paranoid state."

Another evaluation concluded that "psychiatrically, [Campbell] can best be understood as schizoid . . . with mental retardation." On the *Eagle*, Campbell felt that he was surrounded by dangerous drug abusers and homosexuals. He was certain that he was the object of sexual advances. In his testimony to the mutiny investigators, Campbell blurted out that Norm Pettersen, the day-man, tried to grab him. "While I was taking a shower he tried to grab ahold of my penis," Campbell testified. "So either the guy was drunk or on pills, I don't know which one exactly." Before the trip was over, Campbell would tell other crewmen that he was a CIA agent. He repeatedly insisted that the captain log other crewmen for violations that Campbell either imagined or that were standard practice, such as taking a radio on lookout or having a beer off-watch. Wherever he looked, Campbell saw infractions, law-breaking, and attacks aimed personally at him.

APPROACHING THE Philippines, at about seven in the morning, the *Eagle* passed the Mariana Trench, the deepest place in the ocean floor. As the ship moved past Saipan, a fog set in and there was restricted visibility. The captain ordered standby engines. Given the weather conditions, the engine

*Campbell had sued the Columbia Steamship Company after returning home from this trip. The case required that he be evaluated by doctors.

room took her down a few nozzles. The mate on watch periodically blew the foghorn.

Glatkowski and McKay met briefly after breakfast, just before eight o'clock. They only had a few days left. Glatkowski said that McKay brought up the subject of sabotage. What could they do to sink the ship and its cargo? Glatkowski said that he was upset by this; how would the crew survive? McKay said that there would be enough time to get in the lifeboats. Glatkowski wanted more details. He wanted to know what kind of sabotage, which line should be cut, how they would do it. McKay was not sure. Glatkowski said that he was disturbed by McKay's vagueness.

Later, during the morning coffee break, Glatkowski was in the mess hall when the steward, Parker Holt, made a beeline for him and said that some mates and engineers had complained: he had not soogied their showers properly. Glatkowski, about to explode from the pressure he felt McKay was putting on him, shouted at the steward, *You're a fucking company goon. Go fuck yourself!*

"I was in the mess-hall," said the day-man. "I heard Glatkowski tell the steward to go fuck himself and the steward said, 'Let's go see the captain.' The steward said it three or four times but Glatkowski did not want to go."

Holt and Philip Livingston, who was the baker and the steward department's union delegate, finally took Glatkowski up to see the old man. "The captain climbed all over him for using the language that he did," said Holt. "The captain wanted to log him, which means to put him in the book and this would cost Glatkowski a day's pay. I explained to the captain that Glatkowski had apologized and that he was sorry for what he had done. Consequently the Captain let Glatkowski off with a warning."

At midnight, Glatkowski went to the rail aft of the house. "I'm on the starboard side of the ship," said Glatkowski,

> leaning over the rail and smoking a cigarette. Clyde comes up to me and says, Have you made up your mind yet? This is about buying the fucking gun. And I say, "You know, I've got a lot here to consider, and I can't make up my mind in two hours." I said, "I've got a wife, I've got a kid on the way, I've got a family to think about, my parents, my brothers and sisters, I'm looking at my whole fucking situation and you want me to do this in two hours." So he says, "That's just bourgeois idealism." "Bourgeois idealism! What the fuck are you talking about?! You're a fucking bourgeois, you keep throwing this shit up to me and you can't keep throwing this shit up to me!"

Glatkowski felt that it was easy for McKay to risk everything. McKay had nothing, so he had nothing to lose. "You looked at Clyde and you saw someone who was just emptiness," Glatkowski said. "You did not see the humanity. You saw emptiness. And I'm not just saying that. I'm telling you, you looked at him and you saw emptiness."

When Glatkowski looked at himself, he saw someone straddling two worlds: on the one hand, a commitment to join McKay in mutiny; on the other hand, attachment to family. He was different from McKay. He had family. He had something to lose.

As he cleaned the rooms of the licensed men, Glatkowski was plagued by uncertainty. If he went through with it, he knew that he could die. No doubt about it. If he survived the action, he might be tried and executed. Or spend the rest of his life in jail.

Whether he lived or died, he would always be defined by this act, for the rest of his life. Mutineer. Hijacker. Saboteur. A hero of the revolution? Maybe. To some people. To others, a traitor. He knew that throwing a wrench into the war machinery was the right thing to do. But could he go through with mutiny? Mutiny, for Christ's sake! Mutiny! It was like killing a king. Overthrowing a government. A coup d'etat.

One thing was dead certain, the longer this trip went on, the harder it would be to back out.

GLATKOWSKI AND McKay met back aft. McKay said that he wanted to discuss the specifics of sabotage. Glatkowski was full of questions: What kind of sabotage? Sink the cargo? Blow it up? Place a live bomb in with the cargo? Shoot into the detonators, causing a chain reaction?

"He tells me that he wants to go down into the hold to set fire to this fucking ship," said Glatkowski. "And I said, 'How are we going to do it? How?'"

Glatkowski's recollection was that McKay wanted to make an explosive, set it next to the detonators, then have everyone jump off the ship as the crates ignited. Thinking about this later, Glatkowski shook his head in exasperation. "The man wanted to blow the ship up in the middle of the fucking ocean!" Seizing the ship, getting everyone off, then sinking it . . . Glatkowski said he could live with that. There was something clean about it. Something genuinely revolutionary. But blowing the ship up was a different story. "I told him, I said, 'Listen, if you succeed, you're going to jeopardize all our lives, we all may be killed! I mean, it's okay if it's you or I, but what about these other people?' And his argument was, 'Oh, that's just bourgeois idealism, Alvin.' Bourgeois idealism? What the fuck was he talking about?!"

Glatkowski said that he suddenly had a moment of serious doubt about this whole adventure. Who was McKay anyway? A guy who had memorized dozens of passages from revolutionary tracts. A guy with a gun, gold pieces, and the single-minded determination to "do something." But no definite plan. Little or no technical expertise. And a cavalier attitude about their survival.

CE Logbook: Wednesday, March 11. Arrival Lokanin Point.

Navigating through the Philippines: Biri Island, San Bernardino Island, then past Corregidor on its approach toward Bataan. The *Eagle* arrived at Lokanin Point shortly after 11 in the morning. At 11:33 the chief mate told the bosun and day-man to let go the port anchor. At 11:48 the chain was secured with five shots in the water. The ship was anchored at a point 255 degrees off Lokanin Point and 304 degrees off Agnipa Point, very near an oil pipeline. The pipeline was the reason the ship was here: to take on bunkers.

At 12:20 a doctor and other Philippine officials came aboard, at 12:30 a fuel oil barge came alongside. At 1:06 pratique (permission to use the port) was granted, at 1:30 the company agent and immigration officials boarded the vessel. At 2 P.M. a U.S. Navy supply vessel came alongside, bringing a water barge with it. Armed Philippine guards stationed themselves at the gangway, back aft and on the bow.

Glatkowski and McKay did not have much time. They showered, dressed, and went out on deck, ready to take the first launch ashore. The chief mate had already set the sailing board for 7:30 that night, which meant that they had to be back by 5:30. It was now 2:30. Since the round trip itself would take about an hour, they had two hours to buy a pistol.

As they looked toward the water, they saw a slew of bumboats surrounding the ship: whores climbing up a Jacob's ladder back aft, thieves scrambling on to the deck, hustlers selling dope. The usual craziness.

The captain and chief mate—trying to keep whores and dope dealers from running around the fo'c'sles, trying to keep "pirates" from making away with shackles and heaving lines—were on the bridge, yelling: *Go away!*

The old man ordered the bosun to aim fire hoses at the bumboats, and he threatened the head of the Philippine guards: *Keep those damn whores and thieves away or you won't get paid!*

And then, suddenly, in the middle of this chaos, as Glatkowski and McKay were getting ready to take a bumboat ashore, several shots rang out.

7 THIS IS A MUTINY

Philippines/At Sea

Before the ship had come in to Lokanin Point to take on bunkers, the old man had let the crew know that he wanted to avoid the typical chaos that surrounded all incoming vessels. "The word came down that we weren't going to allow bumboats to get close to the ship," said Glatkowski. The captain passed the word on to port security as well. "When I sent my cable in for Filipino watchmen," said Swann, "I said I wanted a sufficient number to keep undesirables off the vessel. I didn't want them to say that I didn't hire enough watchmen to do the job properly."

But once the ship pulled in to Lokanin Point, reality took over. "What happened," said Glatkowski, "was that these bumboats came to us anyway and guys threw lines down. They would steal anything: shackles, lines. Anything! Girls going into the rooms while the others were running around stealing sheets, towels, soap. They could strip a ship in no time. They were called pirates but they were more like gypsies."

"I was trying to avoid whisky coming over, dope or what have you," said Swann. "They knew that they wasn't going to get paid if they didn't keep everybody off. So one of the guards shot a robber or pirate or whatever you want to call it. The guy they shot, he wasn't killed, he was shot in the leg or something."

After the shooting, it became even more chaotic. The old man and chief mate ran around screaming at the guards that they wanted all those people off the ship right now!

While this was going on, McKay and Glatkowski signaled one of the bumboats. They scrambled down the gangway, got inside the boat, and went ashore.

"When the bumboat took us ashore," said Glatkowski, "we landed in the boonies somewhere." A village in Bataan called Lamao. Dirt roads churned into mud by periodic rainstorms. Rice paddies and banana orchards and emaciated dogs roaming, picking at picked-over garbage. Wooden shacks and a couple of makeshift whorehouses. Colorfully painted taxis, called jeepneys, waited for the few seamen who ventured ashore.

"We were in a bar," Glatkowski said,

> beaded curtains, bamboo, dirt floor, right on the beach. What we're talking about is a grass shack. All they had was a cooler with lots of beer and some liquor, and a back room. McKay and I got some beer, some guy came up and McKay asked him if we could get a gun. And the guy [said], no problem, you can get anything you want. And we told him what we wanted. We asked for a .45, the easiest thing because they take them off the military all the time. And the guy came back, oh, twenty minutes later with this old pistol, a .38, an old pistol. McKay had a Walther, I had this old pistol. And it was like a police snub-nose .38. It wasn't, it had bigger bullets, it was just an antique fucking gun. But the action worked on it, everything worked on it. I forget what we paid for it, I think it was 45 or 35 dollars. And I didn't have enough money to pay for it, so McKay paid the rest. And that's how we got the gun.

Glatkowski had already seen McKay's gun and they talked about it.

> [T]his is it, you know, we're both talking back and forth, and this is it. It's against the law to bring those aboard ship. I was scared.
>
> And McKay, I don't really know the guy. How long had I known him . . . two weeks? We'd worked through a lot in those few weeks. . . . We'd talked a lot. He was more sophisticated, he had read more . . . he was older. He was able to manipulate a little bit better. He was far more well-read than I was.
>
> So . . . so we talked about . . . this is it. That's an important step. Imagine . . . as if we were talking about going down to rob a bank. That's the step we were taking when we bought that gun in Bataan. And as soon as you

> have that gun in your pocket, your butt's going to pucker. What went through McKay's head, I don't know. But I know what went through my head. All this stuff I've been talking about, this is it. As soon as that [gun] goes into my hand, that's it.

Glatkowski said that he put the pistol inside of a manila envelope, folded it, and shoved it into his pocket. It was bulky, but since his shirt was loose, it could not be readily seen. The trip on the bumboat back to the ship took about a half-hour, during which Glatkowski and McKay talked. What should they do with the weapons? Where should they be kept? There would probably be a shakedown later, as often happens when leaving port. Should they stash the guns somewhere?

As the bumboat neared the ship, the gangway was lowered. The two young men scrambled on to the bottom step. Glatkowski looked up to the ship. Jesus! He felt his legs shaking. He placed one hand on the gangway rail line and the other hand on his clothes, on top of the gun. *One hand for the ship, one for yourself.* He felt his heart pumping as he went up step by step. At the top of the gangway, he looked around.

"When we got back with the gun," Glatkowski said, "there was a gangway watch, first of all." It was Campbell, of all people. He looked at McKay and Glatkowski carefully as they came up the steps, certain that they were doing something illegal.

"I was terrified," Glatkowski said. "Oh, God, yeah, I just knew we were going to be caught."

At some point, Glatkowski must have given the package to McKay because Jose Caceres, McKay's watch partner, later told Ciamboli that he saw McKay stick his arm in the porthole and throw a paper bag with something heavy inside onto the top bunk. Lying on the lower bunk, awake but not speaking, Caceres then saw McKay come into the room a few seconds later. As McKay grabbed the package from his bunk, he noticed Caceres looking at him, so he quickly shoved the package into his locker and locked it.

McKay turned-to at 7:55 that night. It was a busy watch: making steam, adding water, getting engine auxiliaries ready for sailing. Preoccupied, McKay looked at Caceres for any signs of trouble. Had his watch partner seen him put the gun away? Had the man caught a glimpse of the Walther .38 already in his attaché case? If so, would he tell someone? McKay was more clumsy than usual during his watch; he spilled oil while changing burners.

At 8:30 P.M. the ship pulled up the hook and proceeded out of Manila Bay. By 9 P.M. the *Eagle* was moving full ahead. McKay passed the next three hours of his watch looking at the clock more than at the gauges. At 11:55 P.M., McKay knocked-off and ran to Glatkowski's fo'c'sle.

"Clyde came to me around midnight," Glatkowski recalled, "and he told me that he thought he was 'getting hot.' He thought that another crewmember had seen the stashed weapons. I asked him if he was sure, and he replied that he was 'not certain.'"

They knew, however, that after all the craziness with the bumboats and the shooting in Lokanin Point, there was bound to be a shakedown. If, before the shakedown, Caceres said anything about having seen guns, McKay's fo'c'sle would be ransacked.

Glatkowski offered an alternative plan. "I asked Clyde if he wanted me to take the weapons for safety, that I could probably hide the guns in the officers' quarters." McKay shook off the idea. They decided to go on with their work as if nothing had happened.

CE Logbook: Thursday, March 12, 1970. Clear, smooth sea, vessel steady. Lat. 13°23' N, Long. 116°28' E.

As expected, there was a search aboard the *Eagle* after she left the Philippines. The captain and chief mate came into every fo'c'sle, accompanied by each department delegate. The old man and the mate asked McKay to unlock his locker and open it. McKay stood by, trying not to look tense, as the old man and the mate rummaged around, shelf by shelf. Ciamboli stood nearby, fulfilling his duty as delegate. As they searched his belongings, McKay wondered if his watch partner had seen the guns and reported this to the captain. Why were they spending so much time on his locker? The old man saw the attaché case and looked at it for a moment, but did not pick it up. After a few endless seconds, the old man signaled McKay that he could close and lock his locker. McKay did so. It was a close call. Apparently, McKay's watch partner had not seen the guns.

Meanwhile, in other men's lockers, all that was found was a great deal of booze—the "grog" that the Articles state is not to be brought aboard by the crew. According to Campbell, while the ship was in Bataan there "must have been one hundred cases of beer come aboard for every department and I don't know how many rum and all that." Roger Hammett, the 12–4 AB, said that "there was a whole lot of San Miguel Beer come on board." It was common practice for merchant seamen to bring alcohol on board. As long as the men stood their watches and turned-to on time, the old man was not going to restrict their booze. In the next few days on the *Eagle,* however, while the ship passed through the tropics, the liquor and the soaring temperatures began to take their toll.

Moreover, almost no one had gone ashore in Bataan. Anyone who has ever spent long periods of time at sea knows that something strange happens to seamen if—after more than a couple of weeks at sea—they do not get to unwind in port, at least for one night. Tendencies that have been kept in check suddenly erupt: anger, violence, and sexual tension.

One person whose troubles escalated at this time was Hammett, Campbell's and Smigliani's watch partner. Hammett, age forty-one, was about six foot three and weighed 250 pounds; he was a gentle man, however, and had never pushed his size around. A lover of classical music—he could listen to almost any piece and tell you its name and who composed it—he was the kind of unprepossessing big man whose weight and demeanor invited challenges. And several of these had been thrown at him while he was on board the *Columbia Eagle.*

Born in Greenwood, Louisiana, Hammett worked in Gulf of Mexico oil fields after high school, then served in the army during the Korean War. After this, he moved to the northwest, where he started working on Washington State ferries. Ferryboat work is totally different from deep-sea deck work, but it enabled Hammett to get an AB ticket. In early 1970 Hammett had taken a leave of absence from the ferryboats and caught an AB job on the *Columbia Eagle.* He was not having an easy time of it.

A ferryboat deckhand is essentially a traffic cop, making sure that cars and trucks line up correctly and that they get on and off without a hitch. Ferryboats have no hatches, no gear, no booms. No lines to splice. They do not even tie up the same way as deep-water ships. As a result, Hammett was a middle-aged AB who did not know how to splice lines, and was unfamiliar with booms and tarps and gear.

The two men who constantly harassed Hammett were the most seasoned deckhands on board: the bosun, James Northcutt, and the day-man, Norm Pettersen.

"First the Bosun threatened me 'cause I didn't know how to work gear, then the day-man, Pettersen, tried to beat me up," Hammett reported, "and he threatened me about three different times because I couldn't splice lines.

I went the second time to see the chief mate about it, he told me not to worry about it. He said just to defend myself in case something happened." The day-man, apparently ripe with a case of channel fever, came into the mess hall looking for Hammett. "I was sitting in the mess-hall after hours and Pettersen came in there with a trowel, what you use with cement, you know, and he made gestures with it," said Hammett. "So I was scared and I think that I got a wrench or something to put beside my bed. I felt that there was going to be trouble." Hammett was prepared for the bosun or the day-man to attack him in the middle of the night. He lay in bed waiting. When he saw the door open and heard someone stumbling in, Hammett had his wrench close by, ready to swing it. He saw, however, that it wasn't the bosun or the day-man, but someone whose own mooring lines were breaking loose: Donald Sather. "The electrician," recalled Hammett, "he broke in our fo'c'sle and woke us up several times and bothered Marco Smigliani. . . . I told him to get out." The men of the 12–4 crew wrestled with Sather, trying to get him out of the fo'c'sle.

"Sather's eyes was all glazed and he was blubbering," said Campbell. "So I went up to see the old man and I told him and the chief mate about it and that now he was trying to get into bed with Smigliani, and Smigliani done throwed him out on the floor, so I said come quick, something's gonna happen. So the chief mate and the bosun came down and took the electrician up to the old man's room. Then the electrician tried to jump up and they grabbed him by the door as he tried to run out and they told him to come back and sit down again."

Once they had Sather under control, the captain pieced the story together. While the ship was in Bataan, Sather had gone to see a Philippine doctor who prescribed barbiturates and amphetamines. After Sather returned to the ship, he took massive amounts of both, washed down with hard liquor. By the next day Sather was beyond stoned. He told Mornin to change burned-out light bulbs—the electrician's job—then went back aft to stare at the water. That's where Walter Drabina, the chief engineer, found him. "He was sitting on one of these high-up bitts back there. I went over and had a talk with him." Drabina told Sather that he had abused union privileges by putting the wiper to lamp up the ship, and he warned the electrician to "straighten up" or he was going to take him to the old man.

Drabina said, "Sather answers me, 'Look, I'm the electrician and I work hard and I can have a day off.' And I said, 'Everybody else on the ship is working.' Then he smiles and he says, 'Well, don't worry, everything's going to be all right.'"

The words stuck in Drabina's mind and they would come back to haunt Sather. Late that night, his barriers down, Sather tried to follow up on a passion that had been simmering for a couple of weeks: Marco Smigliani. The electrician went into the 12–4 deck fo'c'sle and started fumbling around, trying to find Smigliani's bunk.

According to Campbell, the old man asked Sather why he couldn't "stay out of Smigliani's room" and Sather answered, "'Well, I'll just tell you the truth, Captain. I'm in love with Smigliani.' The old man said, 'Well, I'll be damned. I wouldn't have thought that about you.' And the electrician said, 'Well, there are a lot of us on here.'"

Campbell said that a flustered captain muttered to Campbell, "I don't know what to tell you, I'm sorry the man woke you up."

Having more or less settled Sather's romantic problem, there was still another issue. The chief engineer told the captain that he was angry that Sather had not turned-to; that was why he told the electrician to take the weekend off, depriving him of sixteen hours of overtime. In front of the old man Sather turned to Drabina and shouted, *You know I got to work Saturday and Sunday, you prick!*

Drabina was astounded that Sather had called him a "prick" right in front of the captain and all the witnesses. The old man came nose to nose with Sather and repeated harshly several times: *I'll put you under confinement!* But Sather did not seem worried.

The old man decided that they could not get rid of Sather's prescription medicine, but they could at least get rid of his booze. They all went to the electrician's fo'c'sle. Campbell recalled, "You should have seen the stuff they throwed over the side. Whiskey, rum, beer, sitting there by the cases. The captain says, 'Go and write it on the bulletin board that nobody is to give this man a drink, because he's taking pills from a doctor.' Well, when this was over, the captain told the electrician not to mess around anymore. So the electrician flat-ass told him 'I'll do what I want to do! I'm tired of you people telling me what to do!' He said, 'I'm chief electrician!'"

At the same time that Sather's drama was playing out, McKay and Glatkowski met to talk over strategy. McKay was having misgivings about the

Burma plan. He was worried about crossing on foot through Thai territory, and he was unsure of the political situation in Burma, which still had ties to the United States. He was afraid that Burmese authorities might turn them over to the Americans

McKay suggested another idea: Cambodia. It was officially neutral, but the country's ruler, Prince Norodom Sihanouk, was openly pro–North Vietnamese, and he was a close friend of China. Sihanouk was a charismatic and independent leader who had a strained diplomatic relationship with the United States over its policy in Vietnam. And Cambodia was an easy country for them to reach. They could sail the *Eagle* right into the Cambodian coast, on the Gulf of Thailand. They would not have to travel on foot through hostile territory. McKay was sure that they would be greeted warmly in Cambodia.

"We decided that if we seized the ship, we would take it someplace where we would be welcomed and then deep-six the cargo," Glatkowski said. Only when the ammo had been sunk, would they feel that they had completed the job. They looked at the map again, and Glatkowski agreed. Cambodia was a good alternative.

DURING THE morning coffee break, the men went to their fo'c'sles, grabbed their life jackets and put on caps because the notice board indicated that there would be an F&B drill at 10:20. The drill began, as it always did, with the fire alarm, sounded by the continuous ringing of the ship's bell. The crew manned fire stations and ran fire hoses out to the lee side of the ship. The mate on watch, George Roush, called the engine room and asked for water on deck. Teams of men held on to hoses and shot powerful streams of seawater over the side, testing the pressure. While this was going on, McKay was on watch in the engine room. The men on watch, or those working in the galley, normally did not participate in drills; they remained in the engine room, the bridge, or the galley.

After the fire drill ended, the abandon ship portion of the exercise began. The alarm was sounded: seven short blasts on the ship's whistle, followed by one long blast, and then the same on the general alarm bell. During this part, the men went to their assigned lifeboats and waited until a mate arrived. The chief mate came to both lifeboats and informed the men that during this drill, they would put the lifeboats into the water.

The *Eagle,* like all Victory ships, had gravity davits—each lifeboat was carried in two cradles mounted on rollers. The rollers rode along two parallel tracks at right angles to the ship's side. A sea-painter was made fast, close to the center to the boat's forward thwart, then led out over the gunwale on the inboard side of the boat. It was rigged so that if the boat needed to move away from the ship quickly, it could easily do so; it was also used to keep the boat alongside the ship in order to allow more men to board the lifeboat.

First the gripes that held each boat to its cradle were released, then the brake. The bosun handled the brake for one boat and the day-man for the other, each one taking a position between the davits, giving slack on the line, taking care to keep the lines from jumping the cleats. Each boat was lowered by removing all but the final round turn and gradually paying out the line. Then each boat and the entire assembly rolled down the tracks by force of gravity, stopping when the lifeboat was suspended over the ship's side.

The men got into the boats. Glatkowski was the last one on. He said that he looked at the deck of the *Eagle* before climbing in. Everyone was either on the boats or on watch. The ship appeared empty. Abandoned. As Glatkowski's boat was lowered into the water, a thought came to him.

In their talks about how to take control of the ship, Glatkowski and McKay knew that it would be next to impossible to hold an entire crew at bay with just two guns. They could take control of the bridge, perhaps hold the captain hostage, and attempt to take the vessel toward Cambodia. But what were they going to do with the rest of the men on board? They could not lock them up. They would have no choice but to let the men roam the ship freely. The crew, no doubt, would attempt to retake the ship, and the more men out there, the harder it would be for Glatkowski and McKay to carry out their plan. It was risky, and they had no idea how to solve the problem.

Until now. Glatkowski suddenly saw a solution. After the drill was over, he went back to his sanitary, soogieing and sweeping impatiently for another hour. Just before twelve—as McKay got off watch—Glatkowski found him in the passageway and the two went quickly to McKay's fo'c'sle, where they were alone.

"I told Clyde that I'd figured out a way," said Glatkowski. "A way to pull it off. We could go to the old man and force him to signal the abandon ship alarm. We could tell him there was an emergency. A live bomb on board. That we'd rigged a live bomb on board. One we can set off at a moment's notice."

Glatkowski suggested that they force the old man to call the bridge and have him order an abandon ship. He was certain that the mate on watch would not question it. He would pull the alarm. Everyone would scramble to his emergency station. That way, most of the crew would be off the ship in one quick stroke, and only a skeleton crew would remain aboard—the captain, three engineers, and two mates.

McKay listened and agreed; it was a good idea. He suggested that they keep Mornin and Gray on board. After they seized the vessel, it was possible these two could be convinced to join the effort.

Later that day, McKay bumped into Dan Mornin and according to the latter's testimony during the mutiny investigation, McKay told him that he thought it was possible that the ship might not reach its destination. "[McKay] made some mention of Cambodia and 50-to-1 odds." Mornin claimed that he did not respond to McKay's statement and gave no sign that he understood where McKay was headed with this. At that point, Bruce Gray walked in and McKay cut it off.

When Mornin told this story to interrogators, they asked him why McKay had confided in him. Mornin told them, "Perhaps he thought I might go along with him." Did McKay ask him to? Mornin said no, McKay never told him what he was planning and never asked him to go along with it. And if McKay had, Mornin said, he would have refused.

That evening, the poker game had more action than usual. The Bataan draw had put fresh cash into the game; money flew back and forth. By midnight, the big winner was Marco Smigliani, who was up two hundred bucks. The game broke up and Smigliani stashed the money in his locker.

Meanwhile, Glatkowski was on the fantail, where he paced and smoked. He had doubts again. At midnight, having just gotten off watch, McKay joined him. "I was standing back aft on the fantail by the ship's railing," Glatkowski recalled, "looking off into the night sea as Clyde approached me. After a few moments of silence, Clyde asked, 'Are you going to be with me when it's time?'"

I don't know for sure, Glatkowski said. *I just can't say at this moment. I need time. This is too quick. I need a little more time.*

McKay wanted to know what was holding him back. Glatkowski, when writing about this incident later, said he told McKay, "I've been doing a lot of thinking, heavy thinking, about how this will affect my life and my family. After coming this far, I don't think that I could live with myself if we *don't* do it; and then, I think of my wife and child. I just don't know. There's so much going through my mind now." According to Glatkowski, "Clyde exploded when he heard this. He said, 'You're a bourgeois! A fucking bourgeois! I'm going to do it, with you or without you.' I tried to talk to him, to make him understand what I was going through, but he didn't want to hear it."

They both smoked cigarettes. "We thought of this mostly in silence," Glatkowski wrote. "Just before he left, he faced me and asked me, 'Are you going to be with me when the time comes?' I told him, 'I don't know. I just don't know.' Then he said, 'Okay. I'll see you tomorrow.' Then, with no further words, Clyde left the fantail."

CE Logbook: Saturday, March 14, 1970. Lat. 6°53'N. Long. 105°34'E. Partly cloudy, vis. good, ship steady in a slight sea & swell.

Clyde McKay came into the mess hall at half past seven in the morning, before turning-to. He had a big breakfast. No bacon or ham or sausages, but he filled up on pancakes and eggs and cereal. He and Glatkowski exchanged a few words and arranged to meet later. Then McKay went on watch. Changed tips on the burners. Gazed at gauges. At the same time, Glatkowski did his sanitary. Cleaned the captain's stateroom. Then the rooms of the other licensed men.

McKay finished his watch just before noon. He ate another big meal, then went to his fo'c'sle. Shortly before one o'clock, Jose Caceres, McKay's watch partner and roommate, was lying in bed when he saw McKay open his locker and reach for something. Caceres did not see what McKay took out. He also saw McKay talk to someone in the passageway, but he could not identify the person.

A few seconds later McKay, with a bulky manila folder under his arm, went out to the main deck, behind the house. Glatkowski, already waiting there, would later write, "The moment of decision had arrived. What had been hypothetical speculation suddenly became reality."

McKay stood with the folder wedged under his armpit. *The time is now,* McKay said. *Are you ready to take over the ship?*

Glatkowski hesitated while McKay glared at him. *I don't know,* Glatkowski finally said. *I don't know.* He paused a moment, then blurted out, *I'm going to be a father!*

Bourgeois! A fucking bourgeois, after all.

Glatkowski was furious. *Don't call me bourgeois!*

Weighing the rest of his life in the balance, Glatkowski said that what was holding him back was a connection to his unborn child. "It's just that I felt I had a moral responsibility to be there when the child was born. Not necessarily to follow that child through its life and every other damn thing, but in my heart I felt that I had this moral responsibility." Glatkowski was considering backing out. He asked McKay for a minute to "think it over," then moved into the house.

"I remember this vividly," Glatkowski said. "I went to the washroom, you know, toilet and sink." Glatkowski flushed the toilet. The whoosh of seawater made a sucking sound. He washed his hands and face, dipped his hands in the water, and slicked back his hair. Glatkowski said that he looked at the mirror and wondered what he should do. He was afraid of going through with it. How would it affect his family? What would it do to the rest of his life? Years later, Glatkowski would say that, besides fear, what he felt at that moment was this: "I looked up in the mirror and I said to myself: you cannot live, you cannot face your children, you will not be able to face anyone if you don't do this." He came out of the washroom and went down the passageway. He reached McKay, who was smoking a cigarette on the rail.

I'm okay, Glatkowski finally said. *It's okay. Let's do it.*

McKay flicked his cigarette over the side, took out one of the guns from the attaché case, and gave it to Glatkowski, who hid it inside his belt. They climbed the ladders, McKay in front of Glatkowski, whose legs were shaking.

Halfway up the ladder, McKay suddenly stopped and turned. *Listen, I have something to tell you. You're married, a kid on the way. If it all goes bust, if this fucks up, tell them I forced you into it. I'll take full responsibility for this.*

Glatkowski was insulted and angered. *What are you talking about! You want me to say you forced me into it? No, man, no way. You got no right to take this from me! You got no right! This is mine too!*

McKay backed off and said, *Okay, okay. Listen. When we go in, keep your gun hidden. Don't show it unless, unless it's absolutely necessary.*

Glatkowski agreed to this, and they continued up. They reached the top of the ladder, then walked up to the captain's office. McKay knocked. No answer. They opened the unlocked door and went inside. No one there. Glatkowski guessed that the old man was either in the radio shack or on the bridge taking the noon fix. They moved quickly out of the captain's office and knocked on the door to the chief mate's room. From inside they heard, *Yeah, what is it?*

Could we speak to you for a moment, Mr. Mate?

Morgan opened his door, saw the BR and the fireman. *Make it fast,* said Morgan, *I want to get some shut-eye.*

You don't have to worry about that, said McKay.

The chief mate waved the BR and the fireman into his room, leaving the door on the hook. His arm shaking, McKay pulled out his gun, and aimed it at the mate.

Jesus, man. This some kind of joke? Morgan's eyes jumped from McKay to Glatkowski and back to McKay.

No joke, said McKay. *This is a mutiny.*

It's a hijacking, said Glatkowski.

McKay glanced at Glatkowski and said forcefully, *It's a mutiny.*

Glatkowski later wrote, "The Mate again asked if we were 'joking.' McKay said that we were not, that his gun was real, that he had filed down certain parts of it so that it would shoot faster and so that the trigger would not have so much resistance."

"McKay's arm was shaking so much," Morgan testified before the mutiny investigators, "I was afraid that the pistol would go off by mistake."

"When Clyde pulled the gun on Morgan," said Glatkowski, "I was afraid he was going to shoot the man because his hand was shaking. Obviously, Clyde was scared. I had dealt with *my* fear before coming up there—me in front of the mirror in the washroom, that was the whole nine yards, that was me confronting myself, saying: 'Are you going to do this or aren't you?' The fear aspect of it. I was scared the whole time, but I dealt with my fear, most of it, before we went topside. *His* fear came out up topside, when confronted with the reality of the situation."

"McKay told me about having a live bomb on board the ship and the fact that he didn't want the cargo to reach Vietnam," Morgan testified. "He said, 'If you do anything rash, there's going to be a lot of loss of lives. Lot of bloodshed. If you don't do what we say, we'll be forced to kill you. We will kill you.' And I also noticed about this time that Glatkowski had a .38 in his belt, right by his belt buckle. He didn't—hadn't pulled it out, not yet."

"The noonday report was due to be delivered to the mate any moment," recalled Glatkowski. "It was this that he was waiting for so that he could go to sleep for a while. We said that we would wait with him, then take him over to the Captain's office."

So McKay pointed his pistol at the mate, Glatkowski stood, and the three waited.

Billy Campbell was the deckhand who was supposed to deliver the noonday report. At that moment he was on the wheel and he was pissed, really pissed. A special deck department meeting was about to take place in the bosun's room—a more private place than the mess hall—and the purpose of it was to oust Campbell from his position as deck delegate. Ostensibly, the reason for doing this was that Campbell was only a B-book, not an A-book in his SIU standing. But in his heart Campbell knew the real reason: they were afraid of him. He was the only one willing to stand up to the drug smugglers and the homosexuals aboard the ship, all of whom would take over if it weren't for him.

Normally, the first wheel watch would have been relieved at about 1:15, but on this day—because of the meeting about to take place—Roger Hammett came up at one o'clock. Campbell told Hammett what course he was steering and that the wheel was on the "iron mike," the automatic pilot. Once Hammett got on the wheel, he grabbed the spokes to give himself support—he had chronic back and leg problems—then shifted his weight this way and that as the ship rolled. His eyes flicked back to the binnacle on occasion, just to make sure the ship stayed on the right course.

Herbert Gunn, the third mate, and Captain Swann came into the wheelhouse from the wing. Gunn wrote up the noon report and gave Campbell copies to distribute. No need for the ordinary to take one to the old man, of course. Clutching copies of the report, Campbell went aft from the wheelhouse to the chartroom, then down the interior ladder.

Once he was outside the chief mate's room, Campbell knocked on the door, which was on the hook—secured to a hook at the top, leaving a narrow opening you can peek through. Campbell tried to look inside, calling out for the mate, saying that he had the noon report. Inside, McKay pointed his gun at the mate, signaling him to keep quiet, while Glatkowski, who was standing near the doorway, shoved his face into the opening and told Campbell to give *him* the report. Campbell, taken aback at seeing the BR in the mate's room, asked for the chief mate. He was supposed to give the report to him only.

It was a standoff.

A few seconds passed, then McKay, his arm shaking, pointed his gun at the chief mate's head. Morgan finally spoke. *Give him the report,* said the mate. Campbell heard him and recognized the voice. *Okay, Mister Mate,* Campbell said.

Campbell handed the small piece of paper to Glatkowski through the opening. "He then left for the radio operator's office further down the passageway," Glatkowski recalled. "So we knew that he would be giving a copy of the report to Sparks and that Sparks would radio in the ship's noon position. That meant that nobody would expect to hear from the ship for another 24 hours. We knew that. We took it into account."

Although giving the noon report to the BR struck him as odd, Campbell had too many things on his mind to worry about it. He had to get to that meeting. He moved quickly to the main deck.

"I came down below and they all gathered in the Bosun's room," Campbell told the investigators. "They was having a deck department meeting. They ousted me as deck department delegate, which was fine and dandy. So Pettersen told me, he was drunk, he said 'Now that you ain't delegate, you won't be runnin' up topside telling any more shit.' I said, 'Well, if you were the union man that you should be, you wouldn't be acting the way you do for people to run up topside and tell shit.'"

The entire meeting took less than five minutes, after which the men went to their fo'c'sles or hung out in the mess hall.

Meanwhile, leaving the chief mate's room, McKay forced Morgan to walk with him and Glatkowski to the captain's stateroom. McKay knocked on the door. There was no answer. He opened it and the three men entered. This was a two-room suite, with bedroom and office. They were in the office. McKay told Morgan to call out for Swann, who might be in the bedroom. Morgan did so but there was no reply. McKay knocked on the bedroom door; but again there was no answer. McKay told Morgan to take a seat. They would wait.

CE Logbook: At 1315 this vessel was seized by Clyde W. McKay and Alvin L. Glatkowski who held captain and chief mate hostage in the master's quarters under threat of setting off a bomb unless the master and chief officer complied with their demands while being held at gun-point.

Swann testified to the investigators, "While proceeding from the bridge to my office I heard Mr. Morgan calling, 'Captain, Captain!' Upon entering my office I found Mr. Morgan, Clyde McKay and Alvin Glatkowski there. Mr. Morgan said, 'They have a gun on me.' This was the very first indication I had of trouble to come."

McKay waved the pistol at the captain. *Move very slowly, close the door and get in the corner,* he told Swann, forcing him to sit down on the settee. McKay then sat on the captain's desk with one foot on top of the desk and the other in the desk chair. His pistol was pointed at Swann's belt buckle. Morgan was standing near the captain and Glatkowski was at the door.

With his gun arm still shaking, McKay declared, *This is a mutiny. Now that I have gone this far, and drawn the gun on you, you and I both know that I can't get in any deeper than I am now, so don't do anything foolish like reaching in any drawers or putting your hands where I can't see them.*

The captain asked McKay to explain himself. *What do you want?*

We don't want to kill anyone but we are nervous and these weapons have hair-triggers so be careful and do exactly as I tell you, McKay said. *Now, first off this cargo is not going to reach Thailand and to prevent this we will go so far as blowing the ship up and everyone aboard and we have the means of doing this in a few minutes. But if you will agree to take the ship to Cambodia with a skeleton crew, maybe no one will be hurt.*

Swann tried to talk to McKay, but he found the fireman to be stubborn. "McKay became extremely irritable almost to the point of becoming hysterical," said Swann. "At this point I was convinced that these men were under the influence of some kind of drug and could not be rationalized with. McKay then said it was up to me. If I wanted to save some of the crew, I must get them in lifeboats immediately as there are some nuts below that will get all of us killed."

Enough talk, McKay said. *Someone is going to come in that door and I'll have to kill him. Go to your phone and tell the mate that he's to sound the abandon ship signal and tell the men that a live bomb is on the vessel and everyone is to leave immediately except two mates and two engineers.*

While McKay was fixed on the old man, the chief mate slowly moved in McKay's direction. His arms were outstretched as if to say: I'm unarmed, harmless, just trying to be helpful. Morgan spoke softly. *You know, what you're doing, it's really not logical. I mean, if you want to protest against the war, there are more logical ways of doing it. There are marches, rallies, logical steps to take.*

Glatkowski saw that Morgan was moving dangerously close to McKay. As if he were watching himself in a movie, a Western, Glatkowski snapped the gun out of his belt and pointed it at the mate. *Shove your logic up your ass!* he shouted, half-frightened, half-angry, as the mate stepped back, putting his hands up in the air.

Glatkowski held the gun in two hands, keeping it steady, the barrel pointing at the mate's head.

Until that moment, the event had not seemed real for Glatkowski. As if he could somehow stop it, turn back, pretend it never happened, suffer no consequences. But pulling out his pistol changed all that. He had crossed the line. There was no turning back now.

With Glatkowski pointing his pistol at the chief mate and McKay pointing his at the captain, McKay repeated his demand that the captain call the bridge. Swann said he "tried to reason" with McKay, telling him that it would take more men than he asked for to get the ship to Cambodia. "So at that time [McKay] said I could have another engineer and that was it," said Swann. "That was supposed to be all I was going to have. I tried to haggle again with him." But McKay was adamant.

Meanwhile, Glatkowski started searching the captain's quarters. "He was looking for weapons," the captain recalled, "throwing things around, opening up the file cabinets in the bedroom." McKay said that he knew the captain had a gun and that he should give it to them, or else. "Knowing it was only a matter of time before they would find it," Swann told the investigators, "I told them where my only pistol was." Glatkowski went to the safe and pulled out the captain's gun and pocketed it, along with a box of ammunition. This infuriated Morgan. "The old man caved in so easily," said the chief mate later. "Just gave them the gun. It was disgusting."

McKay repeated his threat: *If you want to save the lives of the men, get them into a lifeboat immediately.* McKay said that he could blow up the ship in minutes. "McKay stressed that," Captain Swann said. "That it wouldn't take him any time at all to blow up the ship, that they were all set to do that. It sounded to me like they had some fuses laid around that they could light off. I thought it was possible. You know, it's hard to inspect a ship thoroughly, to find out whether there is or not, especially under those circumstances."

McKay again told Swann to call the bridge. "And I thought," Swann testified, "don't panic, don't panic anybody. So I shifted my chair to the telephone."

At 1:27 P.M. the Captain—with a gun pointed at him—made the call to the bridge.

8 ABANDON SHIP

Gulf of Thailand

The Bridge

"I was on the wheel," Hammett testified at the investigation, "and the third mate Mr. Gunn received a telephone call from the captain's room."

Gunn heard Captain Swann, in a shaky voice, tell him to sound the abandon ship signal. Gunn was confused—a drill on Saturday? He hesitated.

Mr. Gunn, Swann said more forcefully, *there's a bomb aboard.*

Captain, there's lots of bombs on this ship, Gunn replied.

It was a brief moment, this phone call, but one that would haunt the captain for the rest of his life. In hindsight, Swann told the mutiny investigators, there may have been an opportunity to warn Gunn, to let him know that something was up, that he and the chief mate were being held at gunpoint and that someone should try to rescue them and take back control of the ship. But Swann never gave Gunn this signal.

"Mr. Gunn had no way of knowing what was going on," Swann told the investigators. "He never came back with anything that I could answer to or give him any indication what was going on."

Instead, the captain said that there was a live bomb on board, and it was set to go off. He demanded that the alarm be sounded and the men go to their lifeboats, all of them except for himself, the chief engineer, and the first and the second assistants. He needed them to run the plant.

"I thought it was odd that [the captain] wanted everybody to abandon ship," said Gunn, "but when he told me there was a live bomb on board, well, that changed the picture, and I understood why, or at least I thought I did at the time."

Gunn sounded the alarm, ringing seven short blasts of the ship's whistle, then one long blast, followed by the same series on the general alarm bell.

Orville Mills—Sparks—was in the radio shack and when he heard the alarm, he put on his life jacket and went directly to the bridge. He was surprised that the only licensed man there was Gunn. Mills asked what was going on and Gunn told him, "There's a live bomb on board."

Mills returned to the radio shack, briefly tested the equipment, then waited for word from the captain.

The Lifeboats

When the alarm sounded at 1:27 P.M., the second mate, Robert Stevenson, was in bed. He put on clothes, hat, gloves, light coat, and life jacket. He then went quickly to his lifeboat station, crossing paths with men who were scurrying in confusion and shooting questions at one another: Why an abandon ship alarm the day after a drill? Why on Saturday? What the hell is going on? Stevenson hurried to the motorized boat on the port side. On the way to the boat deck, he hollered up to the bridge, *What's the trouble?* Gunn yelled back, *It's a bomb scare. Get into your lifeboat and get it into the water!*

A few seconds later, Jeffrey Wright, second assistant, showed up at Stevenson's lifeboat. Wright noticed that Stevenson was "perturbed" and had a "shocked, peculiar look." Wright asked him about the alarm. Stevenson, now worried because of what Gunn had told him, did not answer. Wright said sarcastically, *What is this, a military secret?*

The bosun, James Northcutt, came up at this time. Stevenson told him to uncover the boat and get it ready for launching. Billy Campbell, who had just been ejected from his position as deck department delegate, also showed up and started helping the bosun.

At the same time, men arrived at the starboard boat, the #1 lifeboat, which did not have a motor: the day-man, who started uncovering that boat, and Marco Smigliani, dressed in shorts, T-shirt, and flip-flops. Smigliani had not grabbed any other clothing or his poker winnings. He would regret that.

The Engine Room

When the alarm rang, the engineer on watch was Curtis Ridge.

"The telephone rang," said Ridge, "and the third mate, whose voice I recognized, said that everybody should get into the boats with the exception of the chief engineer, the first and the second assistants. He did not say it the way he normally does when he calls down. When he calls down to tell me about the time change or something, he says, 'Well, old partner,' this and that or something, but this time he didn't. He was all business."

Ridge asked Gunn what was going on. Gunn said that there was a live bomb aboard, that was all he knew. Then Gunn hung up.

At this moment Ridge saw Don Sather come into the fireroom. Ridge did not know it, but Sather had taken prescribed barbiturates, washed down with beer and scotch. Ridge asked Sather to close the extra nozzles on top of the high-pressure turbine. Amazingly, Sather obliged. Then Sather walked over to the log desk, near the throttle platform, and leaned over the desk. He stayed there, smiling.

Walter Drabina, chief engineer, came down to the engine room together with Leopold Tober, the Polish-born first assistant, who was jumping around nervously despite having taken nitroglycerin for his heart condition. "The Chief and the First come storming down the ladder, and they were running around there screaming this and that," Ridge recalled, "and they said that they were going to cut off one boiler and so on and adjust the extra feed and all of this which you would have to do to go from a full ahead to a stop." They all asked one another what the emergency was about, but no one knew.

Ridge told Drabina and Tober what Gunn had said—that there was a live bomb on board. "I wanted a confirmation from the skipper himself on this," Drabina testified. So he called the old man and got through to him. He noticed the "strain in the old man's voice." The captain told Drabina to remain on the ship with the first and the second engineers.

Listen, Captain, if me, the first and the second are the only guys on the ship, said Drabina, *then I want a fireman and an oiler or somebody down in the fire room.*

I'm sorry, said Swann, *that's the order, you guys are going to have to do the best you can.*

Drabina hung up and reluctantly ordered the fireman and oiler on watch to go up to their lifeboats. He instructed the wiper, Mornin, to go up to his emergency station. Drabina saw Sather standing by the throttle platform, staring into space with the pained, painted smile of the truly stoned. The chief reminded the electrician that his emergency station was the lifeboat, not the engine room—what the hell was he doing down here?

"The electrician just looked up and shrugged and sort of grinned and kind of pointed to the switchboard, the main switchboard," Ridge recalled. Drabina told Ridge to go to his lifeboat and to take Sather with him, but the electrician would not budge. Sather said he got "seasick in lifeboats."

Drabina, losing patience, asked Sather to do him a favor: *Go topside,* Drabina told Sather, *find the second assistant, and tell him to come down to the engine room. And while you're up there, find out what's going on.* Sather perked up at the idea of performing a reconnaissance mission and left.

Mornin followed orders and went up to his emergency station, the life raft on the flying bridge, the open-air deck directly above the bridge. There he joined Bruce Gray, who—by coincidence—was also assigned to that station. A few seconds after Mornin arrived there, he and Gray looked down and saw Gunn, on the wing of the bridge, shouting up to them: *Leave the flying bridge and go to a lifeboat!* They followed orders, and went two decks down. When Gray and Mornin got into a lifeboat, most of the men were already inside, and the boats were waiting to be lowered.

At that same moment, Sather arrived at #2 lifeboat, which had an outboard Mercury motor, and told Wright that Drabina wanted him in the engine room. Wright got out of the boat and headed below. Having performed his first task, Sather set off for his next assignment: to find out what was going on.*

Meanwhile, in the captain's stateroom, Swann was trying to convince McKay that the ship would need more men. It would be impossible to take the ship anywhere with just three engineers. At the very least, Swann said, they would need three deckhands. Otherwise, how could they handle mooring lines or the anchor chain?

---

*Wright testified that it was Dan Mornin who told him to go down to the engine room. Other witnesses—including Sather himself—testified that it was Sather who told Wright.

Finally, McKay relented. They could hold the man at the wheel and keep two other men. McKay insisted that the two additional men be Mornin and Gray. Swann was not satisfied. If they were going to sail with a crew this short, they would need a couple of experienced deckhands, not a wiper and a pantryman.

McKay stood firm. He wanted Mornin and Gray, and that was that. Swann called Gunn and told him to make sure that these two remained on board.

Gunn ran from the bridge down to the #1 lifeboat and ordered Gray and Mornin back to the flying bridge. The rest of the men were already on the lifeboats, making sure that there was food and water on board, that the motor on #2 was working, that there was safety equipment, and that the plugs were in place. Gunn ran back up to the bridge and watched, more and more perturbed. The men on lifeboat #2 couldn't get the plug in!

Prodded by phone calls from the captain reminding him that there was a live bomb on board—and caught up in the urgency of the moment—Gunn shouted down from the wing of the bridge, *Get the boats away immediately! There's a bomb on board from the last port in the Philippines, and we don't know where it is!*

When the men on the lifeboats heard that, they too were caught up in the urgency. They hurried, scrambled, finally got the plug into the #2 boat, and were ready to lower away.

"The mate said everybody should get into the boat," the bosun said, "so everybody got in, except myself. I'm the man on the brake. So I was standing by to pick the boat back up after drill was over." Campbell and the bosun both stayed on board.

As the lifeboats were going down, Stevenson yelled up to Gunn on the bridge: *Is this for real?* Gunn replied: *Yes! It's for real! You've got to leave immediately!*

From their post by the brake, the bosun and Campbell lowered each lifeboat the rest of the way, paying out each line, making sure it did not jump the cleat. The water was calm and the boats settled down gently, on an even keel. Ridge got to the rail just as the lifeboats hit the water. He yelled to Stevenson that he was coming and then quickly scrambled down the Jacob's ladder.

Gunn yelled down to the men in the lifeboats again. *Cast off!* He pointed toward the horizon. *Nearest land is Vietnam, 109 miles due north!*

The men on the lifeboats could not believe what they just heard. They were mystified. At this point, most of the men were still under the impression that it was just a drill—a strange one, but a drill nonetheless. The mate had just told them to sail for Vietnam! How could they do that? Only one of the boats had a motor so that boat would have to tow the other. The men on the lifeboats shouted that there probably wasn't even enough fuel to go thirty miles, let alone one hundred!

"The third mate again emphasized that we should clear the ship immediately," Stevenson told the investigators. "We then pulled around to the other side of the vessel and took the other lifeboat into tow. We then moved off a safe distance from the ship and just sat in the water watching."

The Captain's Stateroom

The phone rang in the stateroom and with McKay's assent, the captain picked it up. It was Gunn, who said that the boats had cleared the vessel. The captain repeated this to McKay, who told Glatkowski to look out the porthole and check. Glatkowski confirmed it: the boats were about a quarter-mile away. McKay waved his gun and ordered the captain to get the ship under way: *Right now! Full speed!*

Swann pleaded with McKay to be patient. *We're short-handed, it'll take time to build up steam.* McKay was not in a patient mood. He told the old man to call the engine room. *Goddamit,* shouted McKay, *tell them I want 15 nozzles! Open 'er up all the way! Right now!* Reluctantly, Swann made the call.

McKay then ordered Morgan to fetch the appropriate charts from the chartroom so that they could lay out a course. The chartroom was directly above the captain's office. McKay, his weapon aimed at the captain, warned Morgan to come back immediately and not signal anyone. Morgan stepped out of the captain's office, crossed the narrow passageway in two or three steps to the base of the ladder, then went up the steps to the chartroom, a distance covered in about five seconds. Finding the charts in less than a minute, Morgan came back down to the captain's stateroom.

Meanwhile, McKay told Glatkowski to go out on deck, find out who remained on board and bring Gray and Mornin back with him. Not knowing what to expect, Glatkowski left the stateroom and prowled the deck. Campbell was the first to spot him.

"I saw the BR with a pistol just outside the captain's deck," Campbell testified. "I thought they was play guns, you know. Lots of these guys is crazy anyways, but they wasn't playing no games. They were real guns." Campbell saw the bosun on the other side of the captain's deck and pointed out Glatkowski. The bosun carefully approached Glatkowski, who pointed his gun at him, shouting: *Stay right there! We've got the ship under control.* The bosun asked, *By whose orders?*

My orders, Glatkowski replied. *Go forward and stand by!*

"He pointed this .38 at me and I saw the bullets," said the bosun, "and I obeyed his orders. So, I never done nothing drastic, I just obeyed the man's orders."

Glatkowski ran up to the wing of the bridge, looked up and saw Gray and Mornin on the flying bridge, standing near their emergency post. He called for them to come down the ladder, motioning with his weapon. "We were standing by the liferaft," Mornin testified, "and I looked down and saw the BR. He had a revolver. I had no idea why he was carrying a gun."

Instead of coming down, Mornin and Gray ran across the flying bridge to the other ladder. Glatkowski sprinted through the wheelhouse from the starboard to the port wing of the bridge to head them off. When Gray and Mornin came down the ladder to the port wing of the bridge, they were face to face with Glatkowski, who pointed his pistol and shouted at them, *Goddamit, I almost shot at you! If I had missed you and a stray bullet had hit a box of detonators on deck, the ship would have gone up in flames!*

It was a tense moment. Gray and Mornin had gotten to know Glatkowski well during the trip and considered him a friend. But the man facing them now, holding a gun and furiously screaming at them, was not the man that they knew.

It took several seconds for Glatkowski to calm down, after which he made a strained announcement to his fantail buddies: *Clyde and I have taken over the ship as a protest against the war. If you want to join, you're welcome. If you don't want to, you still have to obey orders.*

"We came into the captain's office," said Mornin, "and Clyde, the fireman, was there and he had a pistol as well. He held the captain and chief mate at gun-point. And he informed us that the ship was going to go to Cambodia."

Mornin and Gray avoided making eye contact with the captain and chief mate, who were aware that the wiper and the pantryman were part of the group that hung out on the fantail with Glatkowski and McKay. Mornin and Gray felt guilty by association. At one point, Mornin—apparently feeling that his and Gray's part in this might eventually need some explaining—turned to Gray and said, "When we get to Cambodia, you do the talking."

The chief mate overheard this. "I don't know what Mornin meant by that," Morgan testified, "but I automatically connected him and Bruce Gray as being in with the flock. We didn't know how many hijackers there were on the ship. It seemed like a group of confederates. It seemed like they were working right with them."

McKay had more important issues than Mornin and Gray. The ship was still at stop engines, which infuriated him. Waving his gun, McKay shouted at the captain, who was still looking at a chart spread out on the dining table: *We're not moving yet! What's going on? Why aren't we moving yet?* The captain again explained that the plant had to build up steam, which took time. McKay accused the captain of stalling. His gun hand started shaking again. McKay appeared on the verge of shooting someone, anyone. There was a feeling of dread in the air, that something terrible could happen at any moment.

Suddenly, there was a noise, a banging sound, coming from the passageway. Everyone in the room froze as the door opened. Glatkowski and McKay pointed their pistols.

Standing there, reeling and unsteady, was Sather. At the behest of the chief engineer, he had been trying to find out what was going on, and his snooping had finally landed him at the door to the captain's stateroom. He saw the guns.

"I happened to pass the captain's office and that's where everyone was at," Sather told the investigators. "Clyde had a gun on the captain and Ski put one on me. And the wiper, he was just standing there." Sather asked, *What's going on?* No one answered. The electrician stubbornly planted himself. He told McKay that he was not leaving until he found out what was going on. Finally, Mornin said, *Take a look around you. It's a hijack. Get the fuck out of here.*

Then McKay barked at Sather, screaming at him to leave or else he would shoot him. Sather was not intimidated. He just stood there. "McKay was getting madder and madder, and he was shaking more and more, and Sather just stays right there," recalled Swann. After a few tense moments, "McKay finally shut the door in his face."

McKay then ordered the captain to call Sparks and order him to come to the stateroom. McKay wanted to silence the ship's radio. Mills came hobbling up to the door.

"When I went to the captain's office," said Mills, "the door was closed, so I knocked. When I entered, I saw the captain sitting at the table in his office, and the chief mate was standing. Clyde McKay was standing with an automatic pistol in his hand and Alvin Glatkowski had a revolver in his hand, and McKay told me to sit down and take it easy. The captain was laying out a course on a chart. McKay was the leader. He was giving all the orders. He was telling Glatkowski to do this and don't do that. McKay seemed to be the man in control."

There were now seven men in the captain's office, a small room with a desk, a table, chairs, and a filing cabinet. It felt claustrophobic. If a pistol went off, on purpose or by accident, the bullet's ricochet would likely find a human being in its path.

The captain showed McKay a route to Cambodia. McKay approved it on the spot and had the old man write the course on a slip of paper. The captain gave the slip to Mornin, who was instructed—by McKay—to go to the bridge and hand it to the third mate. McKay then asked Gray to go fix some sandwiches and coffee.

Mornin and Gray took off in different directions. "The wiper [Mornin] and the messman [Gray]," Mills testified to investigators, "they were taking orders from McKay and Glatkowski and carrying them out. To go down and do this and do that. It seemed like they was friendly with them."

The Bridge

Guns in hand, McKay and Glatkowski motioned the captain, the chief mate, and the radio operator out of the captain's stateroom. Still in shock and unsure of what McKay and Glatkowski would or could do, the hostages did as they were instructed.

In the investigation Morgan testified that throughout the mutiny the crew "feared that the two mutineers would shoot them. They had that solid fear implanted in their minds. . . . They were under fear that if they tried anything they'd be shot."

There is no mention in the investigation documents of how the five men went from the captain's stateroom to the chartroom. Logic dictates that Sparks probably went first, crossing the passageway, then hobbling up the steps toward the chartroom. They would have gone up the narrow ladderway single file. The chief mate, who was holding the charts, would likely have gone behind Sparks, and then the captain. McKay was probably directly behind the old man, holding his pistol at the captain's back, while Glatkowski would have brought up the rear, with his pistol aimed in the general direction of the chief mate. It would have taken about fifteen seconds for the five of them to climb topside to the chartroom. As soon as the five men came into the chartroom, they went through the doorway on the port side that led directly forward to the adjacent wheelhouse.

When they arrived, Mornin had just handed Gunn the slip of paper with the course written on it. Hammett, who was still on the wheel, asked, *What the hell's going on?* Swann replied, as calmly as he could, *Roger, it looks like we've got ourselves a little hijacking here.* "I then saw Glatkowski and McKay, and both had their guns drawn," Hammett said.

McKay left Glatkowski in the wheelhouse while he took Mills back through the chartroom, down the interior ladder to the captain's deck, then to the port side. When they were outside the radio room, McKay told Mills to give him the key. McKay locked the door to the radio shack and the small adjacent bedroom, then pocketed the key, telling Mills, *Don't enter this room or send messages without my permission.* Mills wanted to know where he would sleep. McKay told him to use the steward's room, then he left Mills there and bounded up the ladder back to the wheelhouse.

On the bridge, McKay again demanded that the captain call the chief engineer and ask for full steam ahead. Swann rang up Drabina, who told Swann he was moving as fast as he could. This was not fast enough for McKay. He turned to Mornin and ordered him to go down to the engine room and tell Drabina to proceed full speed ahead. *Now!* Mornin ran out of the wheelhouse. Once the wiper was gone, the captain tried to be the voice of reason. *You have to baby this ship,* he said softly to McKay, who angrily turned away.

The Engine Room

On his way down, Mornin ran into Campbell, told him what he had seen, then both went separately to the engine room. Campbell got there first and told everyone what had happened. A few seconds later Mornin arrived and went straight to the chief engineer. "The wiper, he come down and he says,

'I'm the runner between these gun guys and the engine room,'" said Drabina. "'They're giving me the orders. I'm the only guy that can get to them.' So the wiper says, 'Okay, let's go 15 nozzles now.'"

Drabina told Mornin, *I get my orders from the bridge, not from a wiper.* Drabina testified that Mornin shouted back, *Never mind the bridge! That's the orders! You go 15 nozzles!* Drabina was furious. He walked away and called the bridge.

On the bridge, Gunn answered the phone.

Okay, we're ready to start moving, Drabina informed Gunn.

You have to run her at 15 nozzles, Gunn told him.

Drabina said it was a terrible idea to have the ship go at such a fast clip from a dead stop. Gunn told Drabina that he had no choice.

Drabina hung up, told Tober and Wright what had to be done, and was about to open the ship up all the way when he saw Sather stumble into the fireroom. The last thing Drabina wanted was Sather in the engine room right now. The chief screamed at the electrician: *Get out of here! Get out of the engine room!* But Sather went back to his position by the throttle platform, where he stayed, grinning.

"I give the electrician about two or three times warnings to get out of the engine room," said Drabina. "He refused." Suddenly, Drabina remembered that two days before, Sather had said something cryptic to him. Sather had mumbled, "There's nothing to worry about . . . everything's going to be all right." Maybe, Drabina told the investigators, maybe Sather knew that there was going to be a mutiny. Maybe that was what he was talking about.

Drabina watched as Sather left the throttle platform and went to some rag boxes at the after end of the generator flat and started rummaging around in them. "I didn't know what 'Lectro was doing," Drabina testified. "He was clean down to the end towards the inboard side when I went over to him and I told him, 'What are you looking for?' So he just turned around and looked at me and give me one of these smiles, you know. He was the only guy that never seemed worried about anything on the ship."

The Lifeboats

Meanwhile, about a half-mile away, out on the water, the twenty-four men in the lifeboats looked anxiously toward the vessel. The two boats were tied up to each other.

"First we took stock of the situation," Ciamboli recalled. "We got out the lantern, flare gun, checked the food and water supply. We knew what should be in the lifeboat, we were just making sure it was there."

Jose Fernandez, the chief cook, remembered that "the second mate of our boat gave us instructions in regards to how we were going to ration our food and water and then, all of a sudden, we could see steam coming from the Columbia Eagle."

Curtis Ridge stared at it, stunned. "We were watching the ship and all of a sudden a blast of black smoke came up and the screw started spinning and I mean she was going faster than she ever did go, that I know of."

"And then we saw the prop of the ship went full ahead," Pettersen recalled. "Black smoke came out of her stack and she headed for the horizon."

"She kept going, wide open," said Ridge. "They must have had every nozzle on the block open. We couldn't figure out what was happening."

The Wheelhouse

In the *Eagle*'s wheelhouse, McKay and Glatkowski felt the ship moving, almost lurching forward, advancing quickly from stop engines to fifteen knots. The mutineers looked aft and saw a wake, a little wavy at first, but soon straightening out. They ran out to opposite wings of the bridge and saw enormous, thick clouds of black smoke coming from the stack. It had been a little more than an hour and a half since they had entered the chief mate's room. Three hours ago McKay had been standing watch in the engine room and Glatkowski had been cleaning an officer's toilet. Now they were in control of the vessel and most of the men were out in lifeboats. And the ship was moving!

Glatkowski realized he had two pistols on him—the old one they had bought in the Philippines and the much newer one they had gotten out of the old man's safe. Glatkowski looked at the two and threw the old pistol over the side. It made a light splash and sank quickly.

McKay signaled Glatkowski: let's go topside. Moving from opposite sides, they ran up the ladders and went up to the flying bridge. There, where no one could see them, they allowed themselves a brief moment of celebration: they hugged each other. Then they quickly went back down to the wheelhouse and stationed themselves at either doorway, guns in hand.

9 SKELETON CREW

Gulf of Thailand

CE Logbook: At 1443 we resumed speed on 15 nozzles . . . as directed by the mutineers [who] issued a warning to all the bridge officers that if we did not go direct to Cambodia they were going to kill everyone on board and blow the ship up. . . . Thus the vessel was controlled at gun-point.

Glatkowski and McKay, together with the captain, went into the chartroom, which was directly aft of the wheelhouse. Looking at the charts, they examined the route to Cambodia. Assessing which port would offer the least problems—one with a deep enough harbor, fewest obstacles, and some distance from guerrilla warfare—McKay decided on a bay on Cambodia's central coast, near Sihanoukville, the city named after the Cambodian leader whom the mutineers expected would welcome them. Baie de Ream would be their target. The old man, pencil in hand, started examining the charts and working out a course.

While the captain pored over the charts, McKay and Glatkowski walked out of the chartroom, leaving the captain alone. The mutineers went out on the wing of the bridge, where they could keep an eye on the wheelhouse and the man at the wheel. If they were going to control the ship, they would have to control the bridge, whether the captain was there or not. One or both of them would have to maintain a presence on the bridge, with weapons in clear view of the man on the wheel and the mate on the watch.

For his part, the captain was determined not to jeopardize lives. Although, in his own mind, he did not categorically rule out seizing control of the vessel from the mutineers, during these early stages of the mutiny he was resigned to allow the mutineers to call the shots. Even though the two gunmen were not pointing their weapons at anyone, he felt it would be folly to attempt anything. The mutineers were skittish; a gun could go off. They might let down their guard at some point, or they might fall asleep, which would give the captain and his men the opening they would need. The gunmen could not stay awake forever, Swann reasoned. The best thing was to wait it out.

At the same time, the captain did not want the mutiny to be a successful one. Among other things, it would not look good on his record. But how could he stop the vessel from arriving in Cambodia without risking lives, ship, or cargo? He decided that the best course of action was to buy time, to slow the ship down. He hoped that by so doing, it would allow the U.S. Coast Guard or the Navy to catch up and intercept them. There might of course be a dangerous standoff. The captain was willing to gamble that the mutineers—facing overwhelming naval power instead of seamen with no weapons—might lose their nerve. Or they might simply lose stamina and give up out of sheer exhaustion. It was worth a try, the captain thought.

Therefore, while Glatkowski and McKay stood out on the wing of the bridge, the captain began charting a roundabout course that would not only slow down the *Columbia Eagle*'s progress, but also draw attention. His idea was to proceed directly west as far as possible, and then come back toward Cambodia, in something of a buttonhook pattern. Any aircraft on surveillance, or a Coast Guard cutter or land facility looking at radar, would realize that something was wrong. If the mutineers questioned the wayward course, the captain could point out the shoals that were indicated on the chart of the area, or he could say that fishing nets were detectable on radar.

There was one unpredictable factor, a wild card that might throw his plan into jeopardy. The live bomb. McKay had claimed that a device was planted on the ship and was set to go off. The captain felt that this was a ruse, but there was no way that he could ignore the threat. If there was a bomb, it meant that the mutineers were willing to commit suicide in order to achieve their goals. A standoff with the U.S. Coast Guard could end in a disaster. The captain thought about having a few men conduct a quiet search of the vessel. But the words of the third mate echoed in his head. "There's lots of bombs on this ship, captain." He was right. Even if the mutineers had not placed a bomb on board, a bullet could set off the fuses and detonators on deck, and the explosion could rip through the vessel in no time.

Meanwhile, on the wing of the bridge, Glatkowski and McKay discussed their own problems. How were they going to protect themselves from attacks? Glatkowski suggested that they cover one another as they went around corners, weapons ready. "I told McKay," said Glatkowski, "that we were in a strange situation where there were all kinds of weapons on the ship, knives, guns perhaps, certainly knives, pipes, axes, crowbars, anything. If we went down the ladder, for example, one person would have to be facing the other direction with the gun drawn; then when one gets down to the bottom, whistle and then we would turn around and then the other person would go down. To me that made sense. I didn't want us walking along nonchalantly and then suddenly we find ourselves, wham! We're jumped!"

Glatkowski also suggested that they use Gray and Mornin to keep tabs on everyone. Moreover, these two could bring food and coffee. Glatkowski suggested further that Gray and Mornin taste the food and drinks first. And not before they bring it up, either; taste it in front of them. The crew might put poison in their food. They had to be vigilant.

Finally, Glatkowski pointed out that they had to stay awake. If they fell asleep, even for a moment, they would be vulnerable to attack. Coffee would not be enough. He had overheard Gunn and Drabina talk about their "weight-reducing pills." As BR, he had seen some in their medicine cabinets. Moreover, the chief mate, as the ship's medical officer, might have some in his room or in the hospital. They should take amphetamines to stay up. McKay agreed. The pills could come in handy.

While McKay stayed on the bridge, Glatkowski went down the ladder, following his own advice. Holding his gun out like a cop about to kick in a door, he made each turn carefully, checking out if anyone was laying in wait for him. He started his hunt in the chief mate's room. "He ransacked the place," said Morgan, "he threw medicine all over the deck. He made a shambles of the place looking for pills to keep him awake."

"They were searching every doggone room for pills," said Gunn. "I found some of my weight-reducing pills on the bridge afterward."

Glatkowski came back to the bridge with some triangular pink tablets:

Dexedrine. How many should they take? They decided on two apiece to start. They would probably have to take several more before they reached land.

Glatkowski and McKay re-entered the chartroom. McKay asked the old man when they could expect to reach Cambodia. The captain shrugged and mumbled that it was hard to say because it wasn't a direct route. There were islands and other navigational hazards. "I was trying to fool them," the old man later said. "I told them that we must not get too close to the coastline because of reefs and nets and VC snipers."

McKay repeated tersely, *How far is it to Cambodia?* Together, the three looked at the chart. Glatkowski measured the distance. It was less than three hundred miles. They could be off the coast of Cambodia by early next morning. The captain shook his head and said that there was no way that they could be there that fast. He talked about fishing nets, which, of course, were not on the chart. It was fishing season, he said, and the water was webbed by these navigational hazards. A net could get into the screw and stall the ship for days. McKay did not want to hear any more. He impatiently pointed to the chart, insisting that the old man finish laying out a direct course to Baie de Ream, immediately.

Glatkowski and McKay moved away from the captain, to talk in private. They did not trust the old man. How could there be a deep-water port in Cambodia if there wasn't easier access? The captain was trying to buy time. The problem, of course, was that they had no choice. Neither of them knew how to navigate. For the time being, they would allow the captain to determine the course.

The captain, meanwhile, made a request. He needed to meet with the men on board. It was going to be a while before they reached Cambodia and they would have to set watches among themselves. McKay hesitated for a moment, then agreed. McKay and Glatkowski were apparently so focused on retaining control of the bridge that they were willing to take the risk of allowing the remaining crew to congregate without their supervision. Before the captain left the bridge, McKay issued a warning. He and the others had better not try to attack them or plot some move to retake the bridge. If they did, the whole ship could explode. McKay also reminded the captain to tell the men to announce themselves loudly before coming up.

The captain, the chief mate, Sparks, Campbell, and the bosun met in the captain's quarters. They took count. Besides the five of them, there were three engineers in the engine room: Drabina, Tober, and Wright. Sather was somewhere on the vessel. By all accounts, however, he was not in the most stable condition; he had continued to mix liquor with barbiturates. Gray was bringing the gunmen food and coffee; Mornin had taken on the role of liaison between the mutineers and the engine room. That made eleven. Gunn and Hammett were still on the bridge. That was thirteen. Plus the two mutineers made fifteen men on board. Twenty-four had gotten off in the lifeboats.

"We tried to set up a watch and decide how we were going to run things with the few men that we did have," said Swann. It was going to be tricky. In the engine room, Drabina had problems getting up and down ladders. He huffed and puffed, and it was obvious that he might collapse, especially now that it was getting hotter. Tober was excitable to the point of hysteria, even in normal situations; in the last couple of hours his nervousness had gone through the roof. He was taking heart medicine constantly, but it did not calm him down. Wright was a gritty Aussie, but he was sixty years old; it was hard to tell how long his stamina would hold out. Sather was virtually useless, at least at the moment. Perhaps after he sobered up, he could be counted on to lend a hand.

And then there were Gray and Mornin. Even if they were collaborating with the mutineers, they would be needed in the engine room. There was no other way. It was agreed that Sather, Gray, and Mornin would stand watches but that the engineers should keep an eye on them to make sure they did not help the mutineers sabotage the engine room.

What about the deck watches? The captain and chief mate would relieve Gunn at some point. They decided not to go by the clock, but that each man would stay on watch until a relief came, whenever that would be. They would play it by ear. Whoever had energy would take a watch. The bosun, Campbell, and Hammett would take turns handling the wheel. Once it got dark, they would do the same with lookout on the bow.

The bosun said he did not like the idea of being alone on the bow: *Those guys could come up there and kill me and no one would know about it.* Campbell told the bosun that he had to take his turn. The bosun suggested that they go up to the bow in pairs. That idea was quickly dismissed by the others—they only had so many men.

Campbell, according to Swann, then brought up "all kinds of wild stories rumored around the vessel." He'd heard that the fireman and the BR had rigged a bomb in the hold and that they had set some sort of remote triggering device. Maybe a time-bomb was already ticking and they had only so much time to find it. The old man told Campbell he was letting his imagination run away with him. The bosun, obviously scared, said that the ship *could* blow up. The chief mate, for his part, was not so much scared as angry: *I'd like to crack those assholes over the head.* He would show them what it felt like to be hijacked. The meeting was getting out of control. The captain called for quiet.

Swann told the men that the mutineers could not "last it out." He suggested they be patient. He explained that he was proceeding on a course that would delay the ship's entry into Cambodian waters and draw the attention of any planes passing over the area. Swann wanted to make sure of three things: that no one get hurt; that the ship and its cargo remain intact; and that they complete this voyage and deliver the cargo to its destination. They could try to retake the vessel, said the captain, but they must not jeopardize those three objectives in the process. Swann later said that he told the men, *Until we can devise something foolproof, then we better sit tight. There's too much involved here. They may shoot into the deck cargo.*

"I didn't think they had a bomb on the ship," Swann testified, "but I said that I couldn't rule it out. And also, as I said, I was worried about these other men, especially these three men, the wiper and the electrician and the utility man."

The chief mate later said that he was furious that the captain was taking such a passive attitude. The bosun agreed: the old man had allowed a pair of hippies to take over his ship without a fight. Morgan later said that he challenged the others: *Are you men or mice?* The chief mate's comment opened up the meeting to what Swann later called "wild schemes." Campbell and the bosun suggested that they slip the mutineers poison. Or attack them all at once, since they cannot kill everyone. When it gets dark, jump them with fire axes. Swann called for quiet again and warned them all, including the chief mate, not to go off on their own. The bosun said that if they did not do anything, they would all be dead anyway. So they might as well try something.

"I guess pretty near all of us thought that this might be the end," Swann told the investigators. "That was one reason why some of the things they wanted to do, and some of the plans that were thought up, were desperate. I told them, 'Let's try to keep it down now. Any violence and everybody's going to get killed, once it starts.'"

At this moment, according to what Swann told the FBI, Mornin walked in on the meeting. They all stopped talking. Mornin asked if they wanted some coffee. One of the men asked Mornin what was going on topside, and Mornin, Swann said, "began talking about the generation gap and lack of understanding adults or older people have regarding the young." Swann wasn't paying attention to what Mornin said because "I wanted him to leave so we could continue plotting." Swann asked Mornin if he thought the hijackers "would shoot them," and Mornin stated that "McKay is crazy, that even *he* cannot talk to him, but that Glatkowski is all right." Mornin then told the men that McKay had told him, before the mutiny, that the odds were fifty-to-one that the ship might go to Cambodia. When asked why he did not tell anyone, Mornin replied, "I thought it was a joke."

Mornin left. According to Swann, it was decided "not to attempt anything against the hijackers, since at that time we did not know who else was involved."

After the meeting broke up and everyone had left, Swann locked himself in his office, unlocked the safe, and removed the confidential sailing orders: contingency plans about what to do in case of an emergency such as this. There was too much information in there that the mutineers could use to destroy the ship and its cargo. He crumpled these orders and threw them into a metal waste basket. Then he sprayed lighter fluid and threw a match inside. They flared up immediately, burning down to ash in a few seconds. "I never thought that it was going to happen," Swann told the investigators. "But when I saw there was a possibility of the vessel, when I considered it may be my last opportunity to burn my confidential sailing orders, I burned them, destroyed them by fire."

Campbell, meanwhile, wanted to see "what the situation was on the bridge," so he brought a pitcher of ice water up to the wheelhouse. Just before going up the final ladder, he yelled loudly that he was coming up to the bridge, and that he was bringing water for them. McKay told him to proceed. When Campbell came up the ladder, both Glatkowski and McKay had weapons pointed in his direction.

Campbell told the mutineers that the men had talked it over and had decided that he, Hammett, and the bosun would split the wheel watches and lookout. McKay told Campbell that he did not want the bosun up in the wheelhouse: only Campbell and Hammett should do the steering, and the bosun's sole job should be standing lookout. Campbell argued with McKay about this: there were not enough crew members, they could not afford dropping one from the watch. He said that sooner or later the bosun would have to come up. McKay grew tired of this argument. Exasperated, he waved off Campbell and said that they could work it out any way they wanted. Glatkowski was not happy about this. As far as he was concerned, the bosun was a vicious redneck, a danger to them, and should be kept off the bridge.

Just before Campbell went down the ladder, the mutineers told him to get them some cigarettes. Camels. As many as he could find. Now that they were in control of the vessel, Glatkowski and McKay were smoking tobacco only, no marijuana. "Well, I looked all around them rooms and I ain't found no Camels to this day," Campbell said. "I found some Pall Malls and I carried them back up there and I told him that there weren't no Camels down there. Then he said, 'Well, take an axe and break into the ship's stores.' And I said, 'Not me, man.' And he raised his pistol and I said, 'Man, after all this is over, I might get into trouble over this.' He said, 'No, by God, tell them I sent you.'"

Less than two hours after the ship had resumed speed, a plane flew directly overhead. Swann was on the bridge when it first appeared. The plane made one pass and then came back a few minutes later, this time flying much lower. The mutineers went out to the wing to get a closer look at it. Glatkowski thought that it was a "U.S. reconnaissance aircraft." He said that "it was no great surprise to us when it flew very low over the Eagle, surveying the vessel. We were sure it had noticed that the lifeboats were missing." He and McKay pointed their guns at it.

Gunn—a fervent anti-Communist who later said, "those two little pricks, they was the only live bombs"—swore to himself that if the mutineers shot at the plane, he would do whatever it took to kill them. He had heard the captain's warning, but he was ready to take the chance, even if a stray bullet went off. Short, overweight, in his late fifties, Gunn steeled himself to make a jump at Glatkowski.

Other men saw and heard the plane as well: Tober, Campbell, Drabina, the bosun. Feeling certain that the plane would come back, Tober told Campbell to "rig up some kind of light to signal an SOS." Campbell said that it was useless to rig up a light during daylight hours. And if they tried it at night, the mutineers would see it flashing and "would probably come down and shoot us." Tober suggested that they light a fire in a steel drum. Campbell said that was a crazy idea, it could blow up the whole ship. So what could they do? They decided on several ways.

Campbell went into the mess hall, where the national ensign was folded up tightly and wedged between a rail and the bulkhead, just under the clock.

"I pulled down my britches," Campbell said, "and took the flag and I rolled it up and put half of it down one side of my pants leg and the other down the other half, and I pulled my britches up. So I went down in the engine room and told the first assistant to go over and talk to the wiper so the wiper would be looking the other way."

While Tober distracted Mornin, Campbell hurried into the shaft alley. Waddling like a wind-up bowlegged cowboy, the flag rolled up in his pants, constantly looking over his shoulder, Campbell walked down the shaft alley, toward the stern. There, in the bowels of the ship, he could hear the sloshing of seawater, as well as the constant pings and bangs and creaks and moans of the ship's movement.

Campbell walked all the way through, then went up the emergency escape hatch ladder back aft, until he was out on deck. There, he looked around. Nobody there. The after-house prevented his being seen from the bridge. Quickly, he took the flag out of his pants, unfurled it, clipped each end of it to the line on the jackstaff and hung it upside down. He shook the flag to make sure that it could be seen by a plane. And that it *was* upside down. There was not much breeze but the fifteen-knot speed allowed the flag to spread out full-face every so often.

While Campbell was on the stern, the bosun was midships, just outside the mess hall. He took a piece of chalk, leaned over the rail, reached as far as he could and in thick, fat letters about two feet high, wrote a message that he hoped a low-flying plane would see. "I writes a sign on the gunwale back there," the bosun later testified, "right outside the chow hall: SHIP IS HIJACKED."

Campbell on the stern, and the bosun midships, waited for the plane to return. "Then here come that airplane back over," said Campbell. It took another low pass.

On the bridge, Gunn was ready to leap at Glatkowski, if he shot at the plane. But Glatkowski did not shoot. Not this time. The plane buzzed low and kept on flying.

Back aft, Campbell watched it pass by. "After the plane left that time," said Campbell, "I took the flag down because I was scared to leave it back there, that one of them guys would see it. I took it down, rolled it up and put it inside, over some wires, in the escape hatch. So I went back down the same way I come in, by way of the shaft alley."

The bosun saw the plane pass and wondered if it had done any good. He said, "I don't know whether the plane got the signal I left, whether he read it or not." Campbell hurried back on deck so that "they wouldn't miss me." When Campbell was coming back, he ran into Mornin. According to Campbell's testimony, Mornin asked him where he had been. Campbell said he had been down in the icebox. Mornin asked him what he had been doing. Campbell said, *Kiss my ass!* "Can you imagine, a wiper asking me where I been? So I wasn't going to tell him because all them guys was buddies. They watched us the whole damn time, the wiper, Bruce, and the electrician. Everyone of them watched us and we couldn't do nothing without one of these guys running and telling McKay or Glatkowski. We still didn't know who all was in on it and we was all scared."*

Expecting the plane to come back again, and perhaps fly lower than before, Glatkowski suggested to McKay that they give the recon plane something to look at. His idea was to paint a peace symbol on the U.S. flag, then fly it off the stern. "Clyde didn't want to do it," Glatkowski later said. "He thought it was decadent. Bourgeois. Me, I'm saying, 'What are you talking about? Give them a dose of their own medicine. They're going to fly by and see this, they're going to film it, Clyde.' But he didn't want to do it."

Glatkowski eventually got his way. He told the bosun to get buckets of paint. Under Glatkowski's supervision, the men stretched out the U.S. flag on the starboard wing of the bridge while Glatkowski painted a circle with a crow's foot inside. The paint soaked through the flag and left the symbol

*Mornin later told the FBI that any accusation that he watched the movements of other crew members and reported to McKay and Glatkowski was "completely untrue." He also said that he did not see the upside-down flag and did not report it to McKay or Glatkowski.

on the gratings. The same symbol was painted on the stack, covering the company logo. It was large and could be seen by an approaching plane or ship.

Meanwhile, the bosun sat in the mess hall drinking beer, worried. Sather came in and asked him for a beer. Contrary to the captain's orders, the bosun gave him one. He had to go up to the bridge, the bosun said, but he was afraid that the gunmen were going to kill him.

Sather testified that he went up to the bridge with the bosun, bringing the portable record player with him. "When I went on the bridge," said the bosun, "Clyde McKay was standing there with a gun pointed at me with the hammer cocked." Sather put on a record, but McKay told him to get the hell off the bridge. Clutching the record player and records, Sather staggered toward the ladder and left.

The bosun testified that McKay then turned toward him and said, *I hear you raised the flag upside down, bosun.* The bosun said he was afraid that McKay would shoot him. Instead, McKay told the bosun he was lucky that nothing came of it. *If it had, I'd have killed you.* McKay said that since he, the bosun, had made a lot of enemies during the trip, he did not want him on the bridge either. Hammett, who was on the wheel at the time, probably felt sympathetic with what the mutineer said; the bosun had harassed and threatened him during the whole trip, and had certainly made him into an enemy.

"Clyde flat told that bosun that he didn't want him up there anymore," Hammett said. "He said that if he made one wrong move, he would kill him."

"So I never done nothing drastic," said the bosun, "I just obeyed the man's orders [when he] ordered me to stay off the bridge." Hammett stayed on the wheel and the bosun went down below, then forward to the bow to go on lookout.

At 10 p.m. during that hot, humid, tense night, the old man came up to give Gunn a needed rest. By the time Gunn went to his room, he had been on the bridge since noon and his ankles were grossly swollen; being on his feet so long had affected a chronic case of edema. Gunn was very pleased to be relieved, even if it was only for a short while. Two hours later, at midnight, the chief mate relieved the captain. Instead of going back down to his stateroom, the old man went to the chartroom, where he puttered around with charts of the area, familiarizing himself with the Cambodian coast. Glatkowski and McKay, each holding a gun, kept an eye on the chief mate and on the quartermaster.

As Glatkowski paced around in the wheelhouse, the radar caught his attention. He came closer, watching the green, hypnotic line go round and round. There were shadows on the screen. The radar was picking up something. Glatkowski called McKay to take a look at it. They stared at the screen. Glatkowski thought that the shadows must be ships. The old man came over, stared at the radar, and announced that they were fishing nets, not ships. Glatkowski did not believe this. He was sure that what he saw on the screen were ships. Maybe a Coast Guard Cutter or a Navy carrier. Maybe a gunship. The old man insisted that they were nets.

According to Glatkowski, McKay asked the old man "how to avoid those nets." Glatkowski was stunned. McKay was taking the old man's word for it that they were nets! Swann told McKay that the ship needed to do a zigzag maneuver and head into deeper water. *That's the only way to prevent one of those nets from getting chewed up by the screw.* McKay went along with the old man's suggestion: they would proceed on a zigzag course. The old man gave the change of course to Hammett, who was on the wheel. Glatkowski said that he was astounded that McKay bought the old man's explanation. "I couldn't believe it. I just couldn't believe it. We put ourselves right into their hands."

When the old man left the bridge for a few minutes and went down to the main deck, he ran into Campbell, who was obviously enjoying playing commando. According to Swann, Campbell was "creeping around there in the night-time. He was dressed in black turtle neck sweater and black cap, and he had black grease on his face. He was going to creep around back there among those fuses and detonators and everything like that. There was no reason for it, so I said, hold off, hold off, so it would be a concerted effort if we get them. But he was going to do what he wanted anyway."

Alone, Campbell moved stealthily down to the engine room again, keeping an eye out for Mornin. When he was sure that the wiper was not looking, he went through the shaft alley again. When he was at the fantail, Campbell removed his black sweatshirt, positioned himself above the stern light and then used the sweatshirt to send Morse code. Three shorts, followed by three longs, followed by three shorts again. SOS. "I did this for about fifteen or twenty times till I got tired, so I came back to the escape hatch, through the engine room and when I went back up, I told the bosun what I done."

Campbell and the bosun, looking around at all times, went together to Glatkowski's fo'c'sle. It was unlocked. They were scared but they moved quickly. They turned on the lights, then searched Glatkowski's locker, looking for a gun. They found nothing. They looked under the bunks, behind the lockers. Behind the radiator Northcutt found a box of shells. They looked further but found nothing else. They threw the shells over the side. Then the bosun and the ordinary went out on deck to keep an eye out and see if any plane responded to their SOS signals.

It was a long, slow night. The ship moved on. McKay and Glatkowski stood at each doorway between bridge and wing. The captain, unable to sleep, had come back to the chartroom.

At about 2 A.M., with Hammett on the wheel, Gunn returned to the bridge to relieve Morgan. Just before coming off the bridge, Morgan nodded to Gunn to go into the chartroom. The only opening between the wheelhouse and the chartroom was a doorway that connected them on the port side. Unless one stood in that doorway, it was not possible to be in the wheelhouse and see what was happening in the chartroom.

Once the chief mate and third mate were in the chartroom, Morgan whispered quickly to Gunn: *Find me a crowbar or nailbar and hide it in here.* Gunn—happy to be part of a counterattack—nodded, then went back to the wheelhouse. Morgan then went down the interior ladder, which descended from the chartroom.

Gunn looked out at the dark expanse of the Gulf of Thailand. When he went to sit down, he saw that McKay was now sitting in the captain's chair. The third mate asked McKay if *he* could sit down. McKay, holding his gun tightly, gave the mate a sideways glance. The mate asked him again, *Please. I did ten hours on watch before and my legs are all swollen up,* he said to McKay. *I got to sit down.* McKay got up and moved to the wing. The mate sat down. He leaned and touched his ankles, which were so swollen that they felt as if they were going to burst.

While McKay was out on the wing—and Swann was in the chartroom—Glatkowski came close to Gunn, who told the young man that he had had edema for years. Gunn said, *My legs swell up real large, you know, and if*

I don't, if I don't sit down and relieve, get the pressure off my feet, why, they'll lap over my shoe tops.

Glatkowski had taken a liking to Gunn. During the trip across, Gunn and Glatkowski had talked at times, briefly and superficially, and Glatkowski mistakenly felt that Gunn understood—and had sympathy for—the mutiny.

In the quiet darkness, Gunn encouraged Glatkowski to talk about himself, about his childhood.

During a night-time wheel watch, punctuated by the soft clangs of the wheelhouse clock every half-hour, men on watch occasionally reveal their fears, doubts, insecurities—the opposite of the posturing that flies back and forth in the mess hall. It is like a mutual therapy session, filled with stories about failed marriages and vicious divorces, about broken families, about choices made and not made.

According to Gunn, Glatkowski talked about his life back in Long Beach—the life he had left. Gunn told investigators, "So I had Glatkowski's sympathetic side. We got into a conversation about himself, you know, and he started talking about his wife, his child that's supposed to be born before long." Gunn reported that Glatkowski told him that he would seek asylum in Cambodia and that he hoped that his wife and child would join him there.

Gunn asked, *Do you think that what you're doing is worth the sacrifice?* Gunn said that Glatkowski opened his mouth, but was momentarily speechless.

GLATKOWSKI AND McKay stood at opposite ends of the dark wheelhouse, in the door that led out to the wing: Glatkowski on the starboard side, McKay on the port. Both stared out at the water. They had taken another dose of diet pills to stay awake. They knew that the rest of the crew might be waiting for the chance to attack them, but at this moment it felt relatively calm.

The clock struck five bells, indicating it was 2:30 A.M. The wheelhouse clock was soft and quiet, a reflection of the quiet moment on the bridge. The mutineers hardly spoke now. The ship would be in Cambodian waters in another few hours. Things were proceeding smoothly. It was possible that they were being followed and watched, but at the moment they could see nothing on the radar—even though Glatkowski checked it out every few minutes.

They were still following the zigzag course that Swann had urged. Glatkowski was steamed that McKay had accepted the captain's explanation about the erratic course they were on, but he had swallowed his doubts in the face of McKay's decisions. Whatever anger Glatkowski felt, however, was kept inside.

Hammett steered, propping his bulk on the wheel's delicately curved wooden spokes, feeling for the spliced rope collar around the top rung so he would know when the wheel was in its central position. He shifted his weight to keep his legs and feet from aching. There was no conversation between him and the mutineers.

In the chartroom, the captain was joined by Gunn, who had gotten up from the chair to walk around and stretch a little. Together, they looked at a chart, the same chart the captain had examined a hundred times.

Suddenly, the two licensed men heard a slight noise and looked toward the interior ladder, where they saw a shadow. A moment later a head appeared. It was the chief mate, but he had not yelled up first. Swann and Gunn looked toward the doorway to the wheelhouse. Had the mutineers heard? Apparently not.

Swann was concerned. "It was my big job," said Swann later, "to keep blood from starting to flow. I was afraid. I was afraid that once it started, the mutineers could have destroyed the ship and killed us all and nobody would know what happened."

Gunn nodded to Morgan and pointed toward a corner of the room where there was a clump of rags and cleaning materials. The chief mate dug inside the pile and pulled out a crowbar, which he hid under his arm. Morgan then slunk back down the ladder.

"I felt that this was a good time to sneak into the wheelhouse," Morgan said, "because McKay had a habit of sitting up . . . right by the door. He'd sit there in a half-dazed position with his gun cocked, ready to fire at anything, I guess; but I felt that [using] the moment of surprise, if I could sponk him with a crowbar it would make a nice soft thud. And I could then take the gun away from him and then go after Glatkowski."

Crowbar in hand, Morgan walked around to the exterior steps on the port side of the boat deck and waited. He took a few deep breaths. A couple of minutes passed. A thick gray cloud near the horizon drifted across the moon. Suddenly it was slightly darker. Okay, Morgan thought. This is it.

Slowly, he came up the exterior ladder on the port side. One step at a time. When he got up high enough so that he could see what was happening on the bridge, he noticed McKay standing at the doorway between the port wing and the wheelhouse. Leaning dreamily against the bulkhead, McKay seemed to be staring out into space. But he was still holding a gun in his hand. Morgan inched his way up the rest of the steps very slowly, hearing his own breathing.

"I was still on the wheel, steering the vessel," said Hammett, "and suddenly I saw Chief Mate Herrick Morgan try to slip up on McKay."

"So, I sneaked up with a crowbar," Morgan said, "and I was ready to let it fly and give him a rap on the head." Glatkowski caught the chief mate's movement from the edge of his vision. He shouted, *Look out for the mate!*

McKay wheeled, saw the chief mate heading toward him, crowbar in hand. McKay straightened out his gun arm and fired. The pistol report tore a hole in the night silence. No ricochets. No pings. No further echoes. Just the crack of the pistol shot, which stopped everyone on the bridge.

Hammett said that when he heard it, he "jumped about two feet." The chief mate stopped in his tracks, untouched by the bullet. He dropped the crowbar, which fell down the ladder, down toward the main deck, clanging loudly. Morgan put his hands up, palms forward, as if to say, "Don't shoot again."

When Swann heard the shot, he thought, "that damn fool got himself killed!" He and Gunn rushed from the chartroom to the wheelhouse to see what had happened.

McKay screamed at the mate, *If you try anything else, I'll kill you!*

10 ON THE HOOK

Approaching Sihanoukville Bay

After his failed attempt to ambush McKay, the chief mate scrambled off the bridge, went down to his room, and locked the door. Glatkowski and McKay pursued him, leaving the bridge in the hands of the captain and the third mate. McKay banged on Morgan's door, but the mate did not respond. Glatkowski said that he yelled, asking Morgan if he thought that attacking them was the "Christian thing to do." But there was no answer.

After the shooting, there was increased tension on the ship. Gunn testified that he saw McKay, furious about Morgan's attack, go around the ship and get rid of as many potential weapons as he could find. He threw "two fire axes, a hammer and a crowbar over the side of the vessel."

Some crew members were convinced that it was going to end in bloodshed. The general paranoia apparently affected McKay and Glatkowski. Before they went back up to the bridge, after chasing Morgan, they stopped at the saloon to scrounge some food. They ran into Wright. "I heard somebody come in to the officers' mess, and it was McKay and Glatkowski, both armed," said Wright. McKay opened up the refrigerator door and saw an empty shelf.

McKay said, *There's no night lunch, Second.*

Wright smiled. *Who did you think was going to put night lunch in?*

McKay laughed, but Glatkowski "swung around like a western badman," said Wright. "Real fast like. He didn't say anything, he just pointed his weapon at me."

Concerned that they had left the bridge unattended, Glatkowski and McKay quickly went back up. They found everything as it was when they had left: the third mate on watch, Hammett on the wheel, and the captain in the adjacent chartroom.

Hours passed.

Just before daybreak, as the first faint rays of lighter sky tinged the horizon, the mutineers looked out and suddenly realized that dawn was dead ahead. They were heading east. They did not know for how long they had been moving in this direction.

The mutineers rushed into the chartroom, where the old man was dozing, his head folded in his arms on the chart table, a divider still in his hand. When Glatkowski and McKay entered, the captain jumped up, startled. He gazed up blankly at the mutineers as they confronted him: the ship was now heading east. What the hell was going on? The old man pointed at the chart, dotted with clusters of islands, some no bigger than large boulders. They had names like Iles de Pirates, Ile de Poulo Dama, Iles D'an Thoi. He insisted that the reason that they were now heading east after going west all night was that, besides the nets and reefs, there were these rocky outcroppings and islands.

McKay told the old man to plot a dead reckoning course to Sihanoukville. Swann warned that if they took such a course, they could "hit something." And without lifeboats, it was extremely risky. He pleaded that they slow down while going through these hazards.

"The mutineers apparently sensed our easterly course and ordered the course changed prior to the time we intended," Swann told the investigators. "They made us change the course, they shortened up some of the distance."

In the Gulf of Thailand that day the sea was like glass, a slate-gray mirror, whose surface tension was occasionally broken by long, slow swells. Since there were no land features to break up the horizon, looking out toward the water gave them no sense of relief. As the sun rose higher, it got hotter and more humid and more oppressive, as if there was a damp, smothering blanket over them. Not even the fifteen-knot breeze of their forward progress brought relief.

With the others on the bridge, Glatkowski and McKay talked about their expectations. "I heard them say a couple of times that they hoped that the prince would be in Cambodia for them when we got in," Gunn said. Swann echoed this. "McKay thought that they were going to be greeted by Prince Sihanouk with open arms and everything, and welcomed."

At twelve o'clock, Gunn pulled out his sextant and went out to the wing to take a sunline. Glatkowski and McKay were both anxious to find out their exact position. Gunn told the mutineers, *You told me not to get close to you, so don't get close to me. When I'm taking these sights, I'm going to be moving back and forth real fast, so don't get all excited. Stay the hell out my way, because I'll be going through the door, both doors.*

That's all right, said McKay.

The third mate calculated the ship's noon position and drew a pencil mark on the map in the chartroom. They measured the dead reckoning direction between where they were and Sihanoukville. After that, either McKay or Glatkowski constantly kept an eye on the binnacle to make sure that the right course was maintained.

Bruce Gray shouted up from the deck below. Did they need anything? McKay shouted back, *Food and coffee!*

A short while later Gray brought up some food—Gunn called it "a remarkable job of cooking chicken." Whatever was not eaten was thrown into a corner of the wheelhouse, adding to the growing pile of garbage. "The bridge was a mess," said Gunn. Food, cups, silverware, plastic bags, paper strewn all over. "I never saw a pig sty as dirty as that bridge was. Oh, man, it was a horrible-looking mess."

Sather staggered back up to the bridge, the record player in his arms. "The chief electrician, he was up there and he was drunk," Gunn said, "he was about three sheets in the wind. So, he was playing the record player, that god-awful music, nothing but noise."

Glatkowski went to the radar once more and stuck his head inside the hood. Again, he saw blips, this time clustered in a group to the southeast. Glatkowski counted five blips. He was sure there were vessels following them, probably U.S. Coast Guard or Navy. Swann took a look. In his judgment, they were fishing boats, working a shoal area. He pointed out the spot on the chart. Indeed, it was near a mapped shoal. McKay then checked out the radar screen for himself. He was not convinced by the captain's assessment. The blips were moving in a V-like formation, not a static position. And they were going across the screen. The captain took another look. He conceded that the blips were moving, but that did not mean they were chasing the *Eagle.*

McKay reacted strongly to this. The captain was lying, stonewalling, he shouted. They were being pursued by a flotilla of vessels. It was obvious.

The mutineers were fueled by caffeine, diet pills, and tension. The strain, the fatigue, and the desperation of their act were taking their toll. After zigzagging during a long, tense night and morning, and half-expecting the crew to rise up and attack them, the mutineers were probably worried that they might never reach Cambodia. And now it was clear to them that the shadows they had seen earlier on the radar screen were not fishing nets. They had been ships all along.

According to Glatkowski, McKay not only directed his anger and frustration at the captain, but also at his partner. "He was upset that I didn't know enough about radar or navigation to be able to criticize the captain or whoever," said Glatkowski. "He said I should have known better. I should have taken a reading at night, by the stars, and figured out our position. Then they wouldn't have been able to pull a stunt like that. . . . I have a lot of resentment about the way I was treated. A lot of resentment."

Any conflict between the mutineers was kept hidden from the hostages, who testified that they observed full cooperation between them. Morgan, among others, said that Glatkowski and McKay worked like a well-oiled machine.

"It seemed to me that in the handling of the thing," Morgan testified, "it had been well planned. [They] seemed to know exactly what [they were] doing. There was no hesitation." Morgan said that McKay gave the orders and "Glatkowski followed them explicitly. They worked as a team." Apparently, any anger and frustration between the mutineers was short-lived.

At 1:52 P.M., they spotted land. McKay caught the captain's attention and pointed northeast. The old man went into the chartroom and looked at the noon reading.

"We're in Cambodian waters," the captain wearily acknowledged.

"I pointed out a spot about 4.5 miles west of the lighthouse off

Sihanoukville in 10 fathom water," the captain recalled. "I figured that was as close as I could go."

McKay decided that it was important that both U.S. and Cambodian authorities be notified of their presence and their intentions. McKay and Sparks went to the radio shack. They unlocked the room and turned on the radio, which took several minutes to warm up. According to an entry in the ship's logbook, the mutineers "permitted the following message to be sent: 'FROM S/S COLUMBIA EAGLE. INFO ALL. HIJACKED BY TWO ARMED SEAMEN, PROCEEDING TO CENTRAL COAST OF CAMBODIA.'"

Within thirty minutes, the *Eagle* received a reply. From the U.S. Coast Guard cutter *Mellon*, a fully armed fighting ship, a message informed the *Eagle* that it was standing by in international waters and would provide communications assistance.

The Coast Guard reported that "at about 1530 hours, 15 March 1970, the SS *Columbia Eagle* arrived off Koh Rong Sam Lem Lighthouse." Captain Swann ordered standby engines and continued to maneuver in one direction, then another, half ahead, then slow ahead, then half ahead again, until the ship reached the right location.

Once the ship locked in its position, however, the mutineers decided that four and one-half miles from land was too far away; they wanted to go in closer. The captain said that they needed a pilot to help guide the ship through this area. But McKay ordered the captain to go in anyway.

The old man got McKay's attention and pointed at a chart. *See those rocks over there? What do you want to do? You punch a hole in the ship, you're going to have oil all over.* The captain was still trying to delay their entrance into the harbor. "I said anything I could think of," said Swann. "I was telling them why I didn't want to go over there. Of course, as usual, we had plenty of room over there, but I pointed out everything that I could, that it was too dangerous to go in the coast. I finally turned around and come back to the point where I told them I was going to anchor."

According to the Coast Guard report about the incident, "after much discussion between McKay and Captain Swann, the ship anchored at 1729 hours in 10 fathoms of water at position Lat. 10-32.3N, Long. 103-14.7E."

The *Columbia Eagle* was now, as seamen say, on the hook.

McKay went to the radio room and dictated another message to Sparks, who sent it to the *Mellon* just as he heard it:

SS COLUMBIA EAGLE CROSSED CAMBODIAN WATERS UNDER POINT OF GUN. TWO MEN REQUEST POLITICAL ASYLUM. DESIRE SHIP TO BE INTERNED BY CAMBODIAN AUTHORITIES. REQUEST LAUNCH TO REMOVE CREW.

Glatkowski and McKay began waiting for the launch to arrive.

ONCE THE SHIP was anchored, the mutineers discussed what to do with the lethal cargo. They could not trust anyone, not even Sihanouk, to get rid of it for them. They would have to do it themselves, and soon. But how?

"McKay said that we should build a device to detonate the ship," Glatkowski said. "Put the remainder of crew in a life raft. He and I would stay aboard until the last minute, then get off, using remote charges to sink the vessel." The detonators would set each other off like firecrackers, the explosion eventually spreading to the 500-pound and 750-pound napalm canisters in the holds.

The old man overheard their plans.

According to Glatkowski, "The captain went to McKay and talked him out of this plan." This infuriated Glatkowski. "When the pressure was on," said Glatkowski, "Clyde backed down. He gave in to what the captain wanted."

McKay, however, had a plan of his own that he did not share with his partner.

A short while after the hook was dropped, McKay told Glatkowski that he was going down below to "do something" and that Glatkowski should stay on the bridge. Glatkowski did as he was asked, but after about an hour, he started becoming uneasy.

"While I'm waiting for him to come back," said Glatkowski, "I think, what the fuck is going on, where's Clyde?" Glatkowski left the bridge, searching the decks without success, and then was told by a crew member that McKay was last seen in the engine room.

"So I went down below to see where he was at," Glatkowski recalled. "And in the engine room I hear this pounding. And I see him and he's got this pipe and he's trying to break the sea-valve." McKay was swinging a piece of steel pipe, hammering at part of the elaborate plumbing that carried seawater into the ship's power plant. Glatkowski said that he grabbed the pipe in mid-swing and shouted at McKay, asking him what he was doing.

McKay told Glatkowski that he was trying to sabotage the vessel and sink the *Eagle.*

"At this moment," Glatkowski said, "I felt despair. I mean, I literally wanted to pull my hair out. I thought: What the fuck had I gotten myself into?"

You stand a better chance by taking your gun and blasting a hole in it, Glatkowski said he told him. At this point, according to Glatkowski, McKay did pull out his gun. Glatkowski, panicked, yelled that a bullet could crack the plumbing. This, Glatkowski knew, could cause a flood that could, in turn, create a massive explosion.

Glatkowski said that he tried to stop McKay. *You're not going to be able to just scuttle the ship. It's not going to just sink. It's like a pressure cooker. It's going to explode. So before that happens, let's let the crew get off on the life raft. Okay?*

McKay considered this suggestion, Glatkowski said, then finally put his gun down. Agreeing, McKay said that they should go up and put the crew off in the life raft now.

"Between the engine room and topside, McKay changed his mind again," said Glatkowski. McKay decided that he did not want to scuttle the ship. Not now. Not yet.

Other crew members confirmed that McKay was ready to commit sabotage, yet the investigation also revealed that McKay was reluctant to carry out such a plan. Glatkowski said that on a few occasions, when McKay was ready to blow up the ship, others—including the captain—talked him out of it. Wright testified that McKay had been "sheepish" when he admitted to having attempted sabotage. Dan Mornin testified that McKay told him that it would be "easy to take the ship by killing people. . . . The trick was to take the ship without taking any lives."

While McKay and Glatkowski were sorting out how—and if—to destroy the ship and its cargo, the others on board were trying to figure out how to stay alive.

"They said they was gonna scuttle the ship and everything," Leo Tober, the first engineer, later testified to the mutiny investigators. "I mean, what if they scuttle the ship and they got us locked up in the engine room? And we can't get out. Or they might shoot us. Maybe they didn't want no witnesses."

Tober said that he entered the mess hall and ran into the bosun. The bosun had heard rumors that the mutineers were going to kill some or all of the crew. He was sure that he, the bosun, would be the first one killed. He told the Polish-born first assistant that he was thinking about making a swim for it.

Oh no, Tober told the bosun, *don't do that. Don't do like that. We don't know, maybe there's shark in the water. I know you worried, but might be better for you to stay with the ship. Might be nothing happen or something like that. Just don't antagonize these guys. Like when they hijack a plane, you know? The pilots was instructed to take them wherever they want and they probably won't harm us, you know?*

But Tober did not feel very confident about his own advice, because, according to Glatkowski, he went to the mutineers to plead for his life.

"Everybody was calling us up and saying, 'Please don't kill us,'" Glatkowski would later testify. "Like the first engineer was saying, 'Look, man, I speak five languages. Don't kill me. I could be valuable.'" Glatkowski said he told Tober that they had no intention of killing anyone, to go back and do his work.

Meanwhile, more rumors spread quickly among the men. One was that the Nixon administration had sent a message to the hijackers that they would be given clemency if they returned the vessel intact, and that the hijackers had rejected the offer, saying that they still intended to scuttle the ship or blow it up. Another rumor was that the military, rather than let this ship get into the hands of the enemy, would send frogmen to kill everyone on board and then take the ship back out to international waters.

The bosun, worried by these and other rumors, went to the bow, trying to gauge the distance he would have to swim to get to the nearest craft. He was joined by the man he had harassed and threatened during the trip across, Roger Hammett.

"So I go up on the bow," said Hammett, "And Tennessee Northcutt, he's about to have a hemorrhage up there. He was saying, 'They're gonna kill us all! They're gonna kill us all!'" Hammett was probably not upset that Northcutt, feeling threatened, had finally gotten a taste of his own medicine. "So I tell him, 'Keep a cool head, Tennessee.' So he said, 'I'm gonna jump. I'm gonna put a life jacket on, grab a couple of boards and swim to that ship.' I told him, 'That ship is miles away and there's lots of sharks and poisonous snakes here, so you'll die.' So he didn't jump."

Glatkowski and McKay waited for the Cambodians to show up. And waited. Through the binoculars they could see a town, a port with a couple of piers, ships at the dock, and other vessels anchored nearby, as well as tugboats and what looked like a pilot boat.

Hours passed, and no one came out. It was now dark. They could see the lighthouse flashing in a repeating pattern, and the lights of Sihanoukville, but no boat came out to greet them. This was not the welcome that they had expected. "After we anchored in Cambodian waters," Gunn said, "the mutineers were disappointed because they didn't receive a personal greeting from the prince."

They decided to use the ship's signal light to send a message ashore, but they did not know how to operate it, or what signal to send. Swann showed them how to use it. The message they sent was a request for someone to come out to the vessel. "We blinked the light over there a few times," said the captain. The mutineers used binoculars to keep a constant lookout, but no one responded. McKay and Glatkowski felt they had to do something, anything, to get the attention of the Cambodians.

The mutineers asked the bosun if he had any flares. "I was afraid I'd better not lie to them," the bosun said. "They'd go back there and find them, so I got them some." Flares in hand, McKay and Glatkowski went up to the flying bridge. McKay gave Glatkowski his gun and put a flashlight between his knees to get some light on a flare. McKay could not figure out how to launch it and got increasingly frustrated; he also got angry because Glatkowski did not know either.

"McKay's trying to figure out how to launch them, he's never launched them," Glatkowski said. "Here's a fucking guy who's a fireman, he's got his lifeboat ticket, and he didn't know how to use a fucking flare. The guy's 25 years old. He's been sailing for seven years. Or however many years. So I explain to him, well, if you don't know how to do it, read the instructions. But he didn't know."

At that moment, Sather appeared at the bottom of the ladder. He was even more stoned than before. When McKay saw Sather, he became hysterical, yelling at Glatkowski to hold the electrician at gunpoint to prevent him from coming any closer.

"I'm supposed to hold Sather down," said Glatkowski, "I've got a gun on him. I've got Clyde's gun and my gun, two guns. And I'm standing right there and I'm telling Sather: 'Don't take another step!'" But Sather was too stoned to care. He kept coming up. Glatkowski aimed the gun. "Just as I'm pulling the trigger, suddenly I realize that we need Sather, we need him to show us how to use the goddamn flares! And I say, okay, come up and show us how to use these flares, show Clyde how to use the flares."

McKay became incensed, shrieking at both Glatkowski and Sather to stay back! "Clyde didn't want me to touch him, didn't want me even near him. So Sather wants to intercede between McKay and me and he says, 'I'll show you how to use it, I'm going to show you.' He starts to come up the stairs and McKay tells me to shoot him! And I'm ready to do it, and just as I start to pull the trigger, McKay's standing here, he tells me, 'Keep the son of a bitch down! Keep the mother fucker down!' And then I say to Sather, 'One more step and I'm going to shoot!' And McKay is so angry with me for not shooting, he's got the flashlight between his legs and he's trying to pull the flare down to read the instructions because he won't even listen to me."

Once more, Sather offered to help. "So Clyde takes the damn flashlight and he goes like this, WHAM! He throws it at Sather. And he misses him, but nevertheless it doesn't stop Sather, who's so drugged up, he doesn't know what the fuck is going on. Sather's bawling, 'Aw, man, don't be mad at me.'"

Finally, McKay and Glatkowski settled down, struggled through the instructions, and set off a few flares. But no Cambodian vessel came out. Angry about having to spend another dangerous night on board, McKay told the old man that he and Glatkowski were going to be on the fantail.

"After we got the anchor dropped," the bosun said, "the mutineers went back aft, put up cots back there, and one of them would sleep while the other one was awake."

Swann said, "They warned us, no one was to come back. They were going to shoot into that deck cargo if we were going to give them any trouble. We was up that night watching with glasses and trying to determine when both of them were asleep. And we never could see more than one asleep. It's hard to see how they could stay up and hold us all at bay for so many hours, but that was how."

11 BAD OMEN

Sihanoukville Bay

Just as dawn was breaking in the bay on Monday, 16 March, Glatkowski and McKay left the fantail and went back up to the bridge. The little bit of sleep had done wonders. They were refreshed and alert, far less crazed than they had been the night before. Except that the Cambodians had still not made contact, and that bothered them enormously.

They were about to plan their next move, when a plane zoomed overhead again, fairly low. A few seconds later that plane—which Glatkowski thought was the same recon aircraft that had buzzed them the day before—took another pass, and this time much lower. It flew so low that Glatkowski and McKay, on the wing of the bridge, ducked. Glatkowski said that he "could see the pilot and co-pilot." It was an American plane and it flew over again and again, six, eight, ten times.

Glatkowski and McKay drew their pistols, aiming at the plane as it went by. Gunn, seeing them do this, again swore that he would try to kill the mutineers if they shot at the plane. The old man came up, announcing himself loudly before going up that final flight. Swann heard Glatkowski and McKay scream at the plane as it buzzed the ship.

If the plane comes back, I'm going to take a shot at him! McKay shouted.

Before you shoot, said Swann, *let me try to contact them and warn him off.*

If you want to, go ahead, said McKay.

McKay went with Swann and Sparks to the radio shack. McKay dictated the message that he wanted Sparks to send. "So we got on the radio and we picked up the U.S. Coast Guard Cutter Mellon," said Swann. Sparks spoke with the *Mellon,* ship to ship, asking the *Mellon* to warn the recon plane that if it did not back off in fifteen minutes, the mutineers would shoot at it. McKay ordered Sparks to tell the *Mellon* that "this action was the first of a series of mutinies that was going to take place."

The *Mellon* radioed back, asking what the mutineers wanted and what the position of the ship was. The *Eagle* sent a response to the *Mellon:*

> THE MEN THAT SEIZED THIS VESSEL ARE ASKING FOR POLITICAL ASYLUM IN CAMBODIA, AND THEY WILL GO TO ANY LENGTHS TO KEEP THIS CARGO FROM REACHING ITS DESTINATION, EVEN TO SCUTTLING THE VESSEL. NO INJURIES OR DAMAGE TO THE SHIP THUS FAR. VESSEL IS 4.5 MILES WEST OF KOH RONG SAM LEM LIGHTHOUSE AT LAT. 10°-32' N. & LONG. 103°-15' E. DESIRE LAUNCH TO SIHANOUKVILLE. MUST BE CAMBODIAN VESSEL, AND NO AMERICAN CRAFT TO COME NEAR VESSEL.

After this message went out, McKay went back up to the bridge, where Glatkowski, on the wing, was aiming his pistol at the plane, as it made another pass.

"The plane passed about 50 feet over my head," said Glatkowski. "Again they circled, only this time they apparently saw me aiming my gun at the cockpit of the plane, because they immediately veered the plane away from the ship. I stood there a few minutes longer to see if it would return. Fortunately for them, they never passed over the ship again."

A telegram was sent from the U.S. embassy in Saigon, signed by Ambassador Ellsworth Bunker, to the Secretary of State:

> SURVEILLANCE COURSE WAYWARD VESSEL MAINTAINED BY 13TH AIRCRAFT. COAST GUARD VESSEL MELLON MAINTAINING SURVEILLANCE FROM OUTSIDE 12 MILE LIMIT OF VESSEL NOW ANCHORED 5 MILES OFFSHORE OF SMALL ISLAND WEST OF SIHANOUK-VILLE. COAST GUARD IN VOICE COMMUNICATION WITH MASTER WHO STATES HIJACKERS THREATEN BLOW UP SHIP IF ANYONE FOOLS WITH THEM.

Several hours later, a telegram, signed by Secretary of State William Rogers, was sent to CINCPAC (commander in chief, Pacific), as well as to all U.S. embassies in the Southeast Asia region, asking that approval be obtained from the Cambodian government to allow the *Mellon* to "ENTER CAMBODIAN WATERS TO EFFECT CUSTODY OF SS COLUMBIA EAGLE. THIS WILL BE DONE SO AS TO AVOID ANY SIGNIFICANT RISK TO SAFETY OF MASTER AND NON-MUTINOUS CREW MEMBERS STILL ON BOARD. PRESENCE AND COOPERATION OF CAMBODIAN AUTHORITIES WOULD BE WELCOME." The telegram went on to say that if permission could not be received from the Cambodian government, then the Cambodian government itself should be requested to "APPREHEND PIRATES AND RETURN VESSEL AND CREW TO U.S. CONTROL."

ON THE BRIDGE of the *Columbia Eagle,* McKay told Swann that he wanted the Cambodians to remove everyone from the ship. "McKay repeatedly said that everyone was going to be taken off the vessel and the vessel was just going to be left there," Swann said. "So I says, 'If that's the case, McKay,' I said, 'we might as well secure the plant.' So McKay agreed with me, he said, 'Go ahead if you want to.'"

Swann had an ulterior motive. He wanted to shut down the engines because he was still hoping to be rescued by U.S. forces. "I was just playing it by ear," said Swann. "Shutting down the plant was a good way to delay any movement almost indefinitely."

Drabina and his crew started the emergency generator, then they shut down the gyro, radar, and main plant. Just before the plant was secured, McKay told the captain to "open up the slop chest since some of us need some cigarettes and things." According to Campbell, the old man said, "'Wait, let me get the key, and I'll open it,' and Clyde said 'You don't need the damn key, I've got the key.' So Clyde took a big old fire axe and broke into the old man's slop chest. That's where we buy our cigarettes and shaving lotion and all of that, and he goes in there and busts the lock and gets all kinds of cigarettes out."

Swann said that McKay told him to "leave the slop chest open and tell the men that anything they wanted, that they could go in there and help themselves to it."

Once the plant was shut down and the slop chest broken open, anarchy seemed to take a firm hold. Lockers were smashed open and rooms were ransacked.

The two hundred dollars that Marco Smigliani had won in poker the night after leaving Bataan proved to be too much temptation for Campbell. Hammett testified that when he walked into his fo'c'sle, "Campbell had just taken a fire axe and broken open Marco's locker and taken his money, and I catch him red-handed."

Campbell rejected Hammett's account, and accused nearly everyone else. He claimed he saw Glatkowski, McKay, Gray, and Mornin "bust open lockers," including Smigliani's. He said that Sather broke into a room and McKay grabbed an axe and told Sather, Mornin, and Gray to "find money in them lockers and anything of value they could sell."*

Bruce Gray said that he saw Campbell join with Glatkowski in breaking into lockers. According to Billy Campbell's testimony in his psychiatric report, McKay and Glatkowski stole property from the seamen's lockers. "They just went in to people's rooms and they would see a nice suitcase—they would just take it—and that is what they put the cigarettes in." Other seamen corroborated Campbell's tale in the Coast Guard inquiry. "They stole an awful lot of stuff," Gunn testified in the report. "The second mate's radio, they took that ashore with them."

"One of the guys got the baker's camera," Campbell told the investigators. "A real expensive camera, so he put it over in Clyde's luggage. They was just stealing everything." Hammett also accused Glatkowski of stealing the baker's camera and the second mate's radio. Glatkowski did not deny it. "We went down to the main deck and broke open the lockers," said Glatkowski. "We were looking for . . . hell, I don't know what we were looking for." In a recent interview, Glatkowski admitted that he had taken the camera, saying that he had "liberated it."

A short while later, Glatkowski and McKay, still holding their guns, took the captain to his stateroom. "McKay told me he wanted to be paid off and receive transportation back to the States," said Swann. "So I told him I can't do that. So then this Alvin Glatkowski said, 'Gee,' he said, 'you must have about $30,000 in the safe,' he says. 'That's a nice little haul. We might as well take care of that too.'"

Glatkowski confirmed this. "I said to Swann, you either give it to us, or I take it all."

*During the subsequent investigations, Campbell, Mornin, Sather, and Gray all vehemently denied having broken into other people's lockers.

According to Swann, McKay said, "No, this is not piracy. We'll take just what we have coming to us."

"I felt we had a right to demand all of the money on the ship," said Glatkowski. "I figured, what the hell, we're facing the death penalty anyway. I don't want to go out of here with no money or with an insignificant amount. I told Clyde, 'How are we going to survive on the money you and I have coming? We can take all this money!' And Clyde insisted we leave the money there, that we only take what's rightfully ours. It was a pig company, they were shipping munitions, it didn't matter. Clyde's argument was that we would seem like a bunch of crooks. I agreed only because I didn't want to hassle with him. And that made me real furious. We could have used the money to get to China or North Vietnam."

Swann told the investigators, "I'll have to say that if it wasn't for McKay, that the other fellow, Glatkowski, he would have cleaned out the safe."

MID-AFTERNOON AND there still was no contact with Cambodian authorities. Glatkowski and McKay smoked cigarettes constantly, nervously pacing and flicking the butts over the side. Though the recon plane had not returned, they knew that the *Mellon* was still out there, probably just outside Cambodian waters, waiting for them to let their guard down.

McKay and Glatkowski became worried. Where the hell were the Cambodians? At one point, according to Swann, they looked out with binoculars and thought they saw a periscope in the water. Was a U.S. submarine pursuing them? "They got very worked up over this," said Swann, who told them that there could not possibly be a submarine in ten-fathom water. "You couldn't reason with them at all," said Swann. "We told them, 'Heck, how can a submarine be in such few feet of water and be submerged with the periscope up?'"

McKay told Swann that he wanted another message sent ashore. Word was sent to the *Mellon* that the mutineers "want a boat just as soon as possible."

At about three o'clock that afternoon, Tober said, "this little boat came, like a pleasure cruiser. We didn't even know who it was." There were "six or eight Cambodians" aboard. As the yacht pulled alongside, McKay asked Tober to talk to them, apparently trusting the Pole's French more than his own. McKay told Tober to ask if they could take everyone ashore. Or if not, could they at least "bring Cambodian officials out here, out to the ship." As an inducement, McKay dug into his pouch, pulled out a gold coin. He tossed one toward the yacht, but he missed, and it fell into the water.

McKay then gave another gold coin to Wright, who passed it to the yacht. "It was a twenty-dollar Mexican gold piece," said Wright. "Then McKay wrote a note to the Cambodian authorities." It was a plea, in ungrammatical French, for Cambodian officials to come out to the *Eagle.* McKay gave the note to Mornin, who went below and handed it to the people on the yacht. "I don't know what the note said," Mornin told the FBI.

Swann learned that McKay, in that note, was trying to convince the yacht to take everyone ashore. "I started to argue with him," said Swann. "I said, 'Look, McKay, give me a break. You asked me to bring you here,' I said. 'You're here, you're in one piece. Now,' I said, 'I haven't asked you for anything. Let me stay on the vessel. If you have to, take everybody, but let me stay and don't leave the vessel without anybody on it.' And finally he said, all right, that I could stay on the vessel," said Swann. But in the end, the yacht took no one. "McKay tried to talk them into taking us ashore, but they wouldn't have anything to do with that."

The yacht left and a short while later, Sparks received word from the *Mellon.* The message said that Cambodian authorities would "BE OUT AT ABOUT 1700 HOURS ON 16 MARCH."

At about 6:00 P.M., two Cambodian naval vessels finally arrived. One of them made fast along the starboard side, while the other circled the anchored ship ominously. Several Cambodian naval officers and twenty-four armed enlisted men boarded the *Columbia Eagle.* Swann greeted the officers and invited them to his quarters "to discuss the vessel's situation."

"I told them that the vessel had been taken over at gun-point by two men that desire political asylum in their country," Swann said, "and that the ship had been brought there against the will of everyone else aboard, also the owners and my country."

Swann said that everyone was "very concerned, the U.S. government and the owners of the ship, too. And that we would very much appreciate it if they would take those men and let us go on our way. They listened to the story and then they told me that I had to go down to the gunboat alongside and talk to the Cambodian Naval Chief of staff."

Meanwhile, Glatkowski and McKay boarded the gunboat. There, they informed the Cambodians that they were the mutineers. They turned over their weapons and were asked to wait.

At the same time, on the *Eagle*'s main deck, Campbell told anyone who would listen that he, Campbell, was a CIA agent. Campbell went to several Cambodian officers and showed them some sort of identification.

Swann was escorted to the gunship so he could speak with Capt. Amg Kim Ly, the naval chief of staff. "So I went down there and repeated my story," said Swann. "After discussing the whole thing, he questioned me about the cargo. It had already been brought out on the radio that the ship had been carrying ammunition and I knew that they knew I was carrying ammunition, so I told them that. And, of course, they wanted to know what type it was and everything. How much and where it was going."

Swann was trying to avoid spelling out the specifics of the ship's cargo, when, to his shock, Campbell was escorted into the chief of staff's office. Campbell later testified that officials "gave me and the captain a glass of tea, and this Cambodian asked me how long I had been with the CIA, and I said, 'Man, I ain't with the CIA.' Then he started asking the captain about the bombs, like how long they was, how big they was and things like that. One guy says to me, 'How much do they weigh?' And I told him how much I thought they weighed. And he said, 'Are you sure you don't have small arms or small arms ammunition?'" That was a question that would come up over and over during the next few days and weeks.

The captain pointed out that they were asking questions of an ordinary seaman, while he was the captain. "The captain told him that we didn't have small arms," said Campbell. "He said he had one pistol, and McKay and Glatkowski had that. So then this one Cambodian got on the radio and called Phnom Penh and checked me out and came back in a while and said, 'No, he ain't no CIA man.'" Campbell was escorted back to the *Eagle*.

After Campbell left, Captain Amg told Swann that he was prepared to fire at the *Eagle* if the old freighter decided to make a run for it.

"He was so intense," said Swann. "He said, 'Believe me, Captain, believe me, please, I understand your position and how you think, but do not try to run because I must blow you out of the water. I have to do that.' And he told me that and he kept repeating it and repeating. And I tried to figure out, what's the matter with this guy?"

Amg finally told Swann what the problem was. "Captain Amg thought," said Swann, "when he came to the ship, that the entire crew was seeking political asylum and had requested it." Amg said that was the reason he was prepared to take everyone off the vessel. "So, naturally, I protested as vigorously as I could," said Swann. "I didn't know how far I could go, but in a few minutes he made it clear that it was going to be his way, that he was just going to take us off and that was going to be it. There was nothing to say any farther. I told him that the cargo is very sensitive and there should be somebody there to take care of it. And then he wanted me to bring the vessel inside the bay."

Swann was getting more and more worried. Bringing the ship in closer would cut off his last hope that U.S. planes and ships would swoop in and rescue him. He had to think fast. What Swann wanted to communicate to the chief of staff was the possible danger to the town and the port if this ship blew up. Swann said, "I told him that the cargo was really sensitive, and that my government and my owners and no one aboard the ship wanted to see anything happen to any Cambodians due to the action of these two malcontents and that, for the safety of all concerned, that I thought it was strongly advised that the ship be left where it is."

The chief of staff "became very indignant" and disagreed. Swann bargained with Amg, who finally agreed to let Swann keep his three engineers on board—on the condition that Swann bring the vessel in close at 5:00 A.M. "I thought that was the best I could do," said Swann, "and that served my main purpose, [which] was to delay any action for the time being, which was my main reason for getting the plant shut down anyway." Captain Amg then dismissed Swann.

Swann was assuming that while all this give-and-take with the Cambodians was happening, the U.S. government, by way of the *Mellon,* would be "working on straightening it out through diplomatic channels, perhaps the following morning."

After Swann went back to the *Eagle,* Captain Amg summoned Glatkowski and McKay to his room. Glatkowski said that when they spoke with him, the first thing the chief of staff asked was why they had mutinied. McKay replied in French that it was something they believed in, that they did it "in order to prevent the bombs from being dropped on the Vietnamese people."

Finally, McKay and Glatkowski got a chance to ask questions of their own. They said that they did not understand why Cambodian authorities had taken so long in coming out to the ship. They had been signaling for more than twenty-four hours.

Amg told the mutineers that they had heard about the mutiny on the radio, and the news reports were not clear about how many people were involved or whether the bomb that was set to go off was still active or not. They were afraid, he said, that if they came too close and the ship blew up, it would kill them too.

"Everybody thought we had a bomb set to go off," Glatkowski said. "When we spoke with the officials, we finally convinced them that we had already disposed of the bomb. Then we asked them for political asylum."

Back on the *Eagle,* Swann met in the engine room with his engineers: Drabina, Tober, and Wright. He told them that he had no choice but to reactivate the plant.

While the captain was trying to encourage the men in the engine room, Gunn came down and told Swann that the mutineers were now back aboard the *Eagle.* Not only had they not been taken ashore by the Cambodians, but they had been sent back to the *Eagle* with their weapons. Swann was outraged.

"The Cambodian Naval Chief of Staff returned the pistols to Alvin Glatkowski and Clyde McKay and sent them back aboard the vessel with loaded pistols," said Swann, astounded. Swann could not understand how the Cambodians could do that. Didn't they know that these were the guys who had seized the vessel?

Swann went topside and confronted the Cambodian officers. Campbell heard the captain say to the Cambodians, "'What the hell are you doing, letting these guys carry guns back aboard?' So, the Cambodian says, 'Nothing we can do about it.'"

Days later, when Swann was ashore, he asked a Cambodian official why the mutineers had been sent back to the ship with their weapons. He was told that it was a way of making sure that the *Eagle* would not try to sneak away in the middle of the night.

But the ship was not going to sneak anywhere that night. One Cambodian gunship laid off the quarter and the other one off the bow.

Starting up a plant that has been secured is hard enough, even with a full crew and cool weather. During the night of 16 March, in the bay off Sihanoukville, the situation was much thornier. There were very few people working, and they were either sick, incompetent, inexperienced, unreliable, or drunk. It was a recipe for disaster.

Within an hour of starting to reactivate the plant, the heat in the engine room was in the danger zone—150 degrees. The blowers were not working. Before midnight Drabina collapsed on the steps and had to be carried topside. Then Tober passed out from heat exhaustion, and he too had to be carried up to his room. Wright was the only engineer left, and he depended on three men who were all suspected of being collaborators.

The old man sent Campbell, Hammett, and the bosun to help out. "We had the sailors swinging the valves," said Drabina. "But that engine room without the blowers is really a rough place. At that time, the whole engine room hadn't been shut down long enough to cool down." Then, in the middle of the turmoil, they got help from an unexpected quarter.

"Clyde McKay came down below to give us a hand," said Wright. "The first assistant and McKay were stooped over by the feed pump, and I went over there to find out what was wrong and the three-quarter inch nipple on the steam line had been sabotaged. McKay turned around with a sheepish grin on his face and said, 'I did it.'"

After helping out in the engine room, McKay went back up to the main deck, then to the stern, where he lay on a cot. Suddenly, looking up, McKay saw a meteor shower. One comet was especially bright, as if leaving a trail in the hot, humid air above the Gulf of Thailand.

Hours later, McKay spoke to Cambodian soldiers about what he had seen. The Cambodians shook their heads, very upset. It was obvious to McKay that they took it as an omen. They told McKay what it meant: there would be war this year.

12 DOPE THAT DONE IT

United States, Thailand

When it was Monday morning in Cambodia, it was still Sunday night in California. Flo's father, David Longenecker, was listening to the radio when he heard a news report about the seizure of an ammo ship. He turned up the volume. To his shock, the hijacked ship was the *Columbia Eagle,* the vessel Flo's husband was working on. The next day, Monday, someone from Senator Mark Hatfield's office called Longenecker to give him the bad news: not only was it his son-in-law's ship, but the young man himself was involved in the hijacking. Flo could not believe it. Blocking out Glatkowski's comments about what he would do to foment revolution, she told newsmen that "he could never have done what they say he did."

Clyde McKay's mother did not listen to the radio news on Sunday night. The first she heard about it was when a reporter came to the door on Monday afternoon. She recalled:

> I was working that day. . . . I was working as a substitute mother for families where a mother was in the hospital or in jail or wherever, and they needed somebody there in the home to stabilize the home until dad came home from work, you know, so the kids wouldn't be on their own. So I was doing that kind of work and I was with a family that had five kids, I think. And that day I had a headache, I had a headache you wouldn't believe, and I'm not a person to get headaches. And when I came home I told my husband, oh, I've just got this headache, I've got to rest.

> So I was resting when the reporter came to the door. And he was a nice guy. We had read a lot of his writing in the local paper, so we knew who he was. And he tried to break it gently. He said, "Well, it's been reported that, you know. . . ." Well, I said, there's no way that could be Billy, just no way on earth, it's impossible.

The reporter told her that the information had been released by Senator Hatfield's office. She said she told the reporter, "Senator Hatfield is mistaken. My son is a good, decent man, and a loyal American. He would never do such a thing—never. That is the silliest thing I ever heard."

During the next few hours, however, the phone did not stop ringing. Increasingly scared that it might be true, she and her husband, Colonel Cave, watched every news broadcast they could. It was on all the channels. Walter Cronkite, on CBS, reported: "One of the more bizarre stories from the high seas is slowly coming into focus tonight. It's the case of the successful two-man mutiny aboard the American munitions ship, *Columbia Eagle.*"

Frank Reynolds, on ABC's evening news, reported on "the strange saga of the American ammunition ship, *Columbia Eagle.* Over the weekend, two of the civilian crew members apparently fooled everyone else on board into thinking a bomb had been placed on the ship. Most of the crew went overboard in lifeboats and were soon picked up by another ship. Then the *Columbia Eagle* sailed into Cambodian waters."

Chet Huntley, on NBC, said that "there are still at least 13 men, including the captain, aboard the *Columbia Eagle.* Twenty-four others were put off in small boats and picked up by a second munitions ship, which took them to Sattahip."

Although the Glatkowski and McKay families had already been contacted, the young men's names had not yet been released by the media.

That same day, Monday, 16 March, the *New York Times* reported that "U.S. officials" said they believed there was a "strong possibility that the alleged mutineers might have been linked to a peace group in the United States opposing the war in Vietnam." The Defense and State Departments refused to provide formal comment, but Nixon administration officials said that there was "no 'plausible' explanation for the ship's diversion beyond the antiwar theory."

By Tuesday, news reports began to mention the two mutineers by name. Correspondents flocked to the families. On that night's evening news on ABC, Frank Reynolds set the scene: "Mrs. Glatkowski is 19 years old, she expects a child in two months and was under sedation today. Correspondent [Bill] Wordam asked Mrs. Glatkowski how her husband felt about the Vietnam War."

"He was just against it," said Flo, mascara running as tears flowed. "And he, he didn't want to be drafted, but was never any strong feeling against it, I don't think." Flo was bending the truth, but she felt that Glatkowski's strong feelings were not necessarily about stopping the war. He was more passionate about the Communist forces winning it.

Wordam asked, "He wasn't a member of any peace organization? Did he carry any peace symbols or anything like that with him?"

Flo answered, "No, he didn't, no peace symbols." That also was true.

"So this really, Mrs. Glatkowski, must have taken you fairly by surprise when you heard about this?"

"Yes, it did," said Flo. "It was a big shock, and it's still hard to believe."

Wordam then turned to Flo's father. "How does this add up in your mind to the picture you have of your son-in-law?" Longenecker—who had fought with Glatkowski over "the revolution that's coming"—said, "It really doesn't parallel with him. The only thing I can think of is, if the accusations are true, is probably dope that done it. I don't think he could have taken this action had he been rational and not influenced in some way."

On that same night, Walter Cronkite, on CBS, reported that "an American diplomat met with [Cambodian] government officials in hopes of obtaining release of the ship and the 13 crewmen still aboard. Those crewmen are not technically under arrest, but they are not yet free to leave the country."

In a *Los Angeles Times* article that appeared on Tuesday, Flo said she had gotten three letters from her husband on Saturday, the day of the mutiny. Glatkowski's "red-eyed wife" said that he had written that he was "getting along with the crew, liked his work making beds, and was anxious to get back home before the baby is born."

On an NBC report from the Longenecker home on that night's evening news, a correspondent asked Flo about Glatkowski. She answered, "Well, he's, he's what you could call a wishy-washy person. One minute he's one way, the next minute he's another way."

During those first few days after the mutiny, the media drew a particular image of Glatkowski and McKay. This image appeared in cartoons and editorials and the sarcastic undertone of news reports: that the mutiny and hijacking of a ship with thousands of tons of ammo on board, setting off most of the crew on lifeboats, and holding the skeleton crew hostage until the ship had reached a neutral country, all that had been accomplished by a couple of drugged-out hippies who had carried out an extreme prank. McKay's background as soldier-of-fortune and his having immersed himself in revolutionary tracts, as well as Glatkowski's activist past, were conveniently glossed over in the rush to portray both of them, especially Glatkowski, as confused, pimple-faced hippies with no political grounding or agenda. Chet Huntley, in an NBC report that attempted to sum up the media's emerging picture of Glatkowski, mentioned—with a wry tone—Flo's comment that Glatkowski "sometimes spoke about being against the war, and sometimes about being for it."

A *Los Angeles Times* article quoted the castaways' views on Glatkowski and McKay, conveniently setting aside that many of these were the middle-aged seamen with whom the ship's young crew members, especially Glatkowski, had butted heads for much of the trip. Phil Livingston, the baker, said that Glatkowski was "still wet behind the ears." An "unidentified crewman" said it was "a caper, that's all. Both guys were always high on pot or pills. Hell, they wouldn't know Marx from Lenin." The reporter apparently did not ask this "unidentified crewman" if he knew the difference.

Oddly, the view of Glatkowski that most coincides with his own was in a *New York Times* article that quoted Glatkowski's stepfather, who described Glatkowski as a "'hippie-yippie' who hated the police, the war in Vietnam, and the United States. . . . '[Glatkowski] called the Government a bunch of stupid idiots [and] said every member of the armed forces was a warmonger and that his ambition was to go from coast to coast and kill a cop a day.' . . . 'He's easily led,' the stepfather said, 'he will believe anything anybody tells him.' . . . 'If there was anything to demonstrate against, he was there.'"

The article skipped to the west coast and included quotes from Flo's father, who viewed Glatkowski as immature and befuddled: "'He was a confused young man having troubles growing up,' said the father-in-law, a systems engineer. 'I don't mind telling you, he really didn't know where he was at.'"

A few days later a reporter for the *Times of London* interviewed Glatkowski and McKay. His article described the mutineers as having "fairish lank hair, with wispy beards, and pimples on their faces. Both denied charges they were 'pill-popping marijuana-smoking hippies,' as other crewmen of the ship were reported to have described them."

A newspaper in Norfolk, Virginia, where Glatkowski had grown up, ran an article titled "From Good Scout to Alleged Pirate": "Are Leonard [Hardy], the personable youth who grew to young manhood on Norfolk's Neoma Drive, and Alvin Leonard Glatkowski, who reportedly helped hijack a Vietnam-bound munitions ship to Cambodia, one and the same? Neighbors who knew him find it hard to believe, but it is so."

The *Los Angeles Times* stated, "The alleged metamorphosis of Alvin Glatkowski—from high school dropout, to disenchanted service station attendant, to Vietnam War critic, to family man, to suspected mutineer—came without warning." The article quoted Longenecker. "Politically, Al . . . really wasn't an activist. . . . He told me he believed in nonviolence and, as far as any of us know, he never participated in any peace demonstrations."

By the third day, a more complex portrait of the mutineers began to emerge. Frank Reynolds of ABC reported that the action was carried out by "at least two members of the crew said to be opposed to the war in Vietnam."

Still, each attempt to find depth in the antiwar action was "balanced" by portraying them as a couple of "pill-popping, pot-smoking" hippies just having fun. When an ABC correspondent in Thailand interviewed the castaways, Marco Smigliani said that he had argued with McKay and Glatkowski about the war. This was followed by a comment from a cook: "The crew was pretty good, but nowadays you always get a couple of dingalings."

The castaways were approached by newsmen with cameras and tape recorders. These press people had been camped out in Sattahip, waiting for the castaways to leave the *Rappahannock*. Ciamboli said he was asked if he had had any idea, during the trip, that Glatkowski and McKay were planning a mutiny. He told newsmen that he never had a clue it was coming. He said, however, "Glatkowski was weird and capable of anything. But with my conversations with McKay I had the impression that he was intelligent, level-headed and with good manners."

In the middle of these interviews, Thai soldiers came running toward them and hustled the television crews and reporters off the dock area. Finally, the castaways boarded the bus; when the bus passed the guard shack, there were a half-dozen newsmen shouting questions through the open windows.

Besides the anguish the mutineers' families endured—worrying about their loved ones, fielding reporters' calls and visits—they also received phone calls and letters from strangers who wanted to express their feelings about what McKay and Glatkowski had done. More than a few of these were supportive. A man in Los Angeles wrote to McKay's mother, urging her to "be proud of your son. . . . He is a *real hero*. . . . It takes *real courage* to oppose an unjust war. . . . Your son is no traitor. The real traitors against America and against all humanity are the selfish and powerful men in high places who continue the waste of our men and resources and the slaughter of helpless Asians." Another man in San Francisco wrote a respectful, effusive letter to McKay's mother, asking what time of the day McKay was born, so that he could prepare a horoscope.

13 CONSPIRACY THEORIES

Washington, D.C.

During the first few days after the mutiny, Nixon administration spokespeople, speaking openly at press conferences or leaking information anonymously, made some intriguing comments about how U.S. civilian and military leaders learned about the mutiny and what they planned to do about it.

On Sunday, 15 March, Jerry Friedheim, the deputy assistant secretary of defense for public affairs, briefed reporters at the Pentagon. A *New York Times* article said that Friedheim told the press corps that the first indication that there was something wrong came at "about 1 AM Saturday, Washington time" when the Coast Guard cutter *Mellon,* patrolling in the Gulf of Thailand, "intercepted two radio messages sent from the Columbia Eagle." Friedheim said that one of these messages was transmitted by the *Eagle*'s radio officer, Orville Mills, and it said that "men with guns" had taken over the ship; the second was sent by an "unidentified sender" and this one said, "I have been relieved of the bridge."

When it was 1 A.M. Saturday in Washington, it was 1 P.M. Saturday in the Gulf of Thailand. Thus, according to the Defense Department, the *Mellon* knew about the mutiny just as the mutiny was starting.

Another Defense Department spokesperson, Assistant Secretary of Defense Daniel Z. Henkin, also stated that the *Mellon* knew about the mutiny from the beginning. Henkin told reporters at a Pentagon briefing that "after it had become known 26 hours earlier that [the *Columbia Eagle*] had been captured on the high seas by rebel crewmen," the *Mellon* followed the *Eagle* closely until she sailed into Cambodian waters.

Administration spokespeople then told the press that the *Mellon*—after having intercepted these messages—did not inform the Defense Department about this apparent mutiny until "about two hours" later. The Defense Department supposedly did not pass the word on to the White House and the State Department for another twenty-four hours.

Defense Department spokespeople also said that Nixon's administrative staff learned more details of what had happened on board the *Eagle* by "reconstructing the action from the accounts of the 24 [castaways]" after they were rescued by the *Rappahannock*.

Henkin told reporters, "We have received reports that the crewmen rescued from the lifeboats have implicated two of their former shipmates as the alleged mutineers."

Administration spokespeople also said that the United States had launched a mission to bring the *Eagle* back. Friedheim told reporters that five U.S. ships had been sent to the area because "the emergency might have developed into a search-and-rescue operation."

An article in the *New York Times* expanded on the rescue mission. It said that "the Defense Department confirmed earlier reports that orders had been issued . . . Sunday morning to a United States warship [the *Mellon*] to enter Cambodian territorial waters and bring the Columbia Eagle out by force."

Immediately after issuing orders to the *Mellon* to follow the *Eagle* into Cambodian waters and "escort her out by any available means," Adm. John H. Hyland, commander of the Pacific Fleet, "telephoned Washington from his Pearl Harbor headquarters." Hyland reached Adm. John McCain, the commander in chief, Pacific, who was at a meeting in the Pentagon at 4 A.M. on Sunday morning. According to the Defense Department, McCain consulted with the White House, as well as with officials of the State and Defense Departments, and then countermanded Hyland's rescue order.

"The decision against a move into Cambodian waters was reported to have been based on safety considerations involving the ship and her crew and on diplomatic considerations toward the political situation in Cambodia," said a *New York Times* article. "The Nixon Administration felt that a warlike action by the United States in Cambodian territorial waters . . . could have strengthened the North Vietnamese argument that the United States was an 'aggressor' against whom all Asians should rally."

THERE WERE some odd inconsistencies in these official statements. Administration spokespeople said that the *Mellon* knew about the mutiny because of two SOS-type messages coming out of the *Eagle* and intercepted by the *Mellon* at the start of the revolt: "There are men with guns," and "I have been relieved of the bridge."

During the mutiny investigation, however, Orville Mills, the *Eagle*'s radio operator, carefully went over every transmission he sent during and after the hijacking. He said *nothing* about sending out any message while the mutiny was starting. Quite the contrary. He stated very clearly that he sent his first post-mutiny communication when the *Eagle* entered Cambodian waters, at about 2 P.M. Sunday afternoon, which would have been 2 A.M. Sunday morning in Washington. He also said that the radio shack was locked by McKay at the start of the mutiny, before anyone could send any message out. And after he was allowed to transmit, upon reaching Cambodian waters, Mills sent no messages without the hijackers' approval.

The wording of the second message—"I have been relieved of the bridge"—implies that Captain Swann sent it. Swann, in his testimony, made no mention of any message he sent out as the mutiny was beginning. Had such a message been sent, Swann would have been more than eager to tell the investigators, who were looking for any indication that the men on the *Eagle* had tried to stop the mutiny.

Did administration staff make up this story about intercepted messages? If so, why? And if not by way of these messages, then how *did* the *Mellon* learn about the mutiny?

Defense Department spokespeople also said that the United States learned details of the mutiny because there were reports that the *castaways* implicated McKay and Glatkowski.

When asked about this later, Marco Smigliani, one of the castaways, said, "Don't let anybody tell you that we knew who had done it and what had happened. We didn't. Everything we knew came from the same radio reports everybody else was listening to."

Why was such knowledge assigned to the castaways?

On the one hand, the timeline offered by Department of Defense (DOD) spokespeople clearly implies that the DOD knew about the mutiny from its very beginning. On the other hand, when it came to talking about how the DOD had this knowledge, its spokespeople offered the press suspect stories about "intercepted messages" and information that they incorrectly claimed the castaways had. It would appear that the DOD spokespeople were trying to conceal how they gathered their information about the mutiny. Why?

According to the time mentioned by Defense Department spokespeople, the "search-and-rescue" mission was ordered by Admiral Hyland when the *Eagle* was already in Cambodian waters, even though the *Mellon* had followed the ship for twenty-six hours—since the beginning of the mutiny. Why had the *Mellon* waited so long? Or had the rescue mission been ordered when the *Eagle* was still in international waters?

More important, was the search-and-rescue mission—as implied by Defense Department spokespeople—an authorized operation launched by the commander of the *Mellon* and Admiral Hyland, and then reversed by their superiors?

Friedheim told the press that, after finding out about the mutiny (because of the intercepted messages), the officers on the *Mellon* did not inform the Defense Department for two hours and then the Defense Department did not tell the White House or State Department about it for another twenty-four hours. Friedheim said that there appeared to be "considerable confusion and something of a communications breakdown" in relaying to the secretary of state and the president the fact that an American ship carrying thousands of tons of napalm in a war zone had been hijacked by armed crewmen.

Is it reasonable to believe that there had been such a delay? Government officials were apparently skittish about the hijacked ship, and their comments to the press reflected that. What was going on here?

Sihanoukville Bay

Early on Tuesday morning, 17 March, the *Columbia Eagle*, at anchorage nearly five miles from Sihanoukville, shifted closer inside, then dropped the hook.

At about 10 A.M. a group of Cambodian naval officers came on board the vessel again, this time led by Captain Amg. They demanded to inspect the vessel's cargo. Since Swann was preparing to go ashore and could not take the group himself, he told Morgan to take care of it, and whispered to the chief mate that he should try to discourage their hosts from spending too much time in the holds.

Morgan, following Swann's advice, told Amg that he would take them through the mast-house, down to one of the holds, but he kept insisting that this was very dangerous cargo: he did not want anyone smoking cigarettes near the bombs. On his way down the vertical ladder, Morgan sniffed here and there, as if he were smelling something that was not right. "Pretty soon," said Morgan, "Captain Amg started sniffing, and the second in command, then the lieutenants, pretty soon the whole group was sniffing along like a pack of bloodhounds on the trail of a possum. . . . I nearly busted a gut laughing."

Morgan took them down to the 'tween deck and the lower hold, which was the only area where someone could actually walk around or climb up ladders. The Cambodians, apparently nervous, spent as little time as possible in the hold, quickly taking photos of the bombs before going back up through the mast-house.

Back on deck, the Cambodians took photos of all the crew members. "I didn't know what the photographs were for," said Swann. "We had all our gear packed up because Glatkowski and McKay told us that they were going to take us off the ship. So, you see, I thought that those pictures were for making an entry and exit visa." Swann was convinced that everyone was going to be taken off, but he was advised that only he and the two mutineers were being evacuated. This was an enormous relief to Swann, who told Mills to keep contact with the *Mellon* and let the cutter know what was going on.

Before leaving the ship—forever, as it would turn out—Glatkowski and McKay said good-bye to the crew. According to Glatkowski, a number of crew members shook their hands and thanked them for not killing them and not causing an explosion. Sather shook hands with Glatkowski and gave him a slip of paper with his address. When the investigators later asked Sather why he did this, he answered, "I like Ski. It's hard to believe, and the guy is sick. I mean, he's as good as dead now. But he was, to me, he was pretty damn decent." Sather told investigators that the bosun also shook hands with the mutineers and told them, "May God have mercy on your soul."

Shortly after 10:30 A.M. that Tuesday, Swann, McKay, and Glatkowski boarded a Cambodian navy craft. On the way toward shore, Swann talked with the mutineers. "We got into what you might call a political discussion, philosophies and things like that," said Swann. "I [said], 'If you don't like this so-called establishment now, what would you like to replace it with?' That was my main point to him that—to try to get him to answer that question. And I said, 'Do you know of a better way of life? Do you know any place you're going to be better off? How can we make this a better way of life? What is your ultimate goal?' And McKay admitted that he didn't know."

Glatkowski and McKay did not realize that their goal had already become part of an international conflict that was about to take an odd, dramatic turn.

14 THE COUP

Cambodia

Cambodia had become a French colony in the mid-nineteenth century, and it remained one until World War II, when the Japanese occupied it. After 1945, France once more imposed its authority; by 1949, however, feeling pressured by independence-minded insurgencies throughout Indochina, it granted limited self-government to Cambodia. During this period—which eventually led to nationhood—Prince Norodom Sihanouk emerged as a leader. He solidified his following and by 1955 he was the undisputed chief of state and head of government.

Sihanouk's government was authoritarian and centralized. He maintained his power because he was promoted by the French, and he had the support of Cambodian peasants, who were apparently touched by his charismatic personality, his frequent visits to rural areas, and his continuation of the traditional ceremonies, symbols, and institutions of the Khmer monarchy.

Maintaining a policy of neutrality in the country's international relations, Sihanouk succeeded, for a while at least, in keeping Cambodia relatively free of the kinds of struggles that were engulfing other states in the region. In the late 1960s, however, the country was beset by internal troubles. Cambodia's main export crops, rubber and rice, suffered price drops in world markets; there was growing unemployment among the better educated segment of the population; and students, among others, were fed up with authoritarian crackdowns on political opposition.

Cambodia's international posture was also eroding. During the mid-1960s, trying to appease Communist forces filtering into his country, Sihanouk broke relations with the United States and looked to Beijing for support. Cambodia, meanwhile, became a haven for North Vietnamese and Viet Cong forces, which nearly destroyed Sihanouk's policy of neutrality. Sihanouk would later resume ties with Washington, in an increasingly dangerous balancing act between right and left; by 1969 Sihanouk was walking a tightrope without a net.

As would become evident years later, during most of 1969 and the first few months of 1970—that is, during the time that the *Columbia Eagle* entered the scene—something else was going on as well. American B-52 planes were flying highly secret bombing missions into Cambodia, attacking Viet Cong and North Vietnamese sanctuaries. As William Shawcross points out in his book *Sideshow* (1979), Richard Nixon and Henry Kissinger would both later claim that Sihanouk had acquiesced to these missions. If so, that would mean that Sihanouk, in his constant attempts to try to secure Cambodia's survival, had a secret understanding with both sides: permitting the Communists to establish sanctuaries, while at the same time allowing—or at least not stopping—America's bombing of them.

And something else was going on when the *Columbia Eagle* entered Cambodian waters in mid-March 1970. As a result of Cambodia's untenable neutrality and imploding economic and political situation, the country was in the middle of an internal crisis. In Phnom Penh there were demonstrations, staged by General Lon Nol, Sihanouk's prime minister, against the Viet Cong and North Vietnamese presence in Cambodia. One of these —on 12 March, two days before the *Columbia Eagle* was hijacked—turned violent. In Paris, Sihanouk denounced the almost daily demonstrations. Several analysts opined that Lon Nol's intention may not have been to depose Sihanouk but to force him into a more aggressive posture toward the Vietnamese Communists. However, it has also been pointed out that Lon Nol's cohort in the attempts to force a showdown was a man who did want Sihanouk's rule undermined: Prince Sirik Matak, Sihanouk's cousin. In 1941, Sirik Matak—a conservative nationalist—had been passed over by the French in favor of his cousin, and he had apparently nursed resentment about this afterward.

According to documents in Shawcross's *Sideshow*, the CIA had ample warning that the unrest in Phnom Penh was leading toward a change in government. On 12 March, six days before the coup, CIA headquarters received a report called "Indications of a possible coup in Phnom Penh." It stated that the Cambodian army, still loyal to Sihanouk, was preparing to defend against a coup attempt. A U.S. general told Shawcross that "U.S. commanders were informed several days beforehand that a coup was being planned."

Some observers contend that this was why there was a delay in chasing the *Eagle*, and why the order to seize the hijacked ship was countermanded. If indeed Washington officials knew that a coup was about to take place, it would have been a mistake to have a U.S. military maneuver in Cambodia at that time, off the coast, because it might have jeopardized the legitimacy of the new regime.

It was into this cauldron, ready to bubble over, that McKay and Glatkowski brought the *Columbia Eagle*.

Glatkowski later said that he and McKay—unaware of the political chaos beneath Cambodia's apparent neutrality—thought it would be a relatively simple matter. They would turn the ship over to Cambodia, which would keep it and its cargo. Cambodia would give the mutineers asylum and then the mutineers could find someplace in the world willing to take them in. As far as they knew, they were entering a country led by a left-leaning prince, albeit a temporarily absent one, who had the power to do all that.

On Tuesday, 17 March, Swann, Glatkowski, and McKay were taken by a Cambodian gunboat to the naval base at Ream, near Sihanoukville. From Ream they went by jeep toward the nearby airfield. On the way the mutineers were struck by the beauty of the small village of Ream, just outside the naval base; they savored the simple, colorfully painted shacks on stilts, swaying coconut palms, and streams on which small, sinuous men with small boats gathered shellfish. They had seen similar sights before, in Vietnam. But Vietnam was where the war was taking place, and even though the country had rice paddies and water buffaloes, one was never very far from soldiers and artillery fire. Cambodia, obviously, was different. Their initial impression was of a population more friendly and less sophisticated than other places in Southeast Asia, less polluted by the chase after the American dollar, and by war.

The airfield near Sihanoukville was hot and stark, and the small plane that flew them to Phnom Penh was of obsolete Russian vintage. They arrived in the Cambodian capital at about 2 P.M. There, at the military airport, Glatkowski saw Russian MIG fighter jets for the first time. He was impressed by their sleek, metallic beauty.

During the ride into town, Glatkowski saw relatively few cars. On the streets were cyclo-pousse, bicycle rickshaws that transported cargo and people. Some scooters carried entire families, up to five people if you counted the babies and small children. On the side of the road were indelible images: clusters of young, saffron-robed Buddhist monks carrying yellow umbrellas; stalls selling everything from brightly colored plaster Buddhas to bananas and gasoline. Chic young women in stylish skirts, wearing dark red lipstick. Mango trees and incense. Bullocks and water buffaloes and dogs and billiard tables. Men on bicycles carrying all sorts of improbable loads: piglets in rattan cages, mounds of fruit or vegetables, stacks of egg crates, charcoal.

Swann requested to see the American chargé d'affaires, Lloyd (Mike) Rives. The Cambodians told him, *It's too late now, we'll do that tomorrow.* Instead, the three men from the *Columbia Eagle* were taken by a half-dozen naval officers directly to a restaurant in Phnom Penh, by the Tonle Sap River. The restaurant had garish decorations: bright red and yellow figures from Ramayana Buddhist lore—busty females in sexy dance poses—as well as Buddhas and lanterns. The courses came, one after the other: salad, rice-noodle soup, grilled meats and shrimp, wine, sliced French baguette and butter, espresso, fresh fruit—papaya, mango, green guava, pineapple.

Glatkowski said he told Cambodian officers during this dinner that he and McKay had hijacked the ship because they felt that "war was bad." Glatkowski said that the Cambodians certainly agreed with that, but they pointed out that the North Vietnamese and Viet Cong presence in their country was also very bad.

Swann, on the other hand, recalled no political discussion with the Cambodians. "In the restaurant," Swann told the investigative team, "there was just commonplace talk about different customs and the food and things like that. Glatkowski was asking several times about the TASS [Russian acronym for Telegraph Agency of the Soviet Union] News Agency, he wanted to get in touch with the TASS News Agency. In fact, [Glatkowski] even embarrassed McKay. He was asking the Cambodian commander what his pay was and about the living standards of the country and McKay kind of hushed him up."

To Glatkowski, it was probably just one more instance of the condescending way that McKay treated him. Still, Glatkowski felt good about the dinner. He said, "the Cambodians wined and dined us. We were treated very well." McKay agreed. He would later tell visiting journalists that during the first two days they were in Cambodia, he and Glatkowski "were taken to restaurants and hailed as heroes. It was really thrilling."

After dinner, on that first night, the captain and the two mutineers were taken to navy headquarters, just south of Sisowath Quay inside Phnom Penh. Then they left and headed north.

The convoy passed Wat Phnom—Phnom Penh's oldest Buddhist shrine—and went through the colonial part of the city: two- to five-story French-built pastel- and dun-colored houses and charming public buildings, hundreds of stalls selling newspapers and fruit and used auto batteries. On the bridge, which went over the Tonle Sap and led to riverside villages, the convoy's progress was temporarily slowed by a bullock cart that moved at a snail's pace and took up the entire lane. Vehicles impatiently went around it, forcing the cyclo-pousse going in the opposite direction to swerve away.

The convoy crossed the bridge eastward, on the road to Kampong Cham, past dozens of stalls selling baguettes. Though the Cambodian middle class never took to French bread, the peasants did, and this part of the road had become a roadside bread market. The convoy then turned right—south—into the Chrui Changwar Peninsula, toward the naval base. The peninsula narrowed at that point, so that the base, taking up most of the acreage at the southern end of the peninsula, had easy access to all three of Phnom Penh's rivers: the Mekong to the east, the Tonle Sap to the west and the Bassac to the south. At the entrance to the base there were several navy personnel—teenagers wearing olive-drab military uniforms and rubber flip-flops instead of shoes and socks—who waved the small convoy through.

"When we arrived there," said Swann, "they took us to the officers' lounge, a club more or less. And there we were told we were going to be quartered, and I told them I was extremely tired, that I had been up several days and I would sure appreciate it if I could lay down. But they said, 'soon, soon, soon.'" Eventually the three were taken to a barracks that had obviously not been used for some time. "Everything was real dusty and dirty and water just trickled in there."

The room was large and there were three beds, two at one end and one at the other. "I told them," said Swann, "that I didn't want to stay there, that I didn't want to stay in the same room with these men here, and I wanted some other quarters. Let me go to a hotel, but I wasn't going to stay there. The officer in charge said that that was the orders, and that was going to be it. And I thought, 'Jeez, no telling what's going to happen.' But I was so tired at that time, I didn't care." Swann lay down and was fast asleep within seconds. Later, the guards brought dinner for the three men. They woke up Swann, who told them that he wanted to sleep, not eat. He left his plate of food untouched.

The following morning, 18 March, Swann was given bread and tea, then taken across the bridge, back to naval headquarters in Phnom Penh. There, he was set up in an unused office. A bed and a desk were the only items in that room. "It didn't have any electricity," said Swann. "The window was open permanently, bugs would fly in and out."

That same morning the mutineers were also driven across the bridge into Phnom Penh, toward a building that housed the Foreign Office staff. On the way, Glatkowski asked the driver if they could go by the embassies of North Vietnam and the Viet Cong. The driver obliged. Glatkowski said that "there were mobs in front of those embassies," shouting and yelling. The driver moved quickly past the hubbub. Once Glatkowski and McKay were at the government building, an English-speaking Cambodian official who worked in the secretary general's office asked them to write out what it was they had done. "We filled out a declaration as to what we did," said Glatkowski. "Stuff that we had discussed for hours and hours on the ship. Nuremberg Trials, not being good German soldiers, etc. We said that we believed it was our moral obligation to stop those bombs." Glatkowski and McKay told the Cambodian official that they intended to renounce their U.S. citizenship and they handed over their passports.

In the afternoon they were driven back to their living quarters at the naval base on the other side of the river. They did not know what was going on in Cambodia that day, but later, after dinner, they heard sporadic gunfire.

On that same day, Wednesday, 18 March, aboard the *Eagle,* the chief mate was in charge of the ship's day-to-day operation. That afternoon a ragged-looking gunboat—with MRK-13 in large black letters on its hull—came out. The men on the *Eagle* dubbed this boat the "African Queen." Its commander, Chung Kim, paid a visit to the chief mate.

"The lieutenant came over," said Morgan, "and he was sitting in my office."

Well, said Chung, *We're in the same boat.*

What do you mean?

Well, you're wondering what's going to happen to you and your ship. We're wondering what's going to happen to us—the new government. No one knows what's going to happen.

Morgan thought he had misunderstood what the man said.

Captain Swann, in his room at naval headquarters, on the afternoon of 18 March, again asked to see the American chargé d'affaires; he was told that there would be time for that later. Soon, soon.

"It was funny," said Swann. "They had me in that room there, the captain or commander of the port there, or the base. 'How would you like a beer, captain?' I said, 'that's fine, that sounds great.' He said, 'come on to our club,' they had a club, everything like that, and he said, 'have a beer.'"

But when Swann walked in, he felt an "icy curtain" between him and the officers. "It was just like I had the plague, everybody was standing way away from me, almost, not in a complete circle, but behind the bar and the doorways and things like that, and I was just at this table by myself, drinking beer."

"Well, they put on the radio," Swann recalled. "They says, 'Would you like to listen to the radio?' Sure, I'd like to get the armed services news, from Saigon, you know. So they had it on there and the news come on and that's what they was looking at: to see my reaction."

Armed Forces Radio announced that earlier that day, the Cambodian National Assembly had convened, and they had voted unanimously to remove Prince Sihanouk as head of government. Lon Nol had been granted emergency powers, and Sirik Matak was his prime minister.

Swann was astounded. "Of course, I guess my chin dropped down to my knees. I said, I'll just sit here and wait. Surely diplomacy will take care of this thing, the chargé d'affaires or whatever, and I'll just sit here and wait now. But when that happened, I knew I was in bad, bad trouble."

The news reported that Lon Nol and Sirik Matak had called for the evacuation of all Vietnamese Communist forces from Cambodia; the new leaders were decidedly *not* neutral and they did not want to leave any doubt as to where their political sympathies lay. It was claimed that they themselves had organized the demonstrations outside the embassy of the North Vietnamese and the office of the National Liberation Front.

According to Swann, the officers at this club then changed the radio station so that they could hear speeches in Khmer. Of course, Swann did not understand these, but the officers told him that they were listening to the new leaders of the country. Swann tried to gauge the officers' reaction, which seemed very subdued. "The officers did not clap their hands or cheer," said Swann, "they were very serious . . . clustered together listening to these speeches for hours and hours."

In the middle of this, a Cambodian officer who was proficient in English told Swann that he and his ship had arrived at "the worst possible time." This officer told him that there was going to be "no end of trouble and the new [political] party didn't know just yet what they were going to be, whether they were going to be a republic or who was going to do what. They was more or less scared of one another. Who was going to be pro-Sihanouk and who wasn't going to be pro-Sihanouk."

That night, back in his room, Swann also heard gunfire. He again requested to see Mike Rives, the American chargé d'affaires, but he was told by Cambodian officers that "headquarters hadn't had the time to take this matter up . . . they was having too much internal trouble."

On 23 March, less than a week after being held incommunicado in Phnom Penh, Swann was taken back to Ream and then to the *Eagle,* in order to shift to a different anchorage. On the road to Ream, Swann later told investigators, he saw military convoys and tanks. "The movement of men by trucks was quite prevalent at that time," he said. On the way to Ream the

Cambodians told Swann that the reason for the shift was to place the ship in a location which "was more secure from the V.C. and safer."

At the current anchorage they were four and a half miles from Sihanoukville; though far away, the Cambodians were still afraid that the ship could explode and destroy everything in the vicinity. Swann was determined to exploit that fear in order to try to get the ship back on its way, with its cargo untouched and intact.

The shift took the ship to an anchorage near the navy base at Ream—a few miles southeast, on the coast. Between Ream and the *Eagle*'s new anchorage there were several islands, the largest of which was called Ta Kiev, about a mile square. These islands were beautiful and lush, full of jungle-like undergrowth and palm trees. The men on the ship were close enough to see beckoning beaches and inlets, a paradise with occasional rocky outcroppings all around. They were close enough to see that the Cambodian navy kept small contingents of personnel on the islands, sailors who patrolled and protected coastal waters. Apparently, the point of moving the *Eagle* to this anchorage was to have the ship in an area where Cambodian navy craft had quick access to it, while at the same time the islands would serve as a buffer zone in case of explosion.

Out of stubbornness, Swann did not move the vessel to the exact location that the Cambodians wanted him to, but a short distance away. On the night after Swann first shifted the ship to the Ream island anchorage, he was not allowed to remain on board the ship. Instead, he was taken back to the Ream base to sleep, and in order to prevent any more messages from going out from the *Eagle,* Mills—Sparks—was also taken ashore.

Mills later said that when the Cambodians had taken Swann, McKay, and Glatkowski ashore on the seventeenth, they meant to take him also, to prevent him from sending radio messages. "But they forgot and left me aboard and I was able to spend the next few days in constant contact with U.S. officials in Manila," said Mills. "I told them the hijackers had been removed and the press got the word and began broadcasting it."

This was not the only message that Mills sent to the *Mellon.* He also told them that there were three men, still on board, who were suspected of having collaborated with the mutineers. Within hours, while listening to an international radio news program, the men on the *Eagle* heard an item about three suspected collaborators still on board the *Eagle.* Though their names were not mentioned, Sather, Mornin, and Gray were upset that these allegations were broadcast to the world in this manner.

Sather, down in the engine room with Wright, muttered, *Them bastards are trying to throw me to the dogs here, implicating me in this.* Wright asked Sather if he *was* one of them, and Sather said, *Bullshit, I am not one of them!*

As a result of these news items on the radio, the Cambodians realized that Sparks was still aboard the *Eagle* and transmitting to the *Mellon.* An assistant chief of staff of the Cambodian navy, armed with an automatic weapon, came aboard and ordered Mills off the ship. "He was really angry I'd been making radio contact," said Mills.

The day after the shift, 24 March, the Cambodian officials brought Swann back to the ship to shift it again, having figured out that Swann had not placed the ship in the exact location specified. Each time that Swann was returned to the *Columbia Eagle,* he was warned not to send out any messages. According to Swann, the Cambodians told him that any such messages might "complicate things."

During these shifts, the captain saw that the eleven men who remained on the ship were in a relatively comfortable situation. "During the stay in port," Wright told the investigators, "we fellows that were left on the ship were in a better position than the skipper and the radio operator because ... we had our quarters, we had fans, we had the bay breeze. We ate good. I myself was elected cook."

The main problem on board, the men later said, was that with the temperature hovering around 100 degrees, they were afraid that the detonators and napalm bombs might explode. The holds were not air-conditioned, and several men worried that the temperatures down there might get dangerously high.

Except for radio news, the only contact the men on board had with the outside world was the erratic but almost daily visit of the "African Queen," which kept an eye on the *Eagle.* Smiling naval officers would bring pineapples and coconuts, and the men on the *Eagle* would give them cigarettes and baseball caps in return.

The men on board settled into a routine. There was minimal deck maintenance, which was handled by Northcutt, Hammett, and Campbell, who also washed dishes, pots, and pans. Bridge duties were shared by Morgan and Gunn. The only demanding work was in the engine room.

"During this time, while the captain was gone," Dan Mornin told the investigators, "we had to keep the engine room going in order to maintain ship functions. So I was a fireman, we had the three engineers and made the electrician and Bruce firemen as well. So we kept the engine room going fairly well." Mornin was Drabina's fireman, Sather was Tober's, and Gray did fireman duties for Wright, who had good words to say about how Gray handled the job.

When the old man had finished shifting the ship the second time, he was told that he would not be going back to Phnom Penh that night; he would be spending another night at naval headquarters in Ream. The following day Swann found out the reason for this. While eating breakfast with Cambodian officers, he was told that Captain Amg and other officials were going to accompany him to the ship to inspect the cargo for the third time. One young lieutenant, visibly nervous, said that "he was too young to die." Swann exploited this fear. When Captain Amg offhandedly said that this would probably be the last time he, Amg, would visit the *Eagle*, Swann said, "This may be the last time any of us do anything, gentlemen. I want to stress that this is a dangerous operation."

This did not deter Amg; once aboard the ship, he wanted to see the cargo. Swann said, "They demanded [that we] open the cargo hatches and [they] wanted to go down in the holds and take pictures. Of course I stressed we had sensitive cargo, that it was extremely dangerous, that I was not an ammunition expert." Swann continued his excuses and veiled threats. "I told them 'I know that my government is going to be unhappy if this cargo is disturbed in any way. And also the Cambodian government is going to be very unhappy if a lot of people are killed here.' So I said, 'I'm going to go on record as being one-hundred percent against this operation. I don't have the men to do it and you don't have the men to do it, this is a highly skilled operation, we have to have special men, we have to have cork shoes.' I told them anything I could think of."

The Cambodian officials did not buy it. "Captain Amg became very indignant there several times when I told him I couldn't do it. Again, I was delaying as long as I could." Finally, Amg compromised and agreed that they would inspect just one section. "We opened up one pontoon," said Swann, "and let them look down. They took pictures of this and they didn't know what we had exactly. They wasn't sure whether we just had empty shells or what it was." When Amg asked what was in the boxes, Swann answered, *I don't know, all I do is carry it.*

The Cambodians were apparently satisfied that the rumor they had heard was not true. The rumor—reported in several reputable papers and discussed by journalists and diplomats—was that the *Columbia Eagle* was not carrying napalm or large bombs, but had in fact brought small arms to Cambodia: M-16 semi-automatic rifles and corresponding ammo. The rumor was that these small arms had been secretly removed from the holds and distributed into the hands of commanders and troops loyal to Lon Nol and Sirik Matak, who had then used these arms to overthrow Sihanouk.

Malcolm Caldwell and Lek Hor Tan, in *Cambodia in the Southeast Asian War* (1973), explored this issue. They stated that the *Columbia Eagle*'s arrival three days before the coup "sparked off a wave of allegations that the hijackers were in fact CIA agents sent to supply arms to the Lon Nol group. This was the view of a major part of the world's Communist press, as well as of *Le Monde*."

As might be expected, Prince Sihanouk—in exile—believed the rumor and even helped to spread it. In his book, *My War with the CIA* (1973), the prince discussed

> the mysterious case of the Columbia Eagle, in which just two U.S. sailors "mutinied" and imprisoned the whole crew. Shades of Captain Bligh and the Bounty! Ostensibly these men were war protesters who sailed the Columbia Eagle into Sihanoukville harbor because they objected to carrying napalm bombs to Bangkok. It so happened that some French secondary-school teachers at Sihanoukville took photos of the "hijacked" ship when it arrived, and again when it left. They noted that it had been very low in the water on arrival, and very high on departure.
>
> On the day of the coup, Western correspondents noted that the troops massed outside the national Assembly were armed with brand-new M-16 rifles, weapons our army did not possess. It seems that the Columbia Eagle was one of the CIA's responses to Lon Nol's request [for help].

Neither the before-and-after photos of the *Columbia Eagle*'s Plimsoll Line showing that it was low when it came into Cambodia and high when it left, nor the allegation about the "brand-new M-16 rifles," has ever been corroborated or proven.*

The rumor continued to spread. Mills, while at naval headquarters in Phnom Penh, also got wind of it. "Once, in the officers' club," said Sparks, "one of the officers, I don't remember who, said 'Well, perhaps,' he said, 'on this maybe the Cambodians might get some small arms out of it.'"

A *New York Times* article, dated 26 March, said that Prince Sirik Matak "hinted that the arrival of the Columbia Eagle in the midst of this country's internal crisis and tension with the Vietnamese Communists had acutely embarrassed the [Cambodian] Government by providing Communist propaganda organs and Prince Sihanouk with a pretense for alleging that the United States was helping the anti-Sihanouk forces."

The new Cambodian government, under Lon Nol and Sirik Matak, could not afford to have this rumor spread. If the government wished to gain and keep the approval of the Cambodian people, it would need to show that the coup was a result of the will of the people and not American intervention. The problem for the *Eagle* was that the new Cambodian government was not sure whether its public relations were better served by letting the ship go or by holding on to it. As a result, the decision was delayed, and the ship remained on the hook. Days turned into weeks.

After 25 March, Swann and Mills were flown from Ream back to naval headquarters in Phnom Penh. For Swann it was a godsend to have Mills with him; finally he would have a companion in the room, someone who spoke English. And when the two men talked, it was about their growing anger concerning the situation.

During this period, Swann struggled with officials of the Lon Nol government, pleading with them to release the vessel. At one point, he wrote out a set of grievances. In his statement, Swann said his ship and his crew "were forced in here against our will at the point of a pistol." He also said

---

*The most telling argument against this rumor is that none of the men aboard the ship, while it was on the hook, heard or saw any evidence whatsoever that anything was removed from the ship. Moving heavy cargo off a steamship is extremely noisy; it is impossible to do it without the knowledge of the men on board. Moreover, Morgan, the chief mate—in charge of the vessel while Swann was ashore—is the kind of person who tends to see conspiracies everywhere, including in the case of the *Columbia Eagle;* but he too readily admits that nothing was removed from the ship while it was at anchorage in Cambodia.

that he knew that the U.S. government was "unhappy" that the Cambodians were holding the vessel here for so long, given that it was brought in against the crew's will.

According to Swann, the junior officers who watched over him promised to pass his statement on to headquarters. They also assured him that Mike Rives, the U.S. chargé d'affaires, would come to see him soon.

Finally, on 1 April, Swann received a visit from Rives, who was surprised to see Mills there; he had been told that it was only the captain who was being held. Rives told Swann that he had tried repeatedly to see him, without success. Had Swann received the note he had sent? No, Swann said, he hadn't. "He had written me a note telling me . . . that I hadn't been forgotten," said Swann, "that they were doing everything they could for me." Rives told Swann that he did not know what was holding things up. He thought that the vessel would be permitted to leave soon. After ten minutes, a Cambodian soldier signaled Rives that it was time for him to leave.

The next time that Rives arrived, on 7 April—three and a half weeks after the vessel had first entered Cambodian waters—he had good news for Swann. The ship would be leaving the next day, but not before a cargo inspection and a press conference with diplomats and journalists, including a TASS correspondent, Artur Blinov. Swann asked Rives if there was anything that he "shouldn't say, and [Rives] said no, most of the action is known already." Rives suggested that Swann be as "brief as possible" and try to get these unofficial inspectors off the ship as quickly as he could.

On this same day Lt. Cdr. Philip R. Spiker, head of the mutiny investigation team, flew into Cambodia. In Phnom Penh, Spiker tried to get permission to go to the *Eagle* but failed. Finally receiving permission, he went down to Ream on 8 April. There, he was told that he would not be able to go to the ship. He went straight to Amg to ask permission.

At about the same time, Swann and Mills were taken from Phnom Penh to Ream and then to the ship, joined by dozens of diplomats—including Rives—and reporters. "The newsmen wanted to know how it happened. It was a little bit beyond their understanding how two men could hold the ship for so long," said Swann. "They wanted to know if I would do it over again the same way. They wanted to know if I thought that the type of cargo that we were carrying was the reason." Swann told the newsmen that the mutiny had been a "war protest, entirely." The journalists rattled off one question after another. What type of cargo? How long had Swann been carrying that type of cargo? Where was he going to carry it next trip? Where was the ship going now? What did he think of McKay and Glatkowski?

Swann was not comfortable in this situation, which required a skill with words that he did not possess. He did the best he could, avoiding questions about where the ship was heading. When Swann was asked about what would happen to the cargo, he skirted around that question as well.

According to a *Washington Post* article, Rives told the crowd that the cargo "would not continue on to its original destination . . . nor to South Vietnam, but to another port 'so as not to compromise Cambodian neutrality.' Rives added that the Cambodians had placed no pre-conditions on the ship's release and that the decision to divert the ship was an American initiative."*

Captain Amg then called a halt to the press conference. In a very brief ceremony, Amg told Swann in French, "In the name of my government, I give this ship back to her owners." Rives translated this for Swann, who mumbled, "Thanks." Amg then wished Swann godspeed. Swann nodded, anxious to get the ship out as soon as possible.

But the ordeal was not over yet. Captain Amg told the assembled crowd that they could now inspect the cargo for themselves. "They wanted to have foreign correspondents verify the fact that there was no cargo removed from the vessel," said Swann.

The bosun, Hammett, and Campbell opened up a hatch. "In the hold that [was] inspected," said a *New York Times* article,

> the cargo appeared intact. The only Communist representative, Artur Blinov of TASS, the Soviet press agency, looked at the crates of silvery 717-pound napalm bombs and said, "They're empty."
>
> The Columbia Eagle's first mate, Herrick E. Morgan, replied, "Oh, no, they're full of happy little Czechoslovaks."
>
> The Soviet newsman's expression of disbelief was the only doubt voiced.

After the last journalist left, the *Columbia Eagle* finally steamed out of Baie de Ream and headed out to sea. A Cambodian gunship caught up with the *Eagle*, which was told to stop. The Cambodians had changed their minds

---

*Several *Eagle* crewmen said that they heard that not unloading the vessel in the war zone was the price the Americans paid for having the Cambodians meet their condition: that the ship and its cargo be released intact.

about Spiker and permitted him to come on board. Spiker went up the Jacob's ladder and the *Eagle* steamed onward.

As soon as the ship left Cambodian waters, the rendezvous was made with the Coast Guard cutter *Chase*. Webb, Idleberg, and the other investigators came aboard and—along with Spiker—began interviewing the thirteen crew members on the vessel.

According to the *Eagle*'s logbook, frogmen examined the hull. The *Columbia Eagle* then proceeded toward the southern tip of Vietnam.

At the same time, in Sattahip, Thailand, a bus picked up the castaways at the Swan Lake Hotel, then took them to a nearby U.S. air base. There were now only twenty-three men instead of twenty-four because Maurice Ellis, third assistant, had been flown home due to illness. At the air base they immediately boarded a paratrooper plane. The pilot told the seamen, "Gentlemen, we are short of supplies. No parachutes will be issued. The trip will be all over water. The good news is, if anything goes wrong, you will be right back in your own element." The plane landed at a navy repair base on the southernmost point of Vietnam; ironically, this was the point that Gunn had told them to head toward on 14 March, when they had just gotten into the lifeboats and were unaware of what was happening.

That evening the seamen were put on a Navy picket boat, headed for a rendezvous with the *Columbia Eagle*. When they reached their old ship, there was no gangway down, so they had to use the Jacob's ladder. Once aboard, the castaways fell into their routines as if they had never been away.

While the castaways were getting back to their usual work, the investigators continued the questioning. Sitting in the captain's office, a small room that felt even smaller during these intense interrogations, Webb, Idleberg, Davis, and Spiker asked questions while Wedertz recorded it all for posterity. Suspicion fell on three men—Sather, Gray, and Mornin—who were accused by others of having collaborated with the mutineers. The investigators saved these three interrogations for last. With the NIS men on the Naugahyde settee and the Coast Guard men on the swivel chairs, the two big men of the group—Webb and Davis—leaned in and put pressure on the suspects, looking for evidence that they had helped the mutineers.

Question: Did McKay and Glatkowski ever tell you why they were going to Cambodia?

Sather: They did not. I asked them and they says, "This is swinging. We're having our own little revolution."

Question: When they said "our revolution," did that include you?

Sather: That did not include me, for Christ's sake. I wasn't in on this goddamn bullshit.

Question: Did McKay and Glatkowski ask you to join them in Cambodia?

Sather: They did not. . . .

Question: Why did you make a statement in front of two of the ship's officers that you, quote, "I think I'll go with them"?

Sather: I did not make such a goddamn statement.

Question: I have sworn statements from two reputable men . . . that you did make that statement.

Sather: Well, I'm sorry about that, but they're goddamn liars.

Question: I see we're back to the same thing. Everybody on the ship is telling lies except you, is that right?

Sather: I am willing to take a lie detector test and I want all of them to do it. And then you'll find out who's lying and who isn't. . . .

Question: How come you kept going back [to the bridge]?

Sather: There was always a goddamn chance [to stop the mutiny]. Nobody, I'm trying to explain, there wasn't a goddamn thing being done about this, anywhere, as far as I know.

Question: The flag was flown upside down . . . signs were painted on the back of the ship, the chief mate tried to hit him in the head with a crowbar. What else did you want done? . . . You just lounged around the bridge, playing the goddamn tape recorder.

Sather: I wasn't playing the goddamn tape recorder. It was a record player. . . .

Question: When are you going to start telling the truth?

Sather: I've been telling you the truth, for Christ's sakes. . . . I am innocent of all this, this bullshit. . . . I have nothing to do with this shit, for Christ's sakes, let's get on with it.

Question: Let the record show that this interview was concluded . . . due to the unwillingness of the witness to speak in a frank and open manner.

Sather—according to what was put into the logbook—was found to be "in an extremely nervous condition and to prevent him from doing himself or others bodily harm, he was confined to his quarters with Coast Guard personnel guarding the door."

After extensive interrogation, and playing off one person's testimony against the other, both Dan Mornin and Bruce Gray finally confessed—not to having aided and abetted the mutineers, but to having smoked marijuana. "I did know of it and I did smoke it," said Mornin. "I see no point to even lie about that because with all these damn sworn statements, I don't see how I'm ever going to be able to beat the fuck out of it anyway."

Gray, apparently feeling pressured by Mornin's confession, came back and gave additional testimony in which he confessed to marijuana use. The investigators wanted details. They asked, "Was it a large amount or was it already rolled or did you roll it?" "Were they filter tips repacked or in brown paper or what?" They asked how many times Gray had smoked and with whom and where the smoking was done.

The investigators did not have enough to charge the three suspected collaborators with a crime related to the mutiny; instead, they threatened to bring narcotics charges, an infraction that took place on most ships going to Vietnam. In lieu of any further criminal proceedings, the three agreed to surrender their Z-cards to the Coast Guard. Although they did not find any accomplices, at least the investigators did not leave the *Columbia Eagle* totally empty-handed.

While the napalm was being removed from the vessel in Subic Bay, Sather, Mornin, and Gray said their farewells to the rest of the crew.

Gunn told them, "If you lie down with dogs, you're going to get up with fleas."

Ciamboli stood by the gangway as the three departed. He extended his hand and asked Sather if he had anything to say, or any regrets. "He merely sneered and walked on," Ciamboli said, "not acknowledging my extended hand." Ciamboli started to ask Dan Mornin the same question, but Mornin spoke first. "Mornin—looking drained, helpless, bewildered and dazed—asked me, 'Why are they doing this?' I truly felt sorry for him," said Ciamboli. "He was just out of his teens, good manners, very polite, I could see he thought this was the end of the world. All I could think of to say to him without it sounding like it was a scolding was, 'I'm sorry, there was nothing I could do for you. Next time try to choose your friends more carefully.' He accepted my hand but a dishrag had more life in it than his hand did."

15 THE DESERTER

The mutineers were treated well upon their arrival in Cambodia. According to Glatkowski, they were "wined and dined" the first couple of nights, and after Swann was moved to a different base, Glatkowski and McKay were housed by themselves at the Chrui Changwar naval base. Called an "officers' room," it was stark and bare by Western standards.

Those first few days in Cambodia were the highest moments for Glatkowski and McKay. Together, they had pulled off the impossible. They had done what no else had. Although he had misgivings about the fact that the cargo had not been destroyed, Glatkowski was enormously pleased to have been part of such an important event. He later wrote, "We built quite a legend for ourselves in those few days."

After "those few days," however, things started going downhill. No praise from the leftist press or the antiwar movement. Then, shortly after their arrival, there was the coup. After that, it became obvious that they were being treated like prisoners; they were not free to leave the base and were under constant guard. They received no letters and were not sure that those they sent were actually going out. All contact with journalists was controlled by the regime. Technically, they had been given asylum by the previous regime, so the Lon Nol government felt it prudent to continue that policy, at least nominally.

Glatkowski and McKay did have a radio and they listened to the news.

To their shock, they learned that they had been accused of being covert CIA operatives who had brought small arms for Lon Nol's insurgents. This accusation infuriated them.

During those first few days, in spite of the coup, Cambodian authorities allowed reporters and photographers to come onto the base and interview the mutineers. At times there were several newspeople at the same time, giving Glatkowski and McKay the feeling that they were giving a press conference.

One day, less than a week after they arrived at Chrui Changwar, they were in the yard getting some exercise. Glatkowski looked over at a ship anchored on the Mekong, forty yards from shore. He could not quite believe it at first, but there was another Caucasian.

"I happened to see this white guy on this ship over there," said Glatkowski. "I saw bars on the portholes. I realized it was a prison ship. I asked the guard who he was." With the guards' permission, Glatkowski went up to the fence.

Where you from? Glatkowski yelled.

America! the Caucasian yelled back.

You're a Yankee! What are you doing here, Yankee?

Glatkowski approached the guards, who agreed to bring the prisoner over. "He was from southern California, from Ventura," Glatkowski said. "They took him back that day, he was with us only an hour or two. So I was the first one to see Humphrey on the military base. Humphrey's story was that he was trying to defect and go to the Soviet Union. That he was a Marxist. That was his story."

Twenty-two and a half years old, Larry Humphrey was almost exactly midway between Glatkowski and McKay's ages. Humphrey's parents were from small Oklahoma towns near the Arkansas border. In 1943 his parents, who already had two girls and a boy, moved to Ventura—a coastal community sixty-five miles northwest of Los Angeles—where Humphrey's father continued doing what he had done in Oklahoma: working in the oil fields and as a ranch hand.

Ventura was a mixture of farm, ranch, and oil workers—many of them Okies, like Humphrey's father, or Mexican migrant laborers—as well as surfers and military personnel. It was a cool and foggy place and you could smell the brine and shellfish when the wind blew in from the ocean. Larry, born in 1947, was the youngest of five children. His parents were divorced in 1956 and his mother was given custody of the children.

Humphrey left Ventura High after the eleventh grade, then joined the army in September 1965. Trained as a cook, he served stints in Vietnam and Thailand over the next three years. His personnel record says that he "never showed any signs of being disaffected with the US Army." As far as most of his army buddies and superiors were concerned, "there was no indication of mental or emotional instability; acute alcoholism; addiction to drugs, narcotics or barbiturates; homosexuality; psychiatric treatment; or any other unusual symptoms."

He received an honorable discharge from the army on 4 October 1968, at Fort Hood, Texas. Returning to Ventura, he worked in construction and on the same ranch where his father was working.

Humphrey's sister told the FBI that during the year that her brother spent as a civilian, after he got out of the army in 1968, he studied Thai and Khmer "fanatically," carrying study books in these languages with him everywhere, to the point where his friends and family began calling these books "Larry's bibles."

Humphrey re-upped in 1969, and he was sent back to Fort Hood, Texas. Humphrey was supposedly working as a cook. When his brother went to Fort Hood to try to see Humphrey, however, he was told that Humphrey was not assigned to the facility and was not available for a visit. His brother thought that this was very strange.

In the fall of 1969 Humphrey was sent back to Southeast Asia and assigned as a cook to Company A, 538th Engineer Battalion, Camp Samae San, Thailand, near Sattahip.

According to Humphrey's army records, he had no special clearance and no access to classified information. Moreover, according to the extensive investigation carried out by the army and the FBI following his disappearance, none of his army buddies knew of any irregularity in Humphrey's behavior, except for Ronnie Maynard, another cook in the unit. He remembered an instance in which Humphrey was caught sniffing glue. Humphrey's supervisor, Staff Sgt. Charles Martin, told investigators that Humphrey was a "good worker and a good soldier. He either kept to himself or associated with Thai nationals." Co-worker Clark Kaiser echoed this: "He was quiet and apparently had no close friends in the company." A company truck driver, Frederick Stirnkorb, had a different view. He said that Humphrey was "not well-liked in the barracks because he spoke badly to the housegirls," the Thai women who worked at the base. "He teased them and tried to make them feel bad. Other than the housegirls, [Humphrey] never bothered anyone." Humphrey often told Stirnkorb that "he hated the army." Of course, this in itself was not unusual or subversive.

A few days before Humphrey disappeared, he confided in fellow cook, Robert Borkin, telling him that he had had "trouble with his girlfriend, a Thai national." Borkin asked Humphrey "what the trouble was," but Humphrey did not answer. According to Borkin, Humphrey had a history of girl trouble. Borkin, however, did not think that this was the reason he deserted.

Investigators opened up Humphrey's lockers and found a letter dated 13 October 1969, less than three months before his desertion. Written in Thai, it was translated for the U.S. Army by an unnamed translator:

> Good Morning, My Lovely Brother:
>
> It does not matter at all if you will not be able to see me. Thank you again for thinking of me. I wish you to think of me as one of your younger sisters. I don't want you to think about me in any other way. This does not mean that I hate you, but I respect you as my older brother. I wish to tell you the truth; that I cannot love anyone besides my lovely boyfriend. I hope that you may understand what love is. I love my boyfriend so much that I cannot describe it to anybody, since it would be unbelievable. Please love me as one of your younger sisters. Don't fear the Thai police when you come to see me. The Thai police do not want to apprehend you, but I cannot guarantee the same for the American MP's. Oh, I almost forgot to ask you for two apples. Please bring two apples when you come to see me next time.
>
> This is about all, My older brother always,
>
> Nit Noy
>
> P.S. Don't forget to bring me the apples. I am not greedy, but I love to eat them.
>
> Excuse me, my handwriting is rather poor.

What did Humphrey have to fear from the Thai police? Why would he think that they—or American MPs—wanted to apprehend him? Could he have been so heartbroken at having received this Dear John letter, that it drove him to desertion?

Investigators combing through the area where Humphrey was supposed to have lived with his Thai girlfriend found that the Nit Noy, which means "little sister," who wrote him that letter may also have used the name Nid Umonwanit. Dozens of people in the area were questioned. When Nid was found and shown a photo of Humphrey, she "was observed to be very startled." However, she stated that although she knew a U.S. serviceman named Larry, it was not Larry Humphrey. Nid said she had never written any letters to Humphrey nor had any communication with him.

Thinking that perhaps the Nit Noy who wrote the letter was a different woman from Nid Umonwanit, investigators tried to find a "Nit" or "Nid" who was connected to Larry Humphrey. Finally, a hotel owner, Chalong Wansonor, recognized Humphrey's photo and the name "Nid" struck a bell. He said that he did recall Nid, who was, in fact, a male, a homosexual transvestite who lived in the hotel and who solicited American soldiers for "immoral acts at the hotel." Besides this person and the Nid who was startled at seeing Humphrey's photo, there were no others named Nid or Nit who emerged during the extensive investigation. If indeed Larry Humphrey was involved with a homosexual transvestite prostitute, and there was the chance that the army might find out, it might have motivated him to do what he did next.

The last time anyone saw Humphrey on the base at Samae San was on 7 January 1970. For the next month he hid in Thailand. On 28 January, fellow cook Clark Kaiser spotted Humphrey by chance. "During the afternoon Source [Kaiser] saw Subject [Humphrey] in Sattahip. . . . Source attempted to approach Subject in order to try to convince him to return to duty, but Subject saw him and disappeared."

Three days later Humphrey went to the Soviet embassy in Bangkok. He would later tell McKay and Glatkowski that when he talked with the Soviets, he explored the possibility of defecting to the Soviet Union. Six days after going to the Soviet embassy, on 7 February, Humphrey went eastward and sneaked across the border out of Thailand. Once on the other side, he gave himself up to Cambodian officials.

A telegram from U.S. Army headquarters in Thailand informed the Pentagon that Humphrey crossed the border and was seeking asylum, that he had been arrested in Cambodia for illegal entry, and was being held in Phnom Penh. The wire read:

> A CAMBODIAN OFFICIAL (SAID) THAT HUMPHREY HAD REQUESTED POLITICAL ASYLUM SINCE HE DOES NOT WANT TO FIGHT IN EITHER VIETNAM OR LAOS.
>
> HUMPHREY'S STATEMENT TO THE EFFECT THAT HE DID NOT WANT TO FIGHT IN EITHER VIETNAM OR LAOS AND THE SHORT TIME, AFTER LEAVING THE RUSSIAN EMBASSY, IN WHICH HE CROSSED THE THAI-CAMBODIAN BORDER, INDICATES THAT HE MAY HAVE BEEN BRIEFED BY SOVIET OFFICIALS WHEN HE CONTACTED THEIR EMBASSY ON 1 FEBRUARY 1970.

Less than a week later another army telegram was sent to the Pentagon:

> A REVIEW OF RECENT STATE DEPARTMENT TRAFFIC BETWEEN WASHINGTON, BANGKOK AND PHNOM PENH INDICATES THAT SP4 LARRY D. HUMPHREY IS BEING HANDLED BY THE STATE DEPARTMENT AS A ROUTINE BORDER CROSSER.

Once Humphrey arrived in Phnom Penh, the Cambodians transferred him to a prison ship anchored in the Mekong River, inside the Chrui Changwar naval base. He was there for five weeks before Glatkowski and McKay appeared. Within days of their meeting, the Cambodians moved Humphrey in with the mutineers.

On 25 March, a journalist was permitted to enter the base. Fred Emery of the *Times of London* did an interview with Glatkowski and McKay, and Humphrey was there too. The article he wrote, which was also carried by the *New York Times,* gave the mutineers a chance to state their case.

> Mr. McKay said they had done it because they were against the war in Vietnam: "We are sympathetic with the Asian people and, while I'm not an authority on the war in Vietnam, I respect the opinions of people who are authorities like Bertrand Russell and Jean-Paul Sartre, who said the war in Asia was genocide."
>
> He continued: "I felt myself in the position of a German sailor during World War II and from the example of what the Nuremberg Trials showed, I feel myself guilty if I were just to comply and be a part of threatening the people of Asia. I thought it much better to threaten by force the few people who were around the ship and prevent myself being part of a much

> larger-scale threat against the people of Asia by delivering these thousands of napalm bombs."
>
> He said he realized they had threatened murder and been guilty of mutiny and piracy, but he thought this was "on a smaller scale" than being party to "outright murder of delivering napalm bombs."

Later in the article, McKay touched on the current political climate in Cambodia.

> [McKay] said it was a strange coincidence that "Prince Sihanouk was deposed at this time." It had shaken them a bit when they heard it.
>
> Both looked pained when told that the Communists were saying it was all a plot by the CIA. Proudly Mr. McKay said: "It's an S.D.S. [Students for a Democratic Society] plot," and [Glatkowski] added, "An S.D.S. plot more than anything." They were not members, they said, but Mr. McKay said: "We support the groups we believe in if we hold similar ideas and have common enemies."
>
> Asked about the future, Mr. McKay said: "I have to find what avenues are open to me. If I leave Cambodia in the immediate future to another country, it will probably be Cuba." Mr. Glatkowski's plans were "relatively the same," he said, adding, "I intend to carry on my actions against the American government." . . .
>
> A young American soldier, Cpl. Larry Humphrey, 22, from Ventura, Calif., was also sleeping in the room with the two men. He had crossed the border from Thailand, where he was based, five weeks ago. Corporal Humphrey said he had neither defected nor asked for asylum. "I hope to stay with my partners," he said, "and my heart was with them when they came to Cambodia because I too oppose the war."
>
> He also wanted to go to Cuba, adding: "I think what we are doing is what the silent majority is afraid to do. I don't think any of us expect self-gain. It will be downhill individually all the way. But it's something we must do or we wouldn't be able to live with ourselves."
>
> The mutineers were asked if they thought they had prospects of going back to the United States. Mr. Glatkowski's reply was, "only with a gun." Mr. McKay's, "illegally."

This interview apparently angered Glatkowski. He would later write that he did not want Humphrey linked up with the mutiny, and that he was suspicious of the deserter.

DURING THE first few weeks of April, Glatkowski heard the sickening news that the ship had finally been allowed to sail out of Cambodia and that it had discharged its cargo in the Philippines before making the trip back to the United States. He felt betrayed and resentful: they had almost pulled it off. Almost. He felt that because of the decisions McKay had made—not to scuttle the ship when they had the chance, not to deep-six the cargo, not to explode the ship—they were fools instead of heroes. Glatkowski felt that the mutiny had not had any concrete effect: it had not removed lethal weapons from the war, it had not saved any lives. It had been only a gesture. A futile gesture.

In April and May the Cambodians moved the three men around to different parts of the naval base, at one point even taking them back across the Tonle Sap to naval headquarters. Eventually they were moved to the prison ship, an old, rusty cartel boat that was now being used to house enemies of Lon Nol's regime, the most high-profile prisoner being the half-brother of Monique, Sihanouk's wife.

Settling in the prison ship, they made themselves at home. They used equipment—for cooking and entertainment—that they had bought from the guards or had "liberated" from the *Eagle,* for example, the radio and the camera that had belonged to the *Eagle*'s crew. "They moved us three to a large cell," Glatkowski recalled. "So we were all in there. Stove, short-wave radio. Turn it on every night to listen to Radio Beijing or Radio Hanoi. When Sihanouk sent messages via radio, we turned it up loud so that the guards could hear. McKay and Humphrey didn't agree with my doing this."

In late May, McKay wrote a letter to his mother. He gave it to the guards, who promised it would be mailed. First, however, the letter found its way to the American chargé d'affaires, Mike Rives, who took it on his own initiative to read it. Rives wrote to the secretary of state that he was reluctant to open it because of the "privacy of mails," but he added that he felt that the contents of the letter justified his opening it.

Dear Mom,

I received your letter and G'ma's and also a note from Aunt Ruth.

I'm fine and I'm not in captivity, though I'm not free to travel about Cambodia because of the unrest in the country. I don't know what the newspapers had to say about my taking the ship. An organization in California had asked me to delay or preferably to stop the cargo from reaching its destination and for reasons too involved to go into in this letter, I agreed to accomplish this in some manner. Mindful of the many crewmen who died when the SS Badger State was sabotaged more than a month earlier, I took it on my own initiative to hijack the vessel and accomplish the same result in respect to the cargo without harming the crew.

I had to choose between acting against the U.S. government or refusing to act. If I had not played a part, however small, in opposing the war machine, I would live in inner torment. I had to follow the dictates of my conscience and when the U.S. government acts against God and humanity, I'm bound to oppose it.

I have a beautiful view of the Mekong River and I'm only 2 miles from Phnom Penh. I've been busy trying to learn Cambodian.

I don't know how long I'll be here or where I'll be off to next.

I'm not in need of anything.

Say hello to everyone for me.

Love, Bill

Rives added a comment in his wire to William Rogers:

AS WILL BE SEEN FROM THE CONTENT OF THE LETTER, MCKAY APPARENTLY ACTED ON THE INSTRUCTIONS OF AN UNNAMED ORGANIZATION IN CALIFORNIA WHICH WAS APPARENTLY PREPARED TO SEE SHIP DESTROYED. AT TIMES IN LETTER WRITER SEEMS TO HAVE ACTED WILLINGLY, WHILE AT OTHERS HE WRITES AS IF HE HAD BEEN FORCED TO ACT AS HE DID.

Journalists who visited the mutineers and the deserter on the prison ship in June reported that the three young men felt abandoned, isolated, and cut off from the world. Glatkowski knew that Flo must have had a child already, but he had heard nothing about this. He desperately wanted to know whether it was a boy or girl, and how Flo was, but he did not receive any letters. McKay was now his only family, but he felt that Humphrey's presence had changed the relationship between him and McKay. The two mutineers were drifting apart.

Glatkowski felt that McKay had adapted better to the situation. "When we were in Cambodia," Glatkowski said, "it was familiar ground for McKay. When he got out of Spain, when he got out of the Foreign Legion, when he got out of the Sahara, there were several times he had to escape." Even before they came ashore in Sihanoukville, McKay had told Glatkowski, *Don't worry, they'll put us under house arrest for six months and then we'll get out of that and then they'll put us on a plane and we'll be gone.* McKay had been so calm about it. He still was.

McKay, for his part, spent his days continuously composing and sending letters to Lon Nol, to the naval chief of staff, and to the commandant of the base, requesting some consideration, but he received no answer. His constant complaints were that they were not officially prisoners, yet they were held captive; that they were charged with no crime by Cambodia, yet they were on a prison ship; that they had been given asylum, yet they were not free to move around. They were political prisoners and it was maddening.

Even more maddening was that they felt abandoned and betrayed by the left. McKay wrote letters to various socialist and communist countries, trying to get asylum, but the mutineers never received a response. Perhaps the Cambodians were not sending out these letters. It is also possible that these countries believed that the ship had brought small arms to Lon Nol and they were not about to offer political asylum to men they believed were CIA gun-runners.

The months wore on, they were still being held as prisoners, and the frustrations mounted. Virtually the only food that was given to them was rice, with an occasional vegetable or piece of fat. The rice would often have small stones in it, and since it was impossible to pick them all out, the young Americans would occasionally crack a tooth on one of them. They lost several teeth this way, and the pain could be excruciating. Glatkowski said that they began to smoke opium to ease the pain and frustration. Glatkowski used it regularly. Apparently, the more he smoked, the more suspicious he became of Humphrey. Glatkowski began to feel that the former army corporal was hiding something.

Glatkowski's increasing suspicions of Humphrey may have been fueled, in part, by his opium use and by the feeling that McKay was becoming closer with the deserter. Glatkowski, however, felt that he had good reasons for his suspicions. For example, Humphrey denied that he had a military identification; he said he had left all his documents in Thailand. When Humphrey was in the shower, Glatkowski quickly hunted through the deserter's things and found his i.d. Glatkowski wondered: Why would he deny having one?

There is no doubt that there were aspects about Humphrey that were suspicious. Why would someone who spoke Thai, Khmer, and Vietnamese be working as an army cook? Wouldn't a soldier with that kind of language ability be doing intelligence work? If he hated the Vietnam War so much that he was ready to desert from his post in Thailand, then why had he volunteered for another tour of duty after being discharged?

Glatkowski remembered an incident during which he believed he had met Humphrey years earlier, in Washington. "I told McKay, 'I think I know that guy,'" Glatkowski said. "McKay said, 'What do you mean?' I told him [that] I was on a plane going from Norfolk to D.C. one time, and on the seat in front of me was a military man and on his name tag it said Humphrey. And I happened to ask him: any relation to Hubert? And he said, 'No, no.' And I asked him where are you from and he said, 'From California.' I said, 'That's where I'm from.' That's why I remember him, because I made a joke about Hubert Humphrey. And he said no, he was not related to Humphrey."

McKay dismissed Glatkowski's recollection. "So here we are," Glatkowski said, "I'm telling McKay about this and McKay says I'm wrong. I said I'm *not* wrong. I know this occurred. This is the same man, I'm certain of it. So McKay said he wanted to investigate this further."

Glatkowski said that he conducted an interrogation of Humphrey for McKay's benefit. He asked the deserter if he had ever been to Washington, D.C., and whether they had met there. Humphrey said that he *had* been to Washington but had never met Glatkowski. McKay was still not convinced by Glatkowski's story.

"Clyde's reaction seemed strange," Glatkowski said later. "Why minimize it, why doubt it? I think it was from this point on that my relationship with Clyde began to deteriorate. I felt something wasn't right with Clyde. From that point on, I became more and more isolated. They would talk with one another and exclude me. I was always suspicious of Humphrey, and I became very estranged from Clyde." Glatkowski said that he and McKay "were no longer working as a single force. And that is what led to my emotional state afterward."

As he felt more separated from McKay, Glatkowski's sense of isolation and abandonment increased. He began to feel that the Cambodians were putting poison in his meals, so he ate only canned food, which he bought from the guards. When his money ran out, he sold the radio to buy food and opium.

During this time frame, American troops and war equipment—invited in by the Lon Nol government—were actually *in* Cambodia, fighting Viet

Cong and North Vietnamese units, which had been joined by Khmer Communist troops.

Reporters were still being allowed access to the three Americans. Toward the end of June, they were interviewed by television networks, as well as several newspapers and magazines. The reporters brought word to the mutineers that they had been indicted by a grand jury in Los Angeles, on 25 June, for mutiny, assault, kidnapping, and neglect of duty.

One of the journalists permitted to see the mutineers at this time was Don Shannon of the *Los Angeles Times*. In a telegram sent from the American embassy to the secretary of state, Rives summed up the highlights of a story that Shannon had filed. He stated that the mutineers knew about their indictment and said they would fight extradition "in hope that the Cambodian government might change in the interim"; and McKay told Shannon that he had sought the help of the Soviet consul in "transferring funds to Mexican bank account."

It is clear from McKay's own letters that what McKay had told Shannon is that he wanted to get money *out* of his Mexican bank account, not *into* it. McKay felt he needed money now. Shannon's handwritten note, included in a package of reading materials, suggests to McKay how the money could be transferred: "Friends—can't send you a clipping from the L.A. Times yet but here are some books brought to you courtesy of Fred Emery of the London Times. INADANA JATI will accept transfers in $ or pesos. They will charge a commission of 2% on the transfer."

At the same time, Ruth White received a letter from Shannon. It included a handwritten note explaining how to send money to her nephew and an ad—from a French-language Cambodian newspaper—for Inadana Jati Bank.

McKay also wrote to his aunt:

> Dear A. Ruth,
>
> I was very happy to hear from you. I'm still in a precarious position but, grace de Dieu, still all right. Glad to hear that you're well. I'm still petitioning the prime minister Lon Nol for permission to leave. I was granted political asylum and I should be able to arrange to travel to any country which recognizes it, Mexico particularly.
>
> In the very near future I may need some dinero to buy a plane ticket. Wish that you could cash my bond for me and transfer the

money in pesos to here. Don Shannon of the L.A. Times sent instructions on how to transfer it. It looks like it's going to be a lot of bother getting that done in el Banco de Comercio. I'm really sorry to have to put you to so much trouble but I think it may be really necessary for me to fly out of Phnom Penh in the near future.

Say hi for me to Russ & Martha & Pete. Don't believe everything they write about me in the news; half of the reporters here are trying to link me with a CIA plot and the other half with an anarchist conspiracy.

McKay also sent a letter to his grandmother:

Dear G'ma,

I was very happy to receive your letters. I'm well and indeed very comfortable here. Room and board compliments of the Cambodian government. I'm beside the river.

There's usually a breeze so I don't notice the heat so much as I would in town. The food is very good with all types of tropical fruit.

Lois, mom and A. Ruth wrote. I'll write to them as soon as I can. Say hello to dad for me and tell him I'll send a letter shortly. . . . It's very easy for me to send letters now and of course I'll write very much more often.

When I first came here to Cambodia the people told me that there would be a war this year because there was a comet in the sky. 2 days later I found out that the government had changed and given orders to its troops to attack the Vietnamese in Cambodia. Now the war is really here and so close that I hear a lot of the shooting. Where I sit though is the safest place in the whole country, and I'm not in any danger. . . .

I hope and pray that all is well with you.

Tell everyone not to worry about me, I've been in much worse fixes, such as being lost in the middle of the Sahara without water and with the help of the Almighty came out all right.

McKay was obviously trying to communicate a feeling of optimism to his family, but an Associated Press article, carried by the *New York Times* on 4 July 1970, summed up the mutineers' growing frustration:

More than three months after hijacking a U.S. munitions ship to Cambodia, Clyde W. McKay Jr. and Alvin L. Glatkowski wish they were anywhere

> but in Cambodia. Fortune has not been kind to the two young American civilians who, in the name of revolution, hijacked the freighter Columbia Eagle in March. Instead of being welcomed by a leftist government, they have been jailed by the rightist leaders who overthrew Prince Norodom Sihanouk as Chief of State. . . . They want nothing more than to get away.
>
> During an interview this week at the Cambodian naval base on the Mekong River where they are held, the two men asked several times to have a Soviet correspondent or diplomats from the Soviet or Polish embassies come and help arrange new asylum for them. "We want to leave Cambodia," said McKay. . . . "There is nothing we can do from where we are now. I just can't walk down the street and go away. We are prisoners. And if the United States attempts to extradite us, I don't know what we'll do." . . .
>
> The two do not plan to return to the United States. Glatkowski said: "The only way to go back is with a gun. I'll go back to participate in a guerrilla war." McKay, who directed the hijacking, said: "If the U.S. gets me, they will sentence me to death or at least make life not worth living. I won't go back until the present form of government in the U.S. is overthrown. I am a Marxist. I believe the Marxist way of life," he added. Glatkowski said: "Yes, I do too. You know, political power grows from the barrel of a gun." McKay silenced him with a wave of his hand and said, "Not *that* Marxist."
>
> Also with the two American seamen is an American soldier who defected from his unit in Thailand. The three have some freedom on part of the ship. . . .
>
> McKay said he had received only eight letters and cables in the 3 ½ months since he has been a prisoner. Glatkowski said . . . he had not heard from his family. Glatkowski paused and looked at his hands. "I have a child, one child. But I don't know what it is," he said and smiled shyly. The child was born while Glatkowski was away.

Glatkowski's feeling, aboard the *Eagle,* had been that McKay could be so single-minded about the mutiny because he had no connection to family: he had nothing to lose. Conversely, Glatkowski had felt that his own hesitation was because he *did* have a family connection. But now, it was clear that McKay had a supportive family that was ready to help him and maintain contact with him no matter what he had done, while Glatkowski's families, both by blood and marriage, had cut him off.

THERE WERE some people interested in the mutineers, however. According to FBI documents, on 9 July, the U.S. embassy in Bangkok was contacted by "unnamed individuals" who said they could deliver the mutineers to U.S. authorities in international waters, "upon payment of $20,000." The office of Irving Thayer, president of Columbia Steamship Company in Portland, was also contacted. The people who could deliver the hijackers were ready to accept cash from the shipping company or the U.S. government, or both.

Thayer told the FBI that his company was not willing to put up the money. The U.S. government decided to pass on the offer as well and the mutineers remained in detention. It is hard to imagine that anyone other than those who were holding the mutineers in detention—officers of the Cambodian navy or officials in the Lon Nol government—could have made this offer.

During July and August the monsoon season was in full fury. Often, rain came down in massive sheets, causing floods everywhere. Aboard the prison ship, the monsoon limited those moments of the day that McKay, Glatkowski, and Humphrey could exercise on deck. Inside their jail cell almost continuously, the three Americans had little to occupy their time besides marijuana and opium, which they continued to get from the guards in exchange for McKay's gold pieces.

The mutineers' access to the media was largely restricted again. In mid-August, a United Press International (UPI) reporter managed to get permission to see Glatkowski and McKay, who were escorted ashore to talk with him. Later, the reporter met with Rives, who sent a telegram to the Department of State about what he had learned. He stated in the telegram that the mutineers

> HAVE A NUMBER OF SORES ON THEIR BODIES AND, TO UPI MAN . . . THEY APPEARED TO HAVE LOST WEIGHT. NEVERTHELESS THEY BOTH ASSURED UPI THAT THEY WERE WELL FED AND TAKEN CARE OF.

McKay and Glatkowski had made it clear to the reporter that they had no intention of ever returning to the United States and that they feared crossing any country with which the United States might have an extradition treaty.

> MCKAY, THE OBVIOUS LEADER, SPOKE OF HOPE MOVING TO EASTERN EUROPEAN COUNTRY SUCH AS BULGARIA. THEY APPEAR REALIZE, HOWEVER, THAT THERE ARE FEW IF ANY COUNTRIES THAT WANT THEM.

The reporter also told Rives that the mutineers

STARED INTO SPACE QUITE A LOT, BROKE OFF CONVERSATIONS IN MIDDLE OF WORD OR OF IDEA AND ON WHOLE SEEMED RATHER VAGUE.

The reporter said that McKay and Glatkowski mentioned that they were on drugs and even asked the reporter to get them some. When the reporter asked about Humphrey, the mutineers said that he was down with a bout of jaundice and was being treated by the Cambodians on the ship.

A few days later a reporter for the *Hong Kong Standard* interviewed Glatkowski and McKay. The reporter spoke accented English. Apparently offended that their story had been relegated to second-string journalists writing for Southeast Asia papers, the mutineers tried to shock the reporter by telling him that Charles Manson was their hero and their aim was to "overthrow the pigs. Manson was a good American revolutionary. He picked the right people, the bourgeois." They also said that the guards regularly put marijuana in their soup. "Great flavor," Glatkowski commented.

Asked by the reporter if he wanted to return to the United States, Glatkowski said yes, but "with a gun to participate in guerrilla warfare." When asked how long he thought they would be kept in detention, McKay said that he doubted "whether the Lon Nol government will last, so they can't hold on to us all that long."

That article may well have angered the Lon Nol government. Soon after, the mutineers felt that they were pressured and tortured in a number of subtle and not-so-subtle ways. They would buy canned food, then find that their can opener was missing. They would be denied water. Or be prohibited from taking a shower. Their cell began to smell horribly from the damp, mildewed conditions, but they were not permitted to clean it. They were confined, restricted, and guarded. It was unbearable. They had to get out.

At one point, McKay came up with an idea. They knew where ammo was kept on this ship, so he suggested that they set fire to it and during the ensuing confusion make their escape. There were always small boats tied up to the ship. While the fire was raging, while ammo was exploding, they could climb into a boat and make their way down the Mekong, perhaps getting as far as the Bassac or the Tonle Sap. They could end up in a riverside village.

To Glatkowski, it sounded similar to some of the explosion schemes McKay had proposed while on the *Eagle,* and none of them had been carried out. Glatkowski felt he had no reason to believe that this plan would be carried out either. Moreover, Glatkowski thought that this plan was suicidal; it did not make any sense to kill yourself while trying to get freedom. McKay might be willing to make that trade-off, but not Glatkowski.

Glatkowski said that he again tried to make Humphrey confess that they had met before. He said that, after pressing him constantly, Humphrey finally admitted it, but McKay did not believe it was the truth.

Glatkowski, however, felt that he knew what was going on. Humphrey was here to spy on them. Or kill them. Maybe Humphrey would attack them while they were sleeping. Glatkowski said that one night he heard a noise and shook himself awake. "Humphrey was coming toward me with a meat cleaver," Glatkowski said, "one of those food choppers with a bamboo handle." He said that McKay interceded and stopped Humphrey. Glatkowski said that Humphrey had attacked him because he knew that the deserter was a government agent.

On the night of 30 August Glatkowski evaded the guards, sneaked to a lower deck, and jumped over the side. He went into the water smoothly. There was a rush of freedom as he swam downstream. The feeling lasted only a few seconds. Although he was a strong swimmer, the tide was vicious and submerged him completely several times. He gagged, choked, coughed, and spat up water as he struggled not to drown.

Meanwhile, guards had heard the splash. They got into a boat to intercept Glatkowski as he moved downstream. They shone a light into the water and spotted him as he fought to keep his head above water. Swimming away from the boat, scrambling ashore, gasping for breath after nearly drowning, Glatkowski tried to climb up the muddy embankment toward a fishing village just south of the naval base. The guards hunted him with weapons and flashlights, cornering him. When he saw the blinding lights and the men in green uniforms circling him, Glatkowski—according to McKay—"sort of freaked out."

McKay and Humphrey watched as Glatkowski was brought back to the ship, surrounded by men who pushed and prodded him. "Alvin began to talk incoherently, he didn't know where he was," said McKay. "I tried to get through to him, but couldn't. So our captors took Al and put him in a cage below the deck of the ship."

They brought him to a windowless cell, and put him into a steel box barely large enough to lie down in. Glatkowski later described it as a "tiger cage." The temperature in the cage rose to oven heat, while outside the guards entertained themselves by pounding on the metal walls with pipes. Glatkowski began hearing things, including his wife's voice. To him, it sounded as if the guards were having sex with her. "I was weakened from drugs," Glatkowski said. "I was going through withdrawal from opium."

Glatkowski refused to accept food. McKay was brought in to convince him to eat something. "I was suspicious of Clyde," said Glatkowski. "I thought he had sold out to the Cambodians and was working with them." Humphrey and McKay were permitted by the guards to pay Glatkowski brief visits, during which they tried to cheer him up and offer him hope. Glatkowski said that when he was in the cage, he was not sure whether these visits by Humphrey and McKay were hallucinations or not.

McKay was upset by his partner's condition and treatment: seeing him in a tiny filthy cage, refusing to eat, not being allowed to wash himself, suffering the pangs of opium withdrawal. "The cage was too small to stand up in," said McKay, "and there was almost no ventilation. They left him there for seven days but he didn't get any better. He babbled and screamed and cried a lot for his wife."

At one point, in a kind of grotesque echo of McKay's experiences in the Sahara, Glatkowski began to drink his own urine. It got worse. Guards found him eating his own feces. "It was horrific," Glatkowski said. "I did not know if I was going to come through or not. I kept telling myself, 'You're going to get through this, it's okay, you're going to work it all out.' It was really hard. Physically, it was hard, as well as emotionally."

"After a week [in the cage]," McKay told a reporter, "the Cambodians took Al away. They said they were taking him to a hospital, but we're not sure. They could have moved him to another cage somewhere else, where no one can hear his screaming."

16 YOU HAVE ALREADY LOST

On Wednesday, 9 September, Martha Westover—a young freelance journalist who would later change her last name to Honey—and her partner Tony Avirgan were permitted to see McKay and Humphrey. Before leaving the States months earlier, Honey had met with McKay's family in California and had told them that she would be going to Cambodia and would try to get to see Clyde McKay. McKay's mother gave Honey some letters to take to her son.

Traveling as pacifist, antiwar students under the aegis of the Quakers, Honey and Avirgan went to Southeast Asia and managed to get into Hanoi. From North Vietnam, they went to Laos, then Thailand. From Thailand they "slipped into Phnom Penh," where they managed to play themselves "as very straight college students who were pretty sympathetic to the Lon Nol government and to U.S. policy in SE Asia. We thereby landed an interview with one of the top government officials and [an] invitation to a very fancy, exclusive government party at which all of the top officials (minus, fortunately, the U.S. embassy staff) were present."

Honey would later say that people were dressed elegantly at this party and spoke in French about their imported European clothes, dishes, and silverware. Occurring far away from Phnom Penh, in an area where antigovernment guerrillas were growing in strength and number, it was a surrealistic scene; it was as if these guests were Parisian aristocrats in denial, on the eve of the French Revolution.

After several days of "incredible red tape," Honey and Avirgan finally were allowed to see the mutineers. "I think we were granted the permission," wrote Honey, "because I said I had met the men's families and had messages from them."

For the meeting with Honey and Avirgan, McKay and Humphrey were removed from the ship and escorted ashore. They told the reporters that they were being kept in a cage, the same one Glatkowski had been in.

Humphrey said that the reason they were now in the cage was because he too had tried to escape from the prison ship, three days earlier. "I built a sort of snorkel out of empty ball-point pens," Humphrey said. "At noon I went over the side. The Cambodians didn't see me, but the pens clogged up and I had to come up for air. When I reached shore, there was a happy hunting party waiting for me. I surrendered so they wouldn't shoot me. After that, Clyde and I were put in the cage together."

"We can't stand up in the cage and the beds are boards with blankets," said Humphrey. "There are rats, mice, cockroaches, insects. The cell is filthy with urine and dirt. We've asked for water to wash it down, but they won't give us any."

McKay had been bitten constantly. He showed the reporters his arms, "which were scratched raw from a rash he had. 'I had to ask dozens of times for penicillin shots. Finally a doctor came, but he refuses to return because I told him I'd like to go to China. Now a medic comes by every so often and gives me the shots.'"

"During the past months," McKay told the reporters, "we have repeatedly asked why we are under arrest and our captors have consistently answered that we're not under arrest but simply 'being held for our own protection.' We understand that the U.S. would like to bring us home for trial, but legally the Cambodians have no grounds either to keep us as prisoners or to extradite us."

Honey was struck by McKay's commitment to his cause. Although surrounded by armed guards, some of whom understood English, he spoke openly about his opposition to the U.S. and Lon Nol governments and his support for communist governments. "We certainly don't want to go back to the U.S.," said McKay. "There are many places I can think of I'd rather be. Top priority is Russia or Cuba or China."

Honey asked if there was any hope of being released from the cage. McKay said, "We've begun a hunger strike. We're demanding to be released.

We plan to continue the hunger strike indefinitely. If the Cambodians let us die, it means they weren't planning to release us in the future. So we might as well carry it through to the end."

Honey asked McKay what he would do if released. McKay said, "For the past five months I've been writing letters to Lon Nol, plus the Commander-in-Chief of the Navy and the chief of this Naval Base. All I've asked for is permission to walk into Phnom Penh and see if any of the consulates, particularly the Russian, will grant us political asylum. I don't think any of my letters have reached Lon Nol because there's been no answer."

What McKay did not know was that a week and a half earlier, one of his letters had finally reached a high official in the Lon Nol government. On 31 August, the secretary general of the Cambodian Foreign Office called Rives in to show him a letter from Clyde McKay pleading that he and Glatkowski be permitted to leave Cambodia. McKay requested that they be released from the prison ship and be allowed to visit "consulates" in Phnom Penh in order to arrange asylum somewhere.

Rives sent a wire to Secretary of State William Rogers telling him about this meeting. He said that the Cambodian government was

> DESIROUS BE RID OF MUTINEERS BUT AT THE SAME TIME DOES NOT WISH ITSELF PLACED IN POSITION WHERE COMMUNISTS COULD POSSIBLY CRITICIZE ASYLUM GRANTED.

That, of course, was the Lon Nol government's problem in a nutshell. The mutineers were a nuisance. If the current regime violated the asylum granted by Sihanouk, they would draw fire from communist countries with which they maintained strained relations. At the same time, if the Cambodians helped McKay and Glatkowski go to another country, they might jeopardize their relations with the United States, which wanted the mutineers back to face charges.

Making life terrible for the mutineers and hoping that they would turn themselves over to the Americans voluntarily was one method that the Cambodians had been trying, unsuccessfully. The Cambodians were at a loss, which was why they had asked the advice of the U.S. chargé d'affaires.

Rives told the secretary general that the problem was clearly a Cambodian one. Still, Rives had some advice for the secretary general. He suggested that the Lon Nol government determine which consulates the mutineers wished to visit, and that they ask these consulates to send representatives to the naval base to meet with the young men. This would at least avoid the embarrassment of having the mutineers roaming free in Phnom Penh, where they could enter a consulate "such as Poland's" and immediately request asylum there, which would embarrass both Poles and Cambodians.

Rives probably knew that it was highly unlikely, given the political climate and the accusations of CIA involvement, that the mutineers would actually be offered asylum anywhere. Allowing representatives from various countries to visit the naval base, however, would at least mollify the mutineers and avoid embarrassing scenes.

At the end of his wire to the secretary of state, Rives added that Larry Humphrey was apparently "NOT, RPT [repeat], NOT ACTING WITH MUTINEERS."*

On 2 September, an undersecretary of state sent Rives a telegram. He agreed that it was a Cambodian problem because the "SAME CONSIDERATIONS THAT HAVE KEPT US FROM TAKING INITIATIVE UP TO THIS TIME CONTINUE TO OPERATE." Those considerations were, presumably, that the United States wanted to keep its distance from this case, at least on the surface. The undersecretary said that there would be no objection if Cambodia wished to deport the mutineers "on its own initiative." The U.S. embassy in Phnom Penh would issue the mutineers passports if they requested them. Of course, since the mutineers were subject to outstanding federal warrants, their passports would only be good for a one-way trip back to the United States.

As a final note, the Department of State suggested that the time might be

> RIGHT TO REQUEST TO SEE HUMPHREY SEPARATELY. PERHAPS ASK IF HE WISHES TO BE SEGREGATED FROM THE TWO MUTINEERS, SINCE HE DOES NOT SEEM TO BE ACTING IN CONCERT WITH THEM AT THIS POINT.

On 8 September, Rives sent another telegram to Rogers:

> MEETING HAS BEEN ARRANGED FOR 0900 SEPTEMBER 8 BETWEEN US ARMY DESERTER HUMPHREY AND CONSUL STEIN AT NAVAL BASE. . . . INSTRUCTING STEIN TO ATTEMPT TO SEE MCKAY AND ASCERTAIN WHAT

*It is not clear why Rives had this impression. The UPI reporter, who spoke with Rives after meeting with the mutineers, might have thought that Humphrey's isolation "because of jaundice" was an indication that he no longer wished to be identified with the mutineers. It is also possible that when the UPI reporter asked about Humphrey, Glatkowski made a negative remark, which the reporter misinterpreted.

HIS CONDITION IS AND WHAT IS STORY BEHIND GLATKOWSKI. AS REPORTED EARLIER TELEGRAM, AMERICAN NEWSPAPERMAN WHO HAD INTERVIEWED MUTINEERS STATED THEY WERE TAKING DRUGS. . . . I REALIZE THAT CASES OF THREE AMERICANS ARE RESPONSIBILITY OF CAMBODIA WHICH HAD GRANTED THEM ASYLUM. NEVERTHELESS I FORESEE THAT WE SHALL BE REQUESTED ASSIST IN DISPOSAL OF THESE THREE CASES BEFORE TOO LONG. RIVES

The next day, 9 September, a consular official went to the naval base. In his subsequent wire Rives refers to this person as "Consul," yet Bob Blackburn, a political officer at the embassy, could not recall who it was that went to the base when he was asked later. He said, however, that if it was not John Stein, who is specifically mentioned in the telegram sent by Rives, then it must have been "one of Stein's boys."*

When the consular official arrived at the base, McKay was asked to join in, but he decided he wanted no part of it. McKay had been anxious to talk with someone, but obviously not the American consul. Besides, he had already met with Martha Honey and Tony Avirgan earlier in the day, and he probably felt that he had said what he had to say.

Humphrey, alone, was taken from the cage and escorted by guard to a room where the consular official was waiting. In what must have been a surprising move, Humphrey requested an interpreter. One was brought in, and from then on the young Californian spoke in Khmer.

Rives wired the State Department about the official's meeting with Humphrey:

HUMPHREY IS NOW ON A HUNGER STRIKE, LOOKS THIN BUT IN REASONABLY GOOD HEALTH. CAMBODIAN NAVAL PERSONNEL WHO RESPONSIBLE FOR HIM SAID HUNGER STRIKE WAS ANNOUNCED RECENTLY AFTER HE HAD MADE UNSUCCESSFUL ATTEMPT TO ESCAPE. MCKAY INI-

*John Stein was U.S. consul in Phnom Penh in 1970 and was said to have been with the CIA, according to a source within the consulate. In a correspondence with the authors, Stein wrote: "Involvement with the Columbia Eagle, anyone associated with it, or events resulting from the incident were not among my activities. . . . If, in his telegram, Mr. Rives referred to me by name, he was in error. Mention of my name . . . may have an explanation but I am not about to conjecture about it." Even though telegrams between Rives and the Department of State refer to "Stein" and "Consul" and that could only have been John Stein or someone reporting to him, whoever handled this case is referred to as a "consular official."

TIALLY INDICATED HE WANTED TO SEE CONSUL, BUT THEN BACKED OUT. THUS THERE WAS NO MEETING WITH HIM. . . . WHILE THERE WAS NO ANIMOSITY INVOLVED, HUMPHREY STATED HE HAD NO INTENTION TURNING HIMSELF IN TO US AUTHORITIES.

When the consular official told Humphrey that he was wasting his time in Cambodia, the deserter replied (in Khmer) that—on the contrary—he was "accomplishing a great deal." He told the official that he did not want to see anyone from the U.S. embassy again, but that he did wish to see the Soviet consul. The American official suggested that the Soviet consul might not wish to see Humphrey.

The consular official again told Humphrey that it would be in his interest to turn himself in to U.S. authorities. Humphrey said that if he did, he wanted to be tried not as a deserter, but as a "revolutionary." He also stated that if he were brought to trial for desertion, he would "drag revolution into the proceedings." The official again said that he would be available if the young man wished to see him. Humphrey said that he most definitely did not want to see the consular official again. He added something forcefully in Khmer, which was interpreted as: "I AM WINNING—AND YOU HAVE ALREADY LOST."

Within days, McKay and Humphrey were taken from the cage, moved into comfortable quarters, and given more or less free run of the base. They were not told why their treatment changed so radically, but they were, of course, delighted about the improvement. Although McKay still had his skin problem—his rash had festered and become infected—and both had lost weight, McKay and Humphrey were in relatively decent health, considering what they had been through. They also could now send out letters and telegrams, more or less at will.

When McKay had first arrived in Cambodia in March, his Aunt Ruth —who had taken care of McKay's Mexican bank account over the years— had sent him a wire saying that she loved him and would be there for him, no matter what. He still had that wire and he read it over and over, knowing that it was true and that he could count on her. By way of Don Shannon, he had sent her instructions on how to wire money. It was time to take her up on her offer.

On 19 September, McKay was permitted to go into town with guards so that he could send a wire:

DEAR AUNT RUTH NEED MONEY TO TRAVEL SEND USDOLLARS1000 TO ME INADANA JATI BANK THANKS C W MCKAY JR

As he had done so many times before, McKay sent it collect.

McKay continued to write constantly to higher-echelon government officials, sometimes several times a day, asking them to contact the Swedish government so that they could get asylum there.

The Cambodian Foreign Office, following the advice that Rives had given, contacted the Swedish honorary consul in Phnom Penh, asking if Sweden would consider granting asylum to the three Americans. The Swedish consul never went to see the young Americans but did transmit the request to Stockholm.

U.S. Ambassador Emory (Coby) Swank—who replaced Chargé d'Affaires Mike Rives at this time (thus upgrading the American mission to that of a full-service embassy)—sent a wire to Rogers on 25 September, saying that Cambodia was

OBVIOUSLY AND ADMITTEDLY ANXIOUS TO RID ITSELF OF THESE THREE PERSONS. . . . ALL THREE MOST ANXIOUS DEPART CAMBODIA AND CAMBODIA, IN TURN, DESIROUS RID ITSELF OF THEIR PRESENCE.

The U.S. ambassador had mentioned twice that the Cambodian government was "anxious" and "desirous" to "rid itself" of McKay, Glatkowski, and Humphrey once and for all. The implied question was "What can the United States do to make this goal come true?"

Being treated in a more humane manner by the Cambodians, McKay was optimistic that they would receive asylum in Sweden. He was told by Cambodian officials that the asylum request had been forwarded to Stockholm, and they were hopeful of a positive reply. He wrote his sister Lois, "I'm very comfortable now and expect to be released any day. Cambodia officials assured us that the government is now arranging our affairs and that we may be free within a week. I hope you can make [it] to Europe next summer—I may end up in Scandinavia by that time myself."

One night McKay and Humphrey were even taken out for an evening on the town. "The commanding officer of this base," McKay wrote Lois, "Commandant Vong-Sophano, treated us to dinner & an evening out in Phnom Penh, I really enjoyed it." An evening among Phnom Penh's moneyed class—government officials, military officers, businessmen from Singapore, women, colored lights, cold beer, air-conditioning, barbecued shrimp. Only a couple of weeks earlier, they had been on a hunger strike, cramped inside an abominable, disgusting little cage.

McKay's surge of optimism did not last long, however. On 29 September the Swedish consul told Swank that he had heard from Stockholm. Swedish law required that a person be physically present in Sweden when he applies for asylum. Swank passed the news to McKay.

McKay realized that the chances of receiving asylum were getting slimmer and slimmer.

17 TAKH HMAU

After Glatkowski had spent a hellish week in the cage, he was quietly hustled off to a sanitarium. McKay and Humphrey were not told about the move.

A telegram from Mike Rives on 8 September informed the secretary of state:

> MUTINEER GLATKOWSKI HAS BEEN TRANSFERRED FROM NAVAL BASE TO MENTAL HOSPITAL AT TAKH HMAU ON OUTSKIRTS OF PHNOM PENH SINCE HE HAD BEGUN TO DRINK HIS OWN URINE AND EAT HIS EXCRETA.

Located in Takh Hmau, a village twelve kilometers from the center of Phnom Penh, the hospital was a large, enclosed compound with neat dirt paths, greenery, open space, bougainvillea and palm trees, a few administrative huts at the entrance, and—behind the huts—several yellow two- and three-story buildings with bars in the windows.

Glatkowski was held in one of these buildings, in a room that was much like a cell. The door to his room led out to a dark hallway where the staff parked their bicycles, and it had a slat through which a food tray could be passed. There was a rush mat but no mattress on a flat wooden bed, a hole in the floor for bodily functions, and a pitcher of water. Food was brought to him at regular intervals, usually just a bowl of rice. When he first arrived, Glatkowski refused to eat and shoved the bowls back through the slat in the door. Going through opium withdrawal, food was the last thing on his mind.

During the day, flies swarmed; at night, mosquitoes came out in force. One day, soon after arriving at Takh Hmau, several guards came to get him. He resisted, telling them that he was sick, really sick, his head was pounding, throbbing. The guards lifted him and dragged him to a clinic where a male nurse named Dok Sokhay weighed him, measured his height, and took his temperature. Dok tried talking to him in French, but Glatkowski did not understand. Dok later said that he glanced at this patient's medical file; he saw a comment that this "was an American seaman" whose condition was brought on, in part, by "too much opium and marijuana."

A doctor who spoke English came in and introduced himself as Dr. Chamrowun Sam Eun. Glatkowski said that he told the doctor that all he wanted was something for the pain; he needed to get rid of his headache.

Glatkowski recalled that he looked around and saw a cabinet with glass doors. Inside it were jars with pills. While the doctor and the nurse talked and gestured to him, Glatkowski said, he inched closer to the cabinet, got next to it, balled his right hand into a fist, and then, before anyone could stop him, he smashed the cabinet's glass door.

As hospital personnel reacted, he shouted at everyone to stay back. All he wanted, he told them, was some pills. Something that would make the pain go away. Glatkowski said he saw the guards slowly close in on him. Before they could jump him, Glatkowski said, he quickly reached into the cabinet, grabbed a glass shard and held it to his wrist. Then he held it to his throat, threatening to kill himself—or kill them—if they came any closer. But he could not hold them at bay indefinitely. The guards saw an opening and jumped him, wrestling him to the floor. From the edge of his vision, Glatkowski said, he saw Dr. Chamrowun holding a hypodermic. Then he felt the needle plunge into him.

A *New York Times* reporter—who based his story on information given to him by the U.S. embassy—wrote: "In the hospital, embassy officials said, Glatkowski attempted suicide by cutting himself with broken glass." Glatkowski, however, would later disagree.

"You might have read about me attempting suicide," Glatkowski said, "but it didn't happen that way. There's a simple explanation. I broke a piece of glass and told them I was going to cut myself or stab them, I don't remember exactly, it was one of the two, maybe it was both. I'd always perceived that crazy people are left alone. It may be that my brain said, okay, this is what you have to do in order to get out of this. A self-protective measure."

As the hypodermic took hold, Glatkowski relaxed toward immobility. When he woke up he was in a different cell, one with no sheets or anything else that might be used in a suicide attempt. They had left him there, unclothed and unconscious.

"He was in a special room," said Dok, "where he was naked. There was nothing in the room and he was not allowed to wear any clothes. It was a hospital regulation. When people tried to commit suicide, they would put them in that kind of room."

Whatever Glatkowski's perception of that event, the hospital staff considered it a suicide attempt. They got in touch with the Cambodian Foreign Office, which in turn contacted the U.S. embassy. The next morning, Andy Antippas, who served as a political officer at the U.S. embassy in Cambodia, visited the hospital and was briefed by Dr. Chamrowun before meeting with Glatkowski.

"They would get me so doped up I could hardly stand," Glatkowski would later tell an interviewer, "and then carry me across to this room. They'd open the door and it would be like an office. Somebody from the American embassy would be there. He'd talk to me, offer me cigarettes, and try to talk to me into coming back to the United States."

Antippas tried to make the young mutineer understand that he was now the father of a baby boy. He showed Glatkowski a photo of Flo and the baby and asked if he wanted to see them again. Didn't he want to come back to the United States? But the mutineer, apparently not understanding who and what Antippas was talking about, shook his head no. A *New York Times* article, based on what Antippas told a reporter, said that Glatkowski "showed no recollection of his family and indicated no desire to return home."

When Antippas reported to Rives, he said that Dr. Chamrowun suggested that the best care for Glatkowski would be in the United States. Antippas told Rives that he had not given Dr. Chamrowun any response to this suggestion.

Rives sent a wire to Secretary of State Rogers about these events:

> IT IS NOT INCONCEIVABLE THAT CAMBODIAN GOVERNMENT MIGHT REQUEST MEDICAL EVACUATION OSTENSIBLY ON HUMANITARIAN GROUND, BUT IN FACT TO GET HIM OFF THEIR HANDS.

Rives asked Rogers what he should do if the Cambodian Foreign Office asked the U.S. government to evacuate Glatkowski.

The answer came within hours. A wire, bearing Rogers's name, advised Rives to "REMAIN IN CLOSE TOUCH WITH GLATKOWSKI AND DOCTOR." The secretary of state's telegram also advised Rives to tell the appropriate Cambodian official that the United States would "LOOK FAVORABLY" on Cambodia's request for returning Glatkowski to the United States on "HUMANITARIAN MEDICAL GROUNDS."

Rogers's wire noted that Glatkowski would still be subject to prosecution upon his return and also advised Rives that the Department of State would get in touch with Flo and her parents in order to "ASCERTAIN THEIR WILLINGNESS" to seek Glatkowski's return. In the meanwhile, the Department of Justice would work out "THE ARRANGEMENTS FOR MODALITY OF GLATKOWSKI RETURN."

There appeared to be a convergence of interests about how to get Glatkowski back to the United States. The problem had always existed because the United States did not have an extradition treaty with Cambodia; Glatkowski had to agree to come back voluntarily. If, however, Glatkowski was declared incapable of making that decision for himself, then an evacuation based on "humanitarian medical grounds"—given his wife's approval—could be carried out. Therefore, if U.S. officials could convince Glatkowski's wife and her parents that a medical evacuation was in Glatkowski's best interest, then he could be returned to the United States without his agreement.

Three days later, Flo and her parents received a wire from the State Department, telling them about Glatkowski's condition. Neither Flo nor her family was in any mood to "seek Glatkowski's return." In the wake of the mutiny, Flo's father had lost his job at McDonnell-Douglas. Moreover, the birth of Flo's child, back in early May, had been extremely difficult; she had nearly bled to death. Glatkowski was blamed for this as well, because the family felt that her labor problems were the result of stress. Flo's parents had always disliked Glatkowski. Since the mutiny they had felt that he was the source of all their problems; he had committed an act that destroyed Flo and her family.

Flo's father wrote to the State Department, saying that Flo was divorcing Glatkowski and that they wanted nothing more to do with him. This must have been disappointing to the State Department, which had hoped for an easy way to get Glatkowski back to the United States. Without Flo's participation, U.S. and Cambodian officials would need Glatkowski's acquiescence.

Antippas came to Takh Hmau once more, telling Glatkowski that Flo was filing for divorce. Glatkowski, more coherent than before, now remembered Flo. Vaguely. But he still could not place into rational context what Antippas was telling him about her.

Dok said that Glatkowski often received a package of canned food and candies. Dok assumed that these packages were sent by the U.S. embassy. They apparently cheered Glatkowski; he traded chocolate bars for marijuana, which helped ease the pain of opium withdrawal.

As Glatkowski improved slightly, and Dr. Chamrowun felt that he was not in danger of hurting himself or others, he was permitted to walk around within the compound. He was also moved to a different room, one with a mattress and mosquito netting.

Glatkowski's past was like a jigsaw puzzle whose pieces had become scrambled and were only now starting to fit back into place. He finally grasped what the consul had told him. His wife was divorcing him, and she wanted nothing more to do with him. He realized, suddenly, that he had been rejected and abandoned.

During his stay at Takh Hmau, Glatkowski regularly saw groups of young, saffron-robed Buddhist monks who visited the sick and insane as part of their daily rounds. Glatkowski started following them around. The monks allowed Glatkowski to tag along. He taught them a few words in English and they in turn taught him some Khmer. He had the freedom to walk around on the dirt paths with the monks, a kind of daily exercise, a meditation. The monks would visit patients and he would go with them, even though they knew that he too was a patient.

After those first few horrific days, Takh Hmau had become bearable. It was not an idyllic place, and he was still in pain, but on the whole it was a haven of greenery, monks, flowers, fruit trees, and people smiling and taking care of him. Compared to the cage, it was heaven.

Dok said that one day a group of children visited the hospital. Glatkowski gave them all the chocolate he had. Suddenly, Glatkowski realized that he had nothing left with which to buy marijuana. The guards, feeling sorry for him, gave him some anyway.

As days turned into weeks, Glatkowski found himself praying with the monks. They had no common language, but he did not need one. Lighting incense, placing lotus buds as offerings—that was language enough. It felt good. It felt . . . holy.

Glatkowski had noticed, of course, that all the monks had their heads shaved. He assumed that it had to do with humility or poverty or simplicity. Maybe it was just a way of keeping the lice away. In any case, Glatkowski asked that his head be shaved. The monks found scissors and razor and went to work.

18 ESCAPE

On 30 September 1970, Glatkowski was told that his interlude at Takh Hmau had come to an end. He had returned to sanity, to some degree, and his doctors issued him a clean bill of health. The past month had been a period of almost total disconnection from reality for Glatkowski, and also one of spiritual reawakening. The monks had unlocked something in him and he had achieved a state of peace with himself. "I felt my soul needed that," he would say later of his time spent at the mental hospital. The ride back to the Chrui Changwar naval base, however, re-triggered some of the old anxieties. Glatkowski dreaded having to return to the prison ship; the cage had been the lowest point of his life.

On the prison ship, meanwhile, McKay and Humphrey had been moved from the cage to officers' quarters. Glatkowski was brought in to share these quarters with them when he arrived. McKay and Humphrey were surprised to see him; not hearing from him in a month, they had been unsure of his fate. Glatkowski appeared strange to them, with his head shaved and his Buddhist talk. He was very upset when he learned that there were no letters for him. There was nothing from Flo or his family.

All three prisoners were eventually transferred to a room in the Royal Government of Cambodia's official guest house in the heart of Phnom Penh. The building was an old French colonial palace, with high-ceilinged rooms and impressive chandeliers. It had been used as a place for visiting dignitaries during the Sihanouk regime. It was now nearly vacant, void of guests and furniture. Their room was magnificent, and it completely dwarfed the three small cots, plain table, and three simple chairs that furnished it. A half-dozen guards were stationed in the building. Twice a day guards took them to eat at local restaurants.

The prisoners' circumstances had improved thanks largely to the efforts of Martha Honey, who had lobbied on their behalf with the Cambodian government and had filed stories describing their wretched conditions on the prison ship. Also, Fred Emery's interview with the mutineers had been carried by papers around the world and had drawn much public attention to their sorry plight. Meanwhile, back in the States, McKay's mother was involved in yet another letter-writing campaign to her congressman and others in the U.S. government. These letters put pressure on U.S. and Cambodian officials to treat the Americans more humanely.

Shortly after arriving at the guest house, the mutineers and the deserter received a visitor, a woman named Louise Stone, who was small and oddly striking for a woman whose features were plain. She was the wife of Dana Stone, a news photographer who was missing in Cambodia, along with his partner, Sean Flynn.

Stone and Flynn were a legendary pair of daring, iconoclastic journalists who worked on the front lines of the war in Vietnam, often wearing flip-flops, beads, and floppy bush hats. They were part of a circle of like-minded, ganja-smoking journalists who congregated at a freewheeling apartment on Tu Do Street in Saigon. The group included Tim Page, who allegedly was the model for Dennis Hopper's crazed cameraman in the film *Apocalypse Now;* Perry Deane Young, who later wrote *Two of the Missing* (1972), a popular book about Flynn and Stone; and John Steinbeck IV, son of the great American author.

Flynn was the son of Hollywood actors Errol Flynn and Lili Damita. Like his father, Sean was tall and handsome, a glamorous figure who dropped out of a career in acting to become a freelance war photographer. Stone was the opposite of Flynn, at least physically. He was short, not at all glamorous but incredibly brave, verging on reckless. The grunts called him "mini-grunt" because of his size and his enthusiasm for working in the trenches alongside them. Although he was a freelance photographer for most of his time in Vietnam, CBS offered Stone a job as a news cameraman. After the

Lon Nol coup, CBS then asked him to pick up his still camera again and go to Phnom Penh to stay on top of developments. Flynn followed him there, and so did Stone's wife Louise, who was living in the apartment in Saigon.

Cambodia in 1970 was widely seen as the next domino to fall to Communism, and CBS, as well as most other news services, sent some of their best reporters to Phnom Penh to cover the action. Henry Kamm was there working for the *New York Times*, as was Robert Sam Anson, *Time* magazine staffer, and Keyes Beech, a Pulitzer Prize–winning reporter from the *Chicago Daily News*. T. D. Allman, a twenty-five-year-old freelance journalist who had made a name for himself by discovering Site 85, a CIA base in Laos, and who would later rescue dozens of survivors of a Lon Nol massacre, was also in Phnom Penh, working as a freelancer for *Time* and the *Washington Post*. This group often met at the Royal, an old, rambling colonial hotel in the French part of town. The Royal had a pool that became a social center for the American correspondents as well as for reporters from other parts of the world. After returning from the field, they would gather there at night for a drink and a swim.

On 6 April 1970, while McKay, Glatkowski, and Humphrey were languishing on the prison ship at the Chrui Changwar naval base, Flynn and Stone had taken off from the Royal on a pair of Honda motorcycles to report on the invasion of Chi Pou by the North Vietnamese. Chi Pou was a village in the Parrot's Beak, a portion of Cambodia that juts deep into South Vietnam. The Communist invaders were reportedly being strafed by American planes. This was the first piece of evidence that Communist sanctuaries in Cambodia were being attacked by the U.S. forces, something that the Nixon administration had long denied. A group of journalists, most of whom were staying at the Royal, rushed down highway 1 in Svay Rieng Province to cover the story.

Allman saw Flynn and Stone leave on their journey. "They were on these bright red motorcycles and were heading towards the front," said Allman. "I believe they expected to be back by nightfall." Robert Sam Anson called Flynn and Stone "queasy riders" and described them as they left for Chi Pou as looking like a pair of hippies with cameras. "Sean had long hair and was wearing love beads, shower sandals, shorts and a GI 'boonie hat,'" Anson wrote in his book *War News* (1989), relating a description of the pair by a journalist who had seen them on highway 1. "Dana was similarly scraggy in jeans, a boonie hat and tee shirt." The two journalists were last spotted approaching a roadblock near Chi Pou at the farthest reaches of the Parrot's Beak. Several Western journalists reported seeing them detained by North Vietnamese regulars.

"The great game was to go into Cambodia and see if you could find the American troops," said Andy Antippas. "All the journalists were predictably anti-administration. They were pretty hostile and the embassy resented that. Once this reporter came in and asked for a helicopter to rescue journalists there. We couldn't really do that, but I went to the defense attaché and asked him. 'Fuck him,' he said to me. 'Fuck him. Let them die.'"

Louise Stone, believing that her husband would surely come back as he had always done after dangerous missions, stayed on at the Royal months after his disappearance. She wrote letters to North Vietnamese, American, Soviet, and Eastern bloc officials, and to Prince Sihanouk, pleading for help in securing her husband's return. She contacted Wilfred Burchett, the famous left-wing Australian journalist who had been reporting from the Communist side; Noam Chomsky, who was in Hanoi at the time; and Walter Cronkite, who formed a committee of distinguished journalists that sought the release of captured correspondents. Louise tried just about everything. She even enlisted the assistance of a Dutch adventurer named Johannes Duynisfield, who had been captured in Cambodia along with several French correspondents and later released. Duynisfield told Louise that he had seen her husband in a guerrilla field hospital. Louise was skeptical of his story at first and asked him if he had seen Dana's tattoo. She did not describe it. Dana Stone's tattoo was of an animal—a squirrel or a possum—and it was on his buttocks. Duynisfield could not identify it.

Duynisfield, however, described other physical traits of the man, and this convinced Louise that he had seen her husband. According to Young, Duynisfield boasted to Louise about how easy it was to go out into the countryside, get captured by the Vietnamese or the Khmer Rouge, travel with them, and then inevitably be released. Duynisfield claimed that he was a friend of Regis Debray and had traveled with the famous French Communist on a trip to visit Che Guevara during Che's final campaign in Bolivia. The Dutchman offered to go out and get captured again in order to make contact with Stone. Louise agreed to this plan, put together a package of medical supplies for him to take to her husband's captors as a goodwill gesture, and gave the Dutchman twenty dollars. Duynisfield was last seen on a bicycle heading out of Phnom Penh.

The problem with Duynisfield's boast was that most Westerners who were captured by the Vietnamese at that time were handed over to the local Communist insurgents, the Khmer Rouge, who did not comprehend or simply chose to ignore the Westerners' propaganda value. The North Vietnamese and the Viet Cong were experienced at holding Westerners, treating them well and manipulating them enough so that when they were released, they sang the praises of their captors. The Khmer Rouge regarded all Western prisoners, even journalists, as risks. They could not afford to have eyewitnesses. Angka, the Khmer Rouge's central organization, practiced safety first in these situations. They ordered the execution of most of these unwanted foreigners. At least twenty journalists disappeared in Cambodia following the coup and subsequent U.S. invasion of that country with ground forces, which is officially dated as beginning 30 April 1970, and most of them never returned alive.

When Louise Stone first dropped in on the mutineers—the palatial government guest house was just down the road from the Royal—she came bearing gifts of food and books. Glatkowski was not in the room when she arrived, so McKay and Humphrey told her their story. McKay showed her his scars from the cage; his arms were still raw with bruises and rashes. Both spoke about their attempts to get out of Cambodia. Stone wrote a story about this for the Dispatch News Service. "We would like the North Vietnamese government to take us in, but we heard that Hanoi . . . said we were probably CIA agents. We're wanted by the State Department for kidnapping, piracy and treason, and the Lon Nol government will not give us up to another country. We can't get visas to pass through countries that have extradition treaty with the U.S., so we can't get to countries like Sweden, that would take us."

When Glatkowski finally came into the room, Stone reported that "his movements [were] very slow, his face pale and slack." McKay whispered to Stone: "He had a nervous breakdown after his escape plan failed." Stone asked Glatkowski why he had shaved his head. "He looked down at his hands and said in a low voice, 'In a Buddhist family, when people die in the family, they, the family, shave their heads. My wife is divorcing me and my family won't write to me, so it's like they were dead. I should have a child by now, but I don't know, I haven't heard. Maybe I am a father.'"

Feeling pity for the trio, Stone invited them back to her hotel. Accompanied by their guards, the trio swam in the Royal's pool. She also treated them to a meal at a restaurant. She returned several days later and repeated the gesture. After that, she visited often. Robert Sam Anson ran into Glatkowski at the Royal's lobby bar. He and his fellow correspondents did not have a good impression of the two mutineers and the deserter. The trio tried to strike up friendships at the Royal, but the cliquish group of writers kept them at arm's length. The three were regarded by most of the press corps as misfits and fools, their adventure a surreal footnote to the more important political and military dramas unfolding in Cambodia. Louise Stone, unlike the others, treated Glatkowski, McKay, and Humphrey with sympathy and kindness. Stone was not entirely selfless in this, however. She had a plan.

On 2 October the Cambodians moved the trio yet again. Adm. John McCain, commander in chief, Pacific (CINCPAC), the man who had allegedly countermanded the order to retake the *Columbia Eagle* forcibly when it was heading toward Cambodian waters, was in Phnom Penh. McCain was slated to occupy rooms at the government guest house and no one wanted him to be in the same building as two mutineers and a deserter.

A telegram from Swank informed the secretary of state that the three Americans had been temporarily moved to city hall during the admiral's visit. He also told Rogers why they had been removed from the naval base earlier:

> CAMBODIAN NAVY NO LONGER WISHED BE RESPONSIBLE FOR THESE AMERICANS . . . RESULT IS THAT FONOFF [Cambodian Foreign Office] TRYING TO ARRANGE THEIR ONWARD TRANSIT TO ANOTHER PLACE OF ASYLUM. AS ALREADY REPORTED, SWEDEN HAS INDIRECTLY TURNED SUBJECTS DOWN AS A RESULT OF REGULATION THEY MUST BE PHYSICALLY PRESENT IN SWEDEN WHEN ASYLUM REQUESTED. SECRETARY GENERAL STATES SOVIET EMBASSY HAS ALSO BEEN APPROACHED BY FONOFF BUT THAT NO RPT [repeat] NO REPLY RECEIVED.
>
> SECRETARY GENERAL FURTHER STATED THAT GOC [Government of Cambodia] KEEPING SUBJECTS UNDER STRICT GUARD AS IT TAKES THEM OFF DRUGS ON WHICH AT LEAST MUTINEERS HAVE BEEN EXISTING FOR SOME TIME. DRUGS HAD RESULTED IN EFFORTS ABANDON SHIP [the escape attempts] ON WHICH FORMERLY KEPT.

At this point in the message there is a portion blacked out by U.S. government censors. The telegram picks up in mid-sentence

AND UNPLEASANT INTERVIEW WITH AMERICAN JOURNALISTS. LATTER, ACCORDING FONOFF, HAVE SINCE ATTEMPTED OBTAIN FURTHER INTERVIEWS BUT DECISION TAKEN FORBID THESE SINCE ONLY RESULT IS UNTRUTHFUL PUBLICITY FOR MUTINEERS AND DESERTER AND UNFAVORABLE IMAGE FOR GOC.

Apparently, the reports by Martha Honey, Fred Emery, and others prompted Cambodian officials to restrict press access to the mutineers. However, they did allow an ABC television crew to film the mutineers; the Cambodian government even provided transportation to the location where the interview was to take place.

"They had [some] guards in a car with us," said Glatkowski. "Two of them were unarmed, except for pistols, and one of them sitting in the back had hand grenades on him and a rifle. And he actually let McKay touch the rifle and we talked about it. And when we got to the place to be interviewed . . . at that moment, we had the opportunity to escape."

McKay signaled him to grab the rifle, but Glatkowski hesitated; he could not do it. "McKay got so fucking furious with me because we didn't take the gun," said Glatkowski. "I was not prepared. I was scared, I guess. It just didn't come into my head to do it. McKay wanted to do it, but I was not prepared."

That failure of nerve, combined with Glatkowski's shaky mental state, probably convinced McKay that he could no longer take him into his confidence. "The other two had to talk behind his back, lest he reveal their plans," wrote Perry Deane Young.

By this time it had become clear to McKay and Humphrey that their only option, short of turning themselves in to the U.S. embassy, was to escape. According to Young, Louise Stone talked to them about escaping and suggested the idea of going off into the bush, like Duynisfield, and defecting to the Communists. She apparently told them that it was easy to make contact with the Viet Cong and the Khmer Rouge, who would likely accept them as revolutionaries. Stone probably based her judgment on what Duynisfield had told her about the guerrillas. The Dutchman had been away by that time for several months on his mission to find Flynn and Stone, and there was as yet no word from him. Louise Stone was now optimistically waiting for him as well as for her husband.

Stone was also under the influence of the highly charged atmosphere of the small world she had shared for years with her husband, that of the daring war correspondents who "grooved on the danger." To be captured by the guerrillas was an ambition for many of these journalists. "They had taken that war adventure that final step," Young wrote in *Two of the Missing.* "They had been captured by the enemy and now they would be seeing it all from the other—far more interesting—side." A few journalists, including Robert Sam Anson, Kate Webb of UPI, and Richard Dudman of the *St. Louis Post Dispatch,* would be captured and would survive to tell the tale. They would become the envy of the foreign press corps, who were usually resigned to battlefield press junkets organized by the military. Flynn and Stone were among the first to cross the line. They had walked and talked and slept with the enemy. They had reached the exhilarating height of their profession. McKay and Humphrey were obviously receptive to the heady, gung-ho vibe at the Royal poolside. Louise Stone often told the boys, as she did everyone else, stories about the courageous antics of her husband, and the lengths he would go to and the danger he would put himself into in order to get a good photo.

While Louise Stone may have communicated, intentionally or not, a sense of adventure about going out into the countryside, according to Young she hoped that, like Duynisfield, McKay and Humphrey would attempt to make contact with Flynn and Stone. She strongly recommended that they escape and join Khmer Rouge forces, said Young. Although McKay and Humphrey never revealed Stone's part in their plans, they did not start talking about escape and joining the Communists until after they had met her. Before that, McKay was convinced that their future lay in obtaining asylum in a communist or socialist country, or at least a country that had no extradition treaty with the United States.

On Friday, 23 October, McKay was told that a thousand dollars sent by his Aunt Ruth had arrived. With guards flanking him, McKay went to the office of Inadana Jati to retrieve the money. McKay now had enough to bribe officials and guards. His family had the distinct impression that this was how the money was going to be used.

That same day, the U.S. embassy in Singapore sent a wire to the Department of State stating that Sweden had agreed to accept the three young Americans:

> SUBJECT: COLUMBIA EAGLE MUTINEERS
>
> [censored] RECEIVED QUERY THIS AFTERNOON AS TO USG [United States government] POSITION RE FOLLOWING:
>
> 1. THREE US CITIZEN [sic] MUTINEERS FROM COLUMBIA EAGLE

HAVE BEEN GRANTED ASYLUM BY SWEDEN. THEY WOULD BE FLOWN OUT OF CAMBODIA TO SINGAPORE WHERE THEY WOULD TRANSFER TO AEROFLOT FOR ONWARD TRAVEL TO SWEDEN. THIS INFORMATION WAS REPORTED TO SINGAPORE GOVERNMENT BY ITS EMBASSY IN PHNOM PENH. [censored] DESCRIBED HIS QUERY AS UNOFFICIAL BUT CIRCUMSTANCES LEAD US TO REGARD IT AS BASICALLY OFFICIAL. [censored] ASKED FOR A REPLY BY EARLY MORNING OCTOBER 24.

2. REQUEST GUIDANCE ON REPLY WE SHOULD MAKE.

If the government of Singapore would agree to act as a transit station, the three young men could then go from there to Sweden on a Soviet plane. Three days later, on 26 October, however, the U.S. ambassador in Singapore again wired Rogers, this time to let him know that the government of Singapore had "decided to deny entry permission to McKay and Glatkowski." The wire stated that Cambodian authorities had tried to get Singapore to agree to let them transit through. The message to Rogers from the U.S. ambassador in Singapore made it clear that one more possible avenue of escape had been cut off.

It is likely, given that the mutineers were living in relative openness at the government guest house and were regularly receiving news that pertained to their situation, that McKay learned about Sweden's willingness to accept them and about Singapore's refusal to allow them to pass through.

With all other options cut off and with one thousand dollars in hand, McKay put a plan into action. McKay and Humphrey told Louise Stone that they had heard that there was a strategy in the works, hatched by the U.S. military, to have them executed by Cambodian authorities. They told Stone that they were going to flee from Phnom Penh before that execution could be carried out. Stone wrote that McKay and Humphrey "intended to go to North Vietnam via the Cambodian countryside after making contact with the Cambodian Liberation Front."

According to Stone, McKay said that he had made contact with an intermediary, who in turn had furnished some "Cambodian authority" with the money. This intermediary assured the mutineer that he and Humphrey would get civilian clothes and a means to escape, and they would still have some money left over. The escape plan called for them to slip away from custody during a meal at a restaurant. McKay and Humphrey told Stone that once they were out in the countryside, they would pose "as newsmen."

Martha Honey also heard rumors about a possible execution and an arranged escape. "A reliable source quoted the Cambodian Commander in Chief of the Navy as saying that the American Embassy suggested that the men be released at the South Vietnamese border where they would be 'accidentally' shot by soldiers," Honey wrote in a freelance article that was never published. "The U.S. government has been terribly embarrassed by the entire Columbia Eagle hijacking. As one [Cambodian] official candidly admitted to us, 'The hijackers are only being held to please the United States. It will embarrass the American government if they are set free. Everyone in our government is trying so hard to make friends with the Americans and these boys have become the victims of our policy.'"

Glatkowski later related that it was at about this time that the three of them were taken to a restaurant by their guards. While there, a group of armed soldiers arrived and forced them back outside. The soldiers stood the Americans up against a wall. They cocked their rifles and raised them, execution style. The mutineers' guards came to the rescue, aiming their weapons at the soldiers. "It was a Mexican standoff," said Glatkowski. After a few tense minutes during which the two sides shouted at one another, the guards eventually prevailed. Glatkowski does not know why the guards won this encounter. The soldiers simply pulled back and then reluctantly left. Glatkowski, however, was certain that the soldiers were attempting to collect a bounty. He had heard the rumors that the journalists had heard: someone was offering a reward of several thousands to have them eliminated. They had become a nuisance and an embarrassment to both the Lon Nol government and the United States. There was no doubt in Glatkowski's mind that the U.S. government, or its proxies, had offered that bounty, and that groups within the Cambodian military were scrambling to claim the reward.

On Thursday, 29 October, at about noon, McKay and Humphrey were taken by their guards to a restaurant in the area of the central market. They ordered lunch and then both men visited the toilet separately, but in such a way that they were both there at the same time. While the guards waited patiently, the Americans climbed out of a window, hopped on two motorcycles, which were waiting outside filled with gas and with keys in the ignition, and took off.

From the central market, the closest highway that led out of town was

Route 6A, which started at the Chrui Changwar bridge, crossing the Tonle Sap River, and then over the Chrui Changwar Peninsula, where the naval base was located. Heading northeast the road eventually connected with Route 6, which was only partially paved, and then connected with Route 7, which led into the province of Kampong Cham, an area known as the Eastern Zone by the U.S. military. The Eastern Zone was the principal location of the North Vietnamese and Viet Cong sanctuaries, which were hidden deep in forests of rubber trees and palms. It was also the home of the district headquarters of the Khmer Rouge.

McKay's family, back in the States, had understood that this "escape" had been prearranged and that once free, the escapees would be assisted by the Soviet embassy in Phnom Penh, which would help spirit them away safely to another country. McKay may have gotten such an assurance from the intermediary, or it may have been a story he made up to calm his family's worries. The Soviets, however, apparently steered clear of the affair.

"The recent 'escape' by McKay and Humphrey looks, on the surface, rather suspect," Martha Honey wrote in her unpublished manuscript. "It would seem that, after the two previous escape attempts, the Cambodian soldiers would be on their toes for a third try. Therefore one wonders if the officials (with the approval of the U.S.) did not allow McKay and Humphrey to escape so they could then be shot in the act of flight."

A month later Ambassador Swank met with the Cambodian foreign minister, and in a wire that Swank sent to Secretary of State Rogers, he said he

> GAINED DEFINITE IMPRESSION THAT *CAMBODIAN GOVERNMENT MAY HAVE FACILITATED DEPARTURE OF HUMPHREY AND MCKAY, PROBABLY TOWARD NORTHEAST.* BELIEVE IT QUITE UNLIKELY THEY REMAIN IN PHNOM PENH [emphasis added].

How did the Cambodian government "facilitate" the departure of Humphrey and McKay? Was the mysterious intermediary who obtained the motorcycles for them actually working with Lon Nol's people? And why was the Cambodian foreign minister so eager to share this information with the U.S. ambassador? Was it because he felt that the Cambodian government had done what the United States wanted it to do?

Glatkowski was now alone. According to him, McKay and Humphrey told him about their plans and about the motor scooters, and they gave him the opportunity to escape with them. He refused because he knew that he would only slow them down. He was still sick. On other occasions, Glatkowski has said that he decided not to go because he wanted to return to the United States and publicize what he and McKay had done; he wanted to bring the mutiny to the attention of the American public, which had forgotten about it. He wanted to clear the record: the mutiny had not been a CIA conspiracy, but a legitimate act of protest. According to others, however, Glatkowski had not been made privy to every element of the escape plan. Louise Stone, for example, stated that she was the one who told Glatkowski that McKay and Humphrey intended to join the communist guerrillas, who were now being called the Khmer Rouge.

The dozens of guards—who before the escape had divided themselves up among their three charges—now only had one person to watch. Each night a whole platoon of soldiers would accompany Glatkowski to a restaurant, watch him eat, and then accompany him back to the guest house.

Soon after McKay and Humphrey's escape, Glatkowski was told by Louise Stone what he had been told before but could not grasp: six months earlier his wife, his soon-to-be former wife, had given birth to a baby boy named Charles.

Glatkowski's struggle to regain his sanity was far from over. The reporters who saw him at this time said that he was broke, lonely, and confused. Later, when talking about this period of his life, Glatkowski recalled an event, a memory so hazy, so confusing, so much a part of the state of mind he was in at the time, that he had his doubts about whether it actually occurred or not.

His hands and feet tied, he was driven in a truck for about two hours, past villages and military bases and rice paddies and pineapple plantations. When they finally arrived at their destination, the guards got him out of the truck, untied his feet, and then prodded him to go closer to where a crowd had formed.

As he approached, he saw several bodies hanging from ropes, obviously dead. The guards pointed at the bodies, then laughed at Glatkowski, as if to say: you're next. Then they put him into the truck, tied his feet, and drove back. The event seemed real and hallucinatory at the same time. Maybe he was still suffering from opium withdrawal.

Whether or not it had actually taken place, Glatkowski was scared. Not just because the image of bodies hanging had lodged itself in his brain, but because of what he felt was an almost gleeful reaction by the young soldiers. On the prison ship, on the base, and at Takh Hmau he had been attended by people, men and women, whose smiles were open and beguiling, who had often gone out of their way to be helpful. There was a dark side to the Cambodian character as well. The tortures that he had been subjected to in the cage, for example. A kind of senseless cruelty.

ON 10 NOVEMBER, Swank sent a wire to Rogers advising him that there was still no word on McKay and Humphrey. Then he added,

> GLATKOWSKI HAS BEEN TALKING WITH JOURNALISTS, WHO HAVE TOLD EMBASSY THEY HAVE IMPRESSION HE MAY BE THINKING OF RETURN TO U.S. ON CHANCE THIS MAY BE CASE, EMBASSY ASKED SECGEN [Secretary General of the Cambodian Foreign Office] TO ASK GLATKOWSKI IF HE WOULD CARE TO SEE CONSUL. SECGEN QUICKLY AGREED TO DO SO.

During late November a distraught Louise Stone visited Glatkowski again. She had just learned that Duynisfield, the Dutchman, had been killed in the Cambodian countryside. The cause of his death was a mystery. Glatkowski—feeling, perhaps, that her situation of being cut off from a loved one was parallel to his—wanted to help her find out what had happened to her missing husband. He offered to write a letter to Nguyen Van Hieu, a high-ranking official of the (Communist) Provisional Revolutionary Government of South Vietnam. Glatkowski drafted a letter requesting help in making contact with Dana Stone. In the draft he explained that he, Glatkowski, was one of the two who had hijacked a U.S. munitions ship: *We built quite a legend of ourselves.*

Later in the letter, Glatkowski wrote, *In so far as the American Imperialists are concerned, I understand that they have tried several times to have us, now only myself, either shot or taken to the Cambodia–S. Vietnam border and handed over to the pigs; so much for their fun and games.* Glatkowski outlined some of his problems but did not specifically ask for help for himself.

Glatkowski ended the letter: *I can only hope and pray that something can be arranged so that I can be released. VIVA CUBA! Hasta Vista, Alvin L. Glatkowski.*

Louise Stone saw Glatkowski again in early December. She told him that she feared that the political situation in Cambodia was getting more and more dangerous. Afterward, she spoke with Ambassador Swank and told him that Glatkowski "might be thinking of turning himself in to US authorities." Swank immediately contacted the Cambodian foreign office and said that if Glatkowski gets in touch with them and says that he wishes to talk with the U.S. embassy about repatriating himself, the embassy would be happy to oblige.

Meanwhile, Glatkowski wrote to Flo:

> Dear Florence,
>
> How are you Flo, and baby [Charles]? I don't really know what to say. I suppose that the press really played me up big. Clyde McKay and another man took off to try and reach the North Vietnamese. The Cambodian government and the Soviet Embassy here in Phnom Penh are trying to reach an agreement to help me leave the country without returning to the U.S. If I was to return to the U.S., I would probably have to face charges of mutiny and would more than likely be sentenced to death. I don't want to return to the U.S., Flo. I have never seen the baby, Flo, but I bet he's beautiful. If he looks like you, I'm sure of it. I want to see you and the baby so badly, Florence, but I can't risk returning to the U.S. It would be certain death for me, and you and the baby would face a possible life of fear while the trial is [on]. . . .
>
> I know you haven't had any trouble finding a boyfriend. I'm jealous of him. But I guess that's life, I've missed out. Have you heard anything from my parents? I haven't received any mail for such a long time, I've forgotten what it looks like. I've read that my mother and father have a divorce, and you're in the process of getting one from me. . . .
>
> Once out of the country, I could send for you if you still love me. That's entirely up to you, Flo. I wish that you would send me a picture of yourself and baby [Charles], I sure miss you.
>
> I had my "first" nervous breakdown when I tried to escape from the prison ship I was on and I didn't make it too far and almost drowned. After that I was taken to a hospital until I regained my senses. It's been a long time.
>
> All my best wishes for your happiness, your husband, Al.
>
> P.S. Kiss Baby [Charles] for me. I send him my love.

On Saturday, 5 December, Glatkowski called the U.S. embassy and political officer Bob Blackburn took the call. They arranged to have lunch on Monday at 1 p.m. Swank sent a wire to Rogers about this, saying that he did not know what Glatkowski's intentions were. A southern Californian who had been posted in Cambodia since late 1969, Blackburn had worked under Mike Rives when there were only eight Americans working in the legation. After Rives left, Blackburn—small, wiry, in his mid-thirties—stayed on to work under Swank. After Glatkowski's call, Blackburn joked with Antippas that it was apparently his turn to "take a mutineer to lunch."

On Tuesday, 15 December 1970, early in the morning, carrying two suitcases, Glatkowski was escorted by his Cambodian guards to the U.S. embassy, where he surrendered. Blackburn remembered this process as being rather informal. Glatkowski simply turned himself in. While Glatkowski was under guard at the U.S. embassy, marshals in Los Angeles were dispatched to Southeast Asia to arrest him. Meanwhile, Glatkowski would need a passport to get into Vietnam. There was not enough time to make a passport the normal way, Blackburn recalled, so the U.S. embassy in Phnom Penh quickly slapped one together. Blackburn took a Polaroid photo and pasted it into a blank passport.

Now under American jurisdiction, Glatkowski was no longer accompanied by the platoon of Cambodian troops that had been escorting him everywhere. Blackburn took Glatkowski to his place, a two-floor house off Norodom Boulevard, near the Victory Monument. There, Glatkowski and Blackburn had dinner. Blackburn remembered Glatkowski as being quiet and polite. Subdued. The impression that Blackburn had was that Glatkowski felt that he had gotten in way over his head. In the morning they had coffee and fruit, and then Blackburn himself drove Glatkowski to the airport. It was a quiet, inconspicuous ending to a very strange affair.

A small, eight-passenger T-21 plane was on the tarmac at the airport in Phnom Penh, and two U.S. marshals were waiting in the terminal. Blackburn delivered Glatkowski—and his two suitcases—to them. The marshals immediately snapped handcuffs on Glatkowski. They flew out of Phnom Penh, then changed planes in Saigon. Soldiers placed a casket into the plane's cargo section. On to Okinawa, where they changed planes again, and then to Honolulu. In Honolulu, U.S. Customs checked them through, then they boarded a plane headed for Travis Air Force Base, fifty miles northeast of

San Francisco. Hours later, as the plane was coming in for a landing at Travis, Glatkowski was formally placed under arrest by the marshals. At Travis, the casket was delivered. Glatkowski and the marshals received immigration clearance and then flew to Norton Air Force Base in San Bernardino, thirty miles east of Los Angeles, where they were met by another U.S. marshal, who drove them to the L.A. County Jail.

There, on 19 December 1970, Alvin Glatkowski was booked on one count of Mutiny on the High Seas, nine counts of Assault with a Dangerous Weapon on the High Seas, twelve counts of Transportation of Kidnapped Person in Foreign Commerce, and one count of Neglect of Duty by Seaman.

19 ALVIN IN JUSTICELAND

Southern California

On Sunday, 20 December 1970, Glatkowski was taken to a holding room where he met with two FBI men, Special Agents Ronald Hoverson and John Helfrich. The agents advised Glatkowski of his rights and asked if he would sign a waiver that would allow them to ask questions without the presence of a lawyer. Glatkowski refused. However, he said he would provide them with "background information."

He told the agents that the "CIA and FBI were both instrumental in brainwashing him by sending his friends and relatives from the United States to Cambodia to intimidate him and thereby destroy his brain and cause a nervous breakdown."

Glatkowski said that he recalled "none of the details of the alleged nervous breakdown." He denied ever having attempted suicide. He also said that Larry Humphrey was a "CIA operative and McKay may now be dead." The implication was that Humphrey, in performing his duties for the CIA, had killed McKay. Glatkowski then went on about his attempts to receive asylum in the Soviet Union and North Vietnam. In passing, he mentioned that he was trying to learn Russian and that he was a "Buddhist atheist." He mentioned that he might defend himself in court and "use insanity as defense."

Glatkowski later said that the suggestion that he use this defense strategy came from his L.A. County Jail neighbors. Charles Manson's followers were in the same cell block, according to Glatkowski, and he occasionally talked to them through the bars. They told him that an insanity plea would help him avoid their own likely fate, the electric chair.*

Glatkowski had originally been indicted, along with McKay, on 25 June, while they were both in Cambodia. The bail had been set by the court in Glatkowski's absence at one hundred thousand dollars. No one offered to post bail for him when he arrived in Los Angeles, and no one offered to help him find a lawyer. Indeed, Glatkowski had no visitors while going through his trials. His mother was preoccupied with a wrenching divorce from Sam Hardy, and there was a custody fight that, according to Glatkowski's half-sister Ann, became the family's focus of attention.

On Monday, 21 December 1970, Assistant U.S. Attorney Michael Heuer, from the U.S. attorney's office in Los Angeles, spoke with Glatkowski about his personal effects, which had been held by a U.S. marshal since Glatkowski's arrival in the States. Heuer advised Glatkowski that his property would be held as evidence. It included, among other things, *My First Russian Book,* which contained assignments in Glatkowski's handwriting, a copy of *Ramparts* magazine, as well as a French study journal—with French and Russian language exercises—in which Glatkowski had put his and his son's name.

There was also a small white notepad in which Glatkowski had written, "Thank Karl Marx for my love of life, thank God for my life. I hope and pray, thank the Buddhists that are reborn every so many years and thank the Christians for Jesus and thank Mohammed for Allah is alive. ALG."

Heuer told Glatkowski that he would be arraigned in a week's time and that he expected the trial to begin in April 1971. Glatkowski said that while he was at the jail, he was often marched down corridors protected by a phalanx of guards stretching from wall to wall. When he shaved, a guard held his razor for him. He showered separately from others, with guards accompanying him. Glatkowski asked why he was being treated differently from other prisoners. He was told that it was because they were afraid he would try to commit suicide again.

During Glatkowski's first few days in prison, a lawyer came to see him.

*Some Manson "family" members—Tex Watson, among them—were awaiting trial and already in L.A. County Jail when Glatkowski arrived. Three other men, followers of Manson, were indicted for crimes unrelated to the infamous murders on the same day that Glatkowski was arraigned for mutiny, and they too were placed in the same jail.

Michael Hannon, thirty-four years old, tall, slim, and athletic, was an ex-cop who had made his way through law school while working for the Los Angeles Police Department. Hannon said he would represent Glatkowski for no fee. "I read about it in the newspaper," said Hannon, "and volunteered my services." Hannon did it partly because he was sympathetic to the antiwar movement; more important, he knew that Glatkowski was "going to get screwed" if he tried to defend himself. Hannon also felt that the publicity would be good for his career. "I figured it would keep me working," he said.

On 28 December, after spending Christmas weekend in jail, Glatkowski was taken to the Central District of California's Federal Courthouse, an impressive building. Its floors are parquet marble with symmetrical designs, and it has an atmosphere of imposing seriousness. Except for his meetings with Hannon, Glatkowski spent the day waiting in a holding cell, not knowing if his case was going to come up.

Finally Glatkowski was brought out and appeared in front of Judge David Williams, one of the first black judges on the federal bench, a judge known for his draconian sentences in narcotics cases. The courtroom had a formal feel to it. The section for the attorneys was set far back from the judge's bench. The twenty-three counts of mutiny, kidnapping, assault, and neglect of duty were read out to Glatkowski, who pleaded not guilty to all counts.

Michael Heuer, prosecuting the case on behalf of the federal government, made a motion for the appointment of a psychiatrist to examine Glatkowski. An article in the *Los Angeles Times* described what happened next.

> During arguments on the motion for appointment of a psychiatrist, Asst. U.S. Atty. Michael Heuer said classified information from unnamed sources in Cambodia indicated Glatkowski had exhibited bizarre suicidal conduct in September.
>
> Heuer said the alleged conduct included an attempt by Glatkowski to cut his wrists with window glass . . . and claiming to hear voices commanding him to take his own life.
>
> Glatkowski was quoted by the Cambodian sources as saying that he could not take his own life because he was "the last of the baby Mao Tse-tungs," according to Heuer.
>
> "If these reports are true, it is reasonable cause to doubt his present sanity," Heuer said.

> But Glatkowski's attorney, Michael Hannon, said these reports were of "dubious validity at best." He said the test is whether Glatkowski has the present ability to consult with his lawyer.

According to the *Times*, Hannon told the court that after talking with Glatkowski for several hours during the past week, he considered the defendant competent to stand trial. Hannon said that he instructed Glatkowski to decline to answer any questions put by a psychiatrist, on the ground of self-incrimination. Judge Williams eventually called Glatkowski to the witness stand for a series of questions to determine his awareness of the proceedings.

"The accused man responded in a lucid fashion," the *Times* reported,

> indicating he was familiar with the charges against him.
>
> Glatkowski said he believed he was in a mental hospital or a prisoner-of-war camp in Phnom Penh in September. Questioned by Heuer, he said he was under the care of more than one physician, but it was debatable if they were competent.
>
> "In my opinion, they were absolutely not," he said.

Williams denied Heuer's motion, and he assigned Judge Manuel Real as the presiding judge for all further proceedings. Williams said that Judge Real would "have the opportunity" to assign psychiatric evaluation if it became "necessary."

The *Los Angeles Times* article continued: "Outside the court, Hannon charged the government is trying to 'run down' Glatkowski. The lawyer said it will be easier for the government to explain Glatkowski's actions by showing he is 'some kind of nut.'"

At this early stage, Hannon was convinced that the U.S. government would attempt to portray the mutiny as the act of a lunatic rather than a committed antiwar activist; otherwise, Glatkowski's political motivations would have to be taken seriously in court, which could lead to public sympathy for him. The government apparently wanted to avoid making this trial a public referendum on the Vietnam War. Hannon's comments to the press also appeared to be laying the groundwork for a defense based on a government conspiracy.

Within the next few days, Hannon invited another attorney, Frank Pestana, to join the defense team. In his late forties and known for having views sympathetic to war protesters, Pestana also offered his services at no cost.

Pestana and Hannon were concerned about the fact that Judge Real would preside over the case. Pestana called Real, a former prosecutor who was known for being tough on crime and for a strong pro-police stance, "the worst judge on the federal court." Hannon and Pestana felt that this did not bode well for Glatkowski's case.

While Glatkowski was in L.A. County Jail awaiting trial, he received little support from anyone. He said, however, that one person who did help him was Geronimo Pratt, a Black Panther accused of capital murder. Glatkowski said that Pratt was in another cell at the jail and that they became "friendly." "One time they threw me into a holding cell with nothing but black prisoners. I suppose they figured I'd be attacked. But when Geronimo signaled I was his friend, it was like a parting of the waters."*

During Glatkowski's court appearances, few people came to support him. There were no organized protests outside the courthouse and no marches. A local street character named Peter "Batman" Baxter took up Glatkowski's cause, showing up almost every day on the courthouse steps dressed in a Batman costume, including purple tights. His presence was an odd reminder of the decade that had just ended. Batman made a nuisance of himself, shouting through a megaphone and handing out mimeographed flyers:

ALVIN IN JUSTICELAND

> THREE PARANOID PRESIDENTS have tried and failed to blast their ideology into the minds of men. Congress will not support this presidential mania and THE PEOPLE always drive these madmen from the WHITE HOUSE. ALVIN GLATKOWSKI and another young seaman hijacked a freighter loaded with bombs in March of 1970. This bold, dramatic gesture in defiance and contempt for our president's inane, inadequate, hopelessly naïve policy was carried out with imagination, skill and verve in the teeth of grave personal risk and consequences.

*Pratt and Glatkowski were in L.A. County Jail at the same time, while they were going through their pretrial and trial phases. The Los Angeles murder trial of Elmer Gerard "Geronimo" Pratt, former Black Panther party deputy defense minister, would begin on 1 June 1971. Pratt was also one of the defendants in a conspiracy charge stemming from a shootout between Black Panthers and police.

> Not an egg was cracked in the careful, competent conduct of that cool campaign.

A couple of other characters who paraded around outside the Federal Courthouse were "General Hershey Bar," who wore epaulets made out of candy bar wrappers; and "General Waste More Land," who—like General Hershey Bar—wore an absurd-looking military uniform.

On 18 January 1971, seeing that this case was generating interest from the media as well as the lunatic fringe, Judge Real issued a gag order to the attorneys, thus prohibiting them from talking about the case publicly.

On Friday, 22 January, Judge Real appointed three psychiatrists to evaluate Glatkowski as to his "mental competency and to report said findings" to the court. Real had complete authority as to which psychiatrists to appoint, and he met the fairness guidelines to avoid creating a situation that could be reversed on appeal. He appointed one that each side chose from a list of qualified psychiatrists, plus one that he himself chose. In spite of Hannon's earlier comment, in Judge Williams's court, that he would instruct his client not to answer any of the psychiatrists' questions, Glatkowski talked a great deal during these sessions.

The first two sessions were with psychiatrists who came to the jail. Glatkowski told Dr. George Abe, the prosecution's choice, that McKay was the leader and had forced him into doing it. Then he backtracked by saying that he would have done it later anyway, if they had been able to get more of the crew involved. He said that he hoped their mutiny was the beginning of a trend and that others would follow in their footsteps.

The other psychiatrist who came to the jail to see Glatkowski was Dr. Eric Marcus, who was chosen by the defense team. Marcus's report, based on what Glatkowski told him, stated that "on the day of the alleged crime, McKay approached the defendant and said, 'Are you ready to take over the ship?' The defendant said, 'Yes,' but that he wanted to go to the restroom first. While in the restroom, the defendant reflected on his course of action. He stated that he was afraid not to go along with McKay because either he would be shot; or even if he would shoot McKay, he would be prosecuted. Also, he was afraid that McKay would blow up the ship. He thereupon decided, 'I might as well go ahead and do it—you only live once.'"

This answer, which appeared to minimize his own responsibility, was undermined when he told Marcus that he had thought about trying to stop a war cargo for a long time. "He stated that for approximately two years prior to the crime he had occasional thoughts about stopping a war cargo," Marcus reported. "About one year before the crime, while on board ship, the thought entered his mind but since there were no activists on board nothing happened." The presence of McKay on the *Columbia Eagle* changed things. "Aboard the Columbia Eagle," Marcus's report read, "McKay and others occasionally discussed stopping the ship by means such as setting the cargo on fire. At one point, the defendant said, 'Let's do it,' referring to taking over the ship. But McKay said, 'No.' McKay, instead wanted to set the cargo on fire."

The next day, Glatkowski was taken to see the judge's choice, Dr. John Paul Walters. Glatkowski told the doctor that when the ship left port, he had no intention of hijacking it, and he did not go along with McKay's plan at first because he was a "straight kid with responsibilities." He said that McKay threatened to shoot him if he did not take part in the mutiny. He remembered that when they entered the chief mate's room and McKay said, "this is a mutiny," Glatkowski wanted McKay to use the word "hijack" instead because "he vaguely thought that [hijacking] would be less serious [a crime]." At the time, Glatkowski said, he thought of shooting McKay, but he gave up the idea because "they would still think I was linked with him anyway."

All three court-appointed psychiatrists found Glatkowski sane enough to stand trial. His lawyers were not happy with this conclusion. "Alvin told me," said Hannon, "that the CIA had tried to torture him when he was in a cage on the prison ship, by bringing out his wife from America, and having the Cambodian guards make love to her in the cell next to his. And every time he told me about what had happened on the ship and in Cambodia, the story changed somewhat. Not radically but in certain important details."

Pestana believed that Glatkowski did not fully grasp the fact that he had committed crimes. Therefore, he and Hannon arranged for the mutineer to see still another psychiatrist, this time someone who was not appointed by the court. The lawyers expected Dr. Letticia D. Ciaramelli's opinion would bolster an insanity plea. At the very least it might gain Glatkowski some sympathy.

"Mr. Glatkowski appears to be crying for help and is in tremendous conflict over his own reasons for existence," Ciaramelli wrote in her report, which was submitted to the court on 13 February. “He is unable to fully understand the seriousness of the charges against him. He is incapable of handling the details of his defense.” She concluded: “I do not feel that he was legally sane at the time of the offense charged against him at this proceeding.” Without treatment, she testified, he would likely commit suicide in “the foreseeable future.”

Glatkowski later said that at the time of the psychiatric examinations he was still suffering from “culture shock” and the after-effects of his “nervous breakdown.” He said that his weakened state, and the horrifying difficulties he had endured, made it hard for him to communicate with the battery of doctors whose job it was to decide if he was legally sane or not. Glatkowski said that the psychiatrists had little sympathy for him and for what he had done because they had no background or framework for grasping what he had gone through. For example, he said that when he told them that he had been a political prisoner, they apparently thought that this was a delusion, and an exaggeration of the importance of the mutiny, rather than what he knew it to be: the literal truth.

Glatkowski felt that the psychiatrists tried to stick labels on him, labels that were not valid or accurate and that had nothing to do with what really drove him to hijack a cargo of napalm destined for the war in Vietnam. Glatkowski questioned whether it served any useful purpose at all to examine psychological motivation in situations involving political action. “Mao Tse Tung’s father was a sadist and beat the hell out of his kid,” Glatkowski said. “Did he become a communist because of that? No.” Glatkowski said that a psychological analysis was not important when weighed against historical facts. “When newspapers published the Pentagon papers,” he said, “they didn’t dig into [Daniel] Ellsberg’s psychological motivations.”

Judge Real agreed with the three court-appointed psychiatrists who determined that Glatkowski was sane. Real ordered the trial to begin on 22 March 1971. He estimated that it would last two days.

CONCURRENTLY WITH the psychiatric examinations, Glatkowski and his attorneys had discussed other defense strategies. One that Glatkowski proposed was that he wanted to be tried as a prisoner of war. The mutiny was an act of war, he said, and he had been captured by the enemy. He wanted to be treated like a POW whose case is governed by the Geneva Convention.

POWs are not tried as criminals, he insisted, so why should he be tried as one? Hannon pointed out that since Glatkowski was an American, if he were treated as a soldier or a POW, the government could perhaps prosecute him for treason.

Since the case began, Glatkowski and his lawyers had also discussed what had been widely rumored and written about: that the mutiny had been, in fact, a CIA plot. From what Glatkowski told the psychiatrists and the FBI agents who interviewed him after he came back from Cambodia, it appears that he did not really believe in the CIA plot, at least not at that time. He suspected Humphrey was an agent, but not McKay. Pestana and Hannon, however, were convinced that there had been a CIA conspiracy and that Glatkowski had been the victim of this plot, and they shaped a defense based on this approach. Hannon said that three factors determined their thinking.

First, Hannon was very suspicious of the accounts given to the Coast Guard and NIS investigators by the thirteen men who remained on board, accounts to which both sides had stipulated and which were now part of the trial record. To a man, the seamen had all said that no cargo had been removed from the ship while it was in Cambodia. To Hannon, there was something odd about this testimony. "The depositions from the crew were suspicious," said Hannon. "They all said the same thing, as if they were reciting from a program. It was prefabricated testimony. I didn't believe it."

Second, there were the photographs that had appeared in the *Far East Economic Review* and were brought in by Frank Pestana's investigator. One photo showed the *Eagle* after leaving Cambodia, supposedly still carrying all of its cargo; the other photo showed the *Eagle* as it left Richmond, California, on 9 May 1970, on a subsequent voyage, loaded with cargo.

In the photo of the ship as it left Cambodia, the *Eagle* was very high in the water. The Plimsoll Line was so far off the water level that the screw could be seen. The photo of the same ship a month later, leaving northern California with a full load of ammo, showed its Plimsoll Line very close to the water. As far as they knew, the ship was carrying the same tonnage on both of these voyages. In Hannon's mind, this pair of photos supported the contention that the ship had offloaded its cargo while on the hook off Sihanoukville, and that when it left Cambodia it was empty. (In fact, in these two voyages the *Columbia Eagle* was carrying vastly different loads. On the voyage in which the mutiny occurred, she was carrying 1,750 tons;

on the subsequent voyage she was carrying over 7,200 tons, more than four times as much cargo.)

Third, Pestana's investigator had tried to locate McKay's family and could not. They concluded that McKay may never have existed at all. Maybe McKay and Humphrey were made-up names, aliases taken on by two CIA operatives. To Hannon, these discoveries supported Glatkowski's position that he had been the victim of a CIA conspiracy.

During the first two weeks of January, Hannon therefore filed motions of discovery to have Heuer produce "communications and records within the control of the government of the United States of America." He cited Supreme Court decisions that the prosecution has "an affirmative duty to disclose all evidence which might be material and favorable to the defendant."

"It has been affirmatively stated," read a motion filed on 18 January, "by the governments of the Democratic Republic of Vietnam, the People's Republic of China and government of the kingdom of Cambodia in exile (Prince Sihanouk) that the arrival of the Eagle in Cambodia two days before the overthrow of the government of Cambodia by the Lon Nol rebels was a device used by an agency of the government of the United States of America to provide material to Lon Nol in support of his coup. This theory has also been advanced by eminent journals and reporters in the western world including Phillippe Devielliers, Southeast Asian editor of Le Monde, and the Far Eastern Economic Review."

Hannon's motion said that the government documents were requested because if the conspiracy theory were proven, "then the defendant would be entitled to an acquittal on all counts of the indictment on the grounds that the purported crimes were not crimes at all but an elaborate play staged by an agency of the government of the United States wherein the defendant was entrapped by agents of the said government."

On 1 March, Heuer offered a deal. If Glatkowski pled guilty to the first two charges—mutiny on the high seas and assault with a deadly weapon on the captain—Heuer would drop the other twenty-one charges, including all those of kidnapping. The sentence would be a total of ten years. Glatkowski would be released from prison while still a young man. The offer surprised Hannon, and it made him suspicious. He assumed that someone high up in the Nixon administration had heard that Glatkowski planned to use, as his defense, the idea that he had been the victim of a CIA conspiracy, and then decided that in order to avoid bringing up these issues in open court it would be necessary to plea bargain.

Hannon discussed the deal with Glatkowski, who was reluctant to accept it. Hannon pointed out to Glatkowski that he was facing very long odds. In Cambodia, he had given dozens of interviews saying that he had committed the crimes he was accused of. Besides that, the police had seized drafts of letters he had written, in which he stated unequivocally that he had done it. However much Hannon mistrusted the accounts of the more than a dozen witnesses, there was no question that they had all said that Glatkowski had committed mutiny, kidnapping, and assault with a deadly weapon.

And, of course, they still did not know if Judge Real would permit a defense based on conspiracy theories. Maybe Real would stick strictly to the facts of the revolt and not permit anything that had to do with the political context.

Most important for Hannon, he felt that this deal could give Glatkowski a chance to have a life. He weighed in the balance the possibility that Glatkowski would get out of prison while still a young man, and presumably completely sane by then. "I felt it was better to save my client's rest-of-his-life," said Hannon, "than to take a principled futile stand in court which gets him jail for the rest of his life."

On 2 March, Glatkowski appeared in court on what appeared, to court watchers, another routine day of motions preparatory to the trial. Then came a stunning announcement. The *Los Angeles Times* said that Glatkowski in "a surprise appearance before U.S. Dist. Judge Manuel Real had a sudden change of heart Tuesday and pleaded guilty to mutiny and assault charges."

Real asked Glatkowski if he fully understood what he was doing. Glatkowski said he did. Real accepted the plea on the first two counts and gave Glatkowski the maximum sentence: ten years in prison on count 1 (mutiny), five years on count 2 (assault on Swann). But instead of ruling that these two terms should run concurrently, as had been agreed on with Heuer, Real said the two terms should run consecutively. Hannon was outraged. Real had reneged on the deal that Heuer had made with them.

After a consultation with Heuer, Hannon, and Pestana—in which Glatkowski's lawyers passionately reminded Real about the contents of the deal that Heuer had offered—Real reversed his earlier ruling and said that the two terms would run concurrently.

Glatkowski was sentenced to ten years at Lompoc Federal Prison. "I made up my mind that I was going to die in prison," said Glatkowski, "just as I had on the ship. I went to prison with the idea that I wasn't going to live through it."

During the mandatory ninety-day review period following the guilty plea, Glatkowski finally heard from Flo. In a note that was heartbreakingly brief, she said that the divorce was soon to be finalized. She said she hated him and never wanted to see him again.

Nestled in a small valley in Santa Barbara County, surrounded by fields of flowers as far as the eye can see, Lompoc Prison is a picturesque, sun-bleached cluster of buildings that from a distance appears to be the campus of a well-endowed state university. Approaching this handsome compound, one notices that there is steel fencing around it, with razor-wire shimmering under the hot sun. This federal correction center and penitentiary is surrounded by rolling hills and cash crops of dahlias, poppies, gardenias, and sunflowers. Lompoc Valley is the location of one of the largest flower and flower-seed industries in the country.

Alvin Glatkowski saw this deceptively pristine place for the first time on 12 March 1971, the first day of his incarceration. His first few months in prison were described as normal. "His initial adjustment was satisfactory," read a special progress report written by prison counselors. He worked in the prison sign-making shop and began taking heating and air-conditioning courses offered by the prison.

During his time at Lompoc, Glatkowski submitted to numerous psychiatric evaluations. "He is well-known throughout this institution for his political and moral ideologies, which tend to threaten those not accustomed to dissension," read one progress report. "However, Mr. Glatkowski believes that his treatment here is grossly unfair, that he is being held as a 'political prisoner,' and that he will not receive fair treatment because he is a Communist."

In January 1972 Glatkowski managed to slip an electric drill from the sign-making shop into a laundry bin. Another inmate pushed the bin past the guards and Glatkowski ended up with it in his cell. He hid this drill, along with bits, saw blades, and other paraphernalia, on the ledge by his window, which was high up and barred. "While the Latino prisoners played dominos or sang songs," Glatkowski said, "I would drill holes in the bars, which I plugged up with soap, so that when the guards came in to check them, banging on them to see if they heard hollow sounds, they heard nothing unusual."

Movie night was normally not mandatory. Glatkowski's plan was to escape while most of the other inmates were watching a film. But on the night of the planned escape, the warden required everyone to attend. When the movie was over, and the prisoners were filing out of the theater, there was a large group of federal officers milling around. One of the cell-block captains pointed out Glatkowski. An officer stood in Glatkowski's way, grabbed him, and took him in for questioning. They had discovered the hollow bars. A guard had heard the drilling one day while he was making his rounds outside the prison walls. The prison guards had searched all the cells during the movie.

On 24 July 1972 Glatkowski was indicted for attempted escape from confinement. Again, he was involved in the legal dance: lawyers, writs, filing orders. This time, Glatkowski threw himself into the role of jailhouse lawyer, writing briefs and serving as his own co-counsel. The trial began on 31 October and lasted two days. The deliberations were quick; he was found guilty and sentenced to six years, but the sentence would run concurrently with the one he was already serving. The worst part was that he was put into the intensive treatment unit (ITU), or segregation, for one year. Glatkowski said he fared all right in solitary, but he did feel "occasional sensory deprivations," such as imagining that the cells nearby were not placed squarely but were "at all different surreal angles." He said that he also suffered from hallucinations.

Dr. Barbara Bliss, a prison staff psychiatrist, conducted a routine psychological interview with him at the ITU. Bliss reported that Glatkowski had "markedly lost weight" and he told her that he ate "nothing that grows below the ground, no meat and no grains." She reported that Glatkowski spoke at length "about what he felt to be physical abuse" by prison staff members. "He is basically hostile to 'the establishment,'" Bliss reported, "although he seldom resorts to invective; thus, he has major difficulty understanding why he stimulates a negative response in staff, which leads to his feelings of being unjustly treated."

While in solitary, Glatkowski filed an appeal, which he wrote himself. In it, he contended that "the district judge improperly instructed the jury as to what constitutes an 'attempt' and that evidence was insufficient to sustain the conviction." The appellate judge, using several precedents, rejected Glatkowski's claim and ruled that based upon the legal definition of "attempt," "there was sufficient evidence to justify conviction, because the jury could have concluded beyond a reasonable doubt that, acting with intent to escape, appellant drilled the bars of his cell window and thus committed an overt act toward the commission of escape."

The process of digging into law books was fascinating to Glatkowski. He became absorbed in the process, learning how to write legal language and cite precedents. During the rest of his years in prison he would spend much of his time writing and filing appeals of his original conviction for mutiny and assault.

Glatkowski wanted the U.S. legal system to recognize that it had acted unlawfully. One of his appeals was based on the premise that mutiny, as defined in the statute, is the unlawful usurpation of command. Glatkowski argued that since the United States' involvement in Southeast Asia was unconstitutional, then the mutiny was a lawful act. He also pointed out that, in the statute, assault is defined as an act committed "without just cause and excuse." Glatkowski argued that he had committed assault with just cause. Therefore he should not have been convicted of those offenses.

The appellate court chose to deal with what it felt Glatkowski meant by this: Assuming that a defendant believes that what he did was commendable, even though it is against the law, is this just cause for overturning a guilty plea and conviction?

The court ruled, "The proposition that good motive is a defense where the act done or omitted is a crime has never been accepted. When one commits a felonious act, it is immaterial that he has the highest motive."

Another appeal that Glatkowski filed was to attack the validity of his guilty plea. In his brief, Glatkowski said that—prior to his entering that plea—he had not been fully apprised of the elements of the offense. In answer to this, the appellate court ruled that "a plea of guilty to an indictment is an admission of all facts alleged in the case." This decision quoted another court's ruling on the same issue: "If a plea of guilty could be retracted with ease after a sentence, the accused might be encouraged to plead guilty to test the weight of potential punishment, and withdraw the plea if the sentence were unexpectedly severe. The result would be to undermine respect for the Courts and fritter away the time and painstaking effort devoted to the sentencing process."

Glatkowski's motions were all denied, but he continued making more motions, throwing himself into the role of self-taught lawyer. The process by which he learned how to write legal briefs became, in effect, the higher education he had never received.

When Glatkowski was released from solitary, he approached Dr. C. Scott Moss, the prison mental health coordinator, and asked if he could join a counseling program that Dr. Bliss was spearheading at the prison. Bliss was introducing a method that was new and controversial at the time, in which prisoners counseled each other in groups or one-on-one, often with a teacher from outside the prison. The approach was called Reevaluation Counseling, or RC, and it is very similar to the twelve-step recovery program of Alcoholics Anonymous. The method of allowing prisoners to be alone with each other, helping each other and becoming emotional, ruffled a few feathers at Lompoc, which is perhaps why Glatkowski was interested in it.

"Many of the staff have had difficulty accepting the Reevaluation techniques," Dr. Bliss wrote in a letter to Moss, "because they can seem bizarre or even potentially dangerous in a prison setting; i.e., the physical contact, the encouragement of direct expression of feelings through tears, rage, etc."

Glatkowski thrived on the RC program. "He became thoroughly immersed in RC counseling at every opportunity and became a teacher of the theory and a leader," Bliss wrote in a letter to the prison warden. "On multiple occasions, I have called him in to counsel with another inmate." Glatkowski even earned a limited teacher's certificate, which allowed him to counsel other inmates. He was the first inmate ever to be issued the certificate, according to Bliss. "For a long time," Bliss wrote the warden, "he reminded me of a 'computer' who related to 'other computers' whom he believed had 'good programming' or 'bad programming.' Over the past years, he has become a much more integrated human being, and has been able to relate to others as individual human beings for the most part."

A mental health consultant at the prison named Tina Brady, in a letter to Glatkowski's case manager, also praised his great progress: "I have been impressed, not only with the sincerity and perseverance he has applied to his own problems, but his willingness to assist others throughout the same process."

Glatkowski was finally developing his social skills, but he simply could not shake his fears. "Although Mr. Glatkowski is now able to recognize and respond with personal emotion," wrote psychologist Gordon Morrell in a special counseling progress report, "his 'paranoid' feelings toward authorities and the 'establishment' continues."

WHILE GLATKOWSKI was at Lompoc, an antiwar group made contact with him and took up his cause. The Santa Barbara chapter of the Vietnam Veterans Against the War/Winter Soldier Organization (WSO), with Glatkowski's consent, created the "Columbia Eagle Defense Committee" and published a pamphlet that was intended to drum up contributions for a retrial. The WSO was a group of militant antiwar vets who took their name from a Tom Paine pamphlet castigating "sunshine patriots and summer soldiers" who fought while the weather was good, then would go home once it got cold. The WSO members were, in contrast, winter soldiers, and they were going to continue to carry on the fight even after their enlistment ended. The continuing battle, according to the organization, was a revolutionary one and it would take place at home. Even though Glatkowski had never served in the military, the WSO made him an honorary member. They considered him a freedom fighter. WSO members visited him frequently in prison. In contrast, during the entire length of Glatkowski's stay at Lompoc, more than seven years, no one from his family, including his mother, came to visit him.

For the WSO pamphlet, Glatkowski wrote about the mutiny. Although he characterized McKay as a fellow freedom fighter in the document, he was actually leaning toward a different view.

Suspicions that Glatkowski had resisted for a long time had begun to take hold. Glatkowski was aware of the accusations and rumors that McKay had been a CIA agent. He had even suggested using them as a defense in his original trial. His lawyers had also believed that there might have been a conspiracy. At that time, however, Glatkowski did not really believe that McKay was a CIA agent, not in his heart.

But now, in prison, these suspicions—fueled by discussions with WSO members and an unidentified fellow inmate—Glatkowski began to believe it. Glatkowski began to suspect that when McKay was released from prison in Spain, it was due to the intervention of U.S. intelligence agencies, which also helped him regain his citizenship and his Z-card. Glatkowski even suspected that CIA agents helped McKay get his fireman rating on ship. That would explain why he knew so little about the way the engine room worked.

Glatkowski worked it out in his head. The U.S. government helped McKay out in Spain, then they waited for the right time. Two years went by. He got a call to meet them in the Bay Area. They told him to hijack a ship and get one or two guys to help him. Even one guy would do. A fall-guy. A dupe. Someone who would end up taking the rap. A naïve twenty-year-old.

So maybe the ship did bring small arms, after all. Maybe the Communist press was right: the rifles that were used to overthrow Sihanouk did come from the *Eagle*.

Or maybe it was something else. Perhaps the ship did not bring small arms. The mutiny could have been a diversion. While everyone was tracking the mutiny over there, the CIA engineered a coup over here. A sleight-of-hand trick, a feint, making the audience look in the wrong direction.

Glatkowski began to believe that Humphrey joined them in prison because he was McKay's contact. That's why he knew Khmer, Thai, and Vietnamese. Humphrey did not kill McKay, as Glatkowski had implied to the FBI agents who interviewed him when he arrived from Cambodia. Humphrey was there to *save* McKay, to spirit him away to safety. McKay and Humphrey were probably hiding somewhere in the world, using different names, new identities, new passports, plastic surgery, all paid for by the CIA.

"During my visit with the members of the defense committee," Glatkowski wrote in 1974 while at Lompoc, "we talk of the possible reality of my co-defendant and/or comrade-in-arms, Clyde William McKay, Jr., being an agent-provocateur. I have been talking with a close friend here about the above possibility. Many things that I was told by McKay and some things that I was told by Larry D. Humphrey seem to point in an odd direction. Of course, it would be foolishness for me to say, off-hand and without investigation, that McKay is an agent-provocateur; there has to be a lot of evidence discovered. But, on the other hand, if I accept the view that McKay was an agent, many previously unanswerable questions are now given an answer."

"I feel much pain when I think of this possibility," Glatkowski wrote, "but I can also find much relief if it is true. I shake when I think of this. I think that this is one of the major reasons I went mad while in Cambodia."

He concluded: "There is so much that points in the direction of both McKay and Humphrey being agents, besides their multi-lingual abilities. I just don't know, I've given this much thought since I have been here but there is no method I can use to check this out. So, you can see, I still think of this possibility, and I still shake."

Years later, when he was out of prison and living a normal life in a community where he had friends and neighbors, Glatkowski would still be shaken by doubt. "I try not to see myself as a dupe or to see McKay as a CIA agent," he said. "But I've always lived with this monkey on my back. All my life I'm going to carry around this idea: was he or wasn't he? In my heart I want to believe that he was not an agent and that I was not a dupe. I want to believe that. But I cannot believe that until I'm satisfied. This is something I'm going to live with all my life."

20 TWO MORE OF THE MISSING

The province of Kampong Cham is well-known for its red earth. In the dry season, clouds of henna-like dust rise from the roadways forcing moto (motor scooter) drivers to wear bandannas across the mouth in order not to choke on it. Not only the land is red, but the water too. The Mekong River, which twists and turns through the province after a long straight run through the lowlands up north, flows a brownish claret. In this region, probably more than anywhere else in the country, the Khmers' bloody history seems to have created a permanent stain.

Well before the horrors of Toul Sleng, the Khmer Rouge's torture chamber, and Choeng Ek, the infamous killing field outside Phnom Penh, this eastern province, some 150 kilometers north of Phnom Penh, was racked by brutality. There is a legend that the citizens of the provincial capital were so enraged at the coup against Sihanouk in 1970 that they captured one of Lon Nol's brothers, cut out his liver, forced a restaurant owner to fry it, and fed pieces to the angry mob.

The Khmer Rouge movement was born in this region, called the Eastern Zone during the war. Protected and supported by the Viet Cong, South Vietnamese communist guerrillas, and the North Vietnamese Army (NVA), which set up operational bases here, the Khmer Rouge, or Khmer Communists (KC) as they were called then by the U.S. military,* developed a

*All quoted documents in this chapter retain the original reference to the "KC." Otherwise, the Khmer Communists are identified as the Khmer Rouge.

precocious reputation for cold-blooded murder. To the outside world, events in the Eastern Zone provided the first glimpse of the nightmare that would eventually engulf the entire country. It was a place where people disappeared and were never heard from again. The Eastern Zone was in fact the location of the Khmer Rouge's first killing fields; the people who died here were the first victims of what later became known as "The Genocide."

THE FIRST sightings of Clyde McKay and Larry Humphrey on the run, after they had escaped from Phnom Penh in late 1970, occurred in Kampong Cham, the heart of the country's rubber-producing industry.

The office within the U.S. government that investigated and analyzed these sightings, as well as other sightings of POWs and MIAs in Southeast Asia, was located at Arlington Hall in Washington, D.C. Originally a girls school, the Arlington Hall campus was taken over by the government during World War II and became the first home of the National Security Agency and the Army Intelligence and Security Command. The PW/MIA department occupied temporary buildings, Quonset huts that had worn out their welcome by the time of the Vietnam War. "Our office was like a barracks," recalled John T. Berbrich, the section's intelligence supervisor. "It looked like it was made out of cardboard on the outside." Though the Arlington Hall station was small and shabby-looking, according to Berbrich this office was "leveraging all of the information out there among all the service intelligence organizations."

Berbrich, twenty-seven years old, was a civilian, a self-described "jack-of-all-trades." He became director of the PW/MIA department by chance, after marrying the daughter of a U.S. Navy captain who introduced him to Cdr. Charles F. Trowbridge Jr., the man in charge of the intelligence department. Trowbridge needed someone to fill a vacant position, and Berbrich qualified for the job. "We were all youngsters," said Berbrich. "They got a lot of people out of college." One of his top analysts was Margaret Van Beck. "She had a keen analytical mind," said Berbrich.

Van Beck was a twenty-four-year-old who had graduated from the University of Madrid in Spain with a degree in Spanish, worked for the U.S. embassy in Peru, and then was offered the job at Arlington Hall after returning to the States. Like Berbrich, she was young and bright, and had fallen into the position by chance. Her job was to look at the reports, the sightings of POWs and MIAs in Cambodia, and analyze how valuable these reports were, as well as to connect them to other sightings to see if they referred to the same person or people.

"John [Berbrich] was my supervisor," Van Beck recalled, "and he had been in there for some time. We collectively worked on the reports. If there were harder cases, we'd work together and we'd work with other agencies."

The first sighting that may have referred to McKay and Humphrey was dated 3 November 1973. It was sent as a cable to Arlington Hall from a branch of the Air Force Intelligence Group (AINTELGP) based in Thailand.

A witness reported that, under orders of the Khmer Rouge, a village leader in Anlung Thma—a forest hamlet about one hundred kilometers northeast of the town of Kampong Cham—had given shelter to a pair of Americans. Anlung Thma was in an area where the Khmer Rouge held South Vietnamese prisoners, who were normally bound together. The report said that in contrast to the Vietnamese prisoners, "the U.S. POWs were not tied and did not live in the POW camp. On June 14, 1973, the two U.S. POWs were taken away from Anlung Thma and were last seen traveling north on Route 75." The witness who provided this information said that the village leader told him that from Anlung Thma the Americans were going to be taken to Laos. Route 75, however, does not lead toward Laos, but toward the rubber plantations of the Eastern Zone.

Van Beck examined this Anlung Thma sighting. "Based on the treatment afforded the two PWs, as well as their relative freedom from any type of restraints," she wrote, "the PWs source heard about were probably collaborators. There are two Caucasian individuals missing in Cambodia who might correlate with the two PWs sighted: Mr. Clyde McKay, U.S. civilian and SP4 [Specialist 4th Class] Larry Humphrey, U.S. Army deserter. Both were last seen in Phnom Penh in 1970 when they escaped from the protective custody of the Cambodian government with the stated intention of joining the Communist forces."

Van Beck felt that this was a reasonably reliable sighting, having occurred only five months before the report taken in November 1973. Besides, this was a close-contact sighting, the source having received his information from the village leader who had intimate knowledge of the Americans, having sheltered them for two months.

Van Beck reached her conclusion that it referred to McKay and Humphrey because she knew that the mutineer and the deserter had headed in a northeasterly direction when they left Phnom Penh and that Kampong Cham Province, according to what Louise Stone told the U.S. ambassador, would have been their likely destination. Even if McKay and Humphrey had been intercepted by Communist forces just outside of Phnom Penh, they would likely have been brought to Kampong Cham Province, which was the location of the Eastern Zone headquarters of the Khmer Rouge.

One year later, in 1974, a second important sighting came into Arlington Hall, this time from the U.S. Defense Attaché Office (USDAO) in Saigon. "The following information concerns two Caucasian deserters operating with Khmer Rouge forces in Cambodia," the report read. It was based on the interrogation of a source described as a "rallier." (A rallier was a defector, in this case one who defected from the Viet Cong.) He was debriefed in Saigon on 26 July 1974, and testified that in 1971 he had seen two Americans in Sangke Kaong, a village in Kampong Cham Province. The source was grinding rice in a villager's house for Vietnamese troops that were in the village. "[The source] was told by the house owner," read the report, "that two U.S. advisors to the Republic of Cambodia forces had defected to the Khmer Rouge after being punished by their superiors. They were taking shelter in nearby Cambodian villager's house. . . . Source and a friend went to the house and saw the Caucasians. One was sitting in a chair and the other one was lying on a bamboo bed. They then asked the Caucasians in Cambodian language their marital status and age. The Caucasian sitting on the chair replied in Cambodian that he and his friend were single, and were 21 and 23 years old."

The Caucasian's Khmer was limited, read the report, and so the conversation ended. The source and his friend left the house but lingered and watched. A Cambodian woman walked in and gave the men "a tray of food consisting of beef, rice, fresh sliced bananas and fish sauce." The source said that the man sitting on the chair spoke limited Khmer, was six foot four, with blond short hair; he was wearing black pajamas and was the younger of the two. The other man, lying on a bamboo bed, was about six foot six with short blond hair, and was wearing trousers. According to the source, the older man spoke French.

In a document dated 2 August 1974, Van Beck concluded that this sighting could be of McKay and Humphrey. "The descriptions provided by source somewhat fit both individuals except that neither has blond hair," she wrote. In fact, McKay's hair was light brown. Van Beck was relying on photos that made the hair appear darker than it actually was. Neither Humphrey nor McKay was as tall as the source stated, but they were both over six feet tall and would have appeared very tall to the short Cambodians.

Van Beck knew that data was often ambiguous. "We never had a complete picture," she said. "We were trying to make the associations that fit the best."

In another response to this report, a cable sent from the Arlington Hall office and signed by Van Beck and Trowbridge, the authors expressed greater confidence that the sighting was of McKay and Humphrey. "The source was told that the two Caucasians had defected to the Khmer communists," read the cable, which listed several other reasons why the sighting might correlate with McKay and Humphrey.

1) McKay and Humphrey were last seen in Phnom Penh when they escaped protective custody with the stated intention of joining the communists;
2) both individuals are Caucasians;
3) McKay and Humphrey are tall (6'1" and 6');
4) Their ages are comparable to the information provided by source (27 and 24 years old respectively, in 1971); and
5) The two Caucasians sighted were collaborators, not PWs.

The USDAO in Saigon followed up with another report two weeks later, after a re-interrogation of the rallier, who was shown photos of McKay and Humphrey. "Source restated that he had observed the two Caucasians in a CB [Cambodian] villager's house about ten days after his arrival at another CB villager's house in the same area. Before seeing the Caucasians, source had never heard about them and after seeing them he stayed in the area for almost 20 more days, but did not see them again. During this time he overheard the owner of the house where he was staying say that the two Caucasians had escaped from jail in Phnom Penh to join the KC, and were taking shelter in the area pending their trip to Hanoi for schooling."

The source positively identified a photo of Larry Humphrey as the Caucasian who was sitting in the chair at the villager's home. The source also said that a photo of Clyde McKay showed a slight resemblance to the American who was in the bamboo bed.

The Arlington Hall analysts were now convinced. "It appears that the source does, in fact, have information on Humphrey and McKay," read a report prepared by Van Beck and Berbrich on 23 August 1974. The most telling reasons for this belief, besides those mentioned already, were that these two Caucasians were "viewed as 'collaborators' not PWS. The treatment and lack of physical restrains on either Caucasian would be consistent with the sympathetic attitude toward the communists." And that the two Caucasians sighted in this village had "escaped protective custody in Phnom Penh."

Escaping custody clearly pointed to McKay and Humphrey. There were a number of missing Americans in Cambodia at that time. But there were only two who were known to have escaped from a jail in Phnom Penh with the stated intention of joining the KC. Assuming the investigators did not influence the testimony by feeding the witness leading questions, this report from Sangke Kaong, as Van Beck stated in her report, was strong evidence supporting the hypothesis that McKay and Humphrey were living among the Khmer Rouge in 1971. Also convincing was the positive photo ID of Humphrey, especially coming from a source who had been shown photos of other Americans. Van Beck was convinced enough to ask USDAO Saigon to investigate further.

ON 8 JANUARY 1975, a cable crossed Van Beck's desk that was perhaps the most compelling—certainly the most disturbing—document related to the case. The report was titled, "Capture, containment and execution of two American journalists by Khmer Communists in Kampong Cham Province, Southeastern Cambodia."

"Two male American prisoners were delivered to the Khmer Communist administrative center in Sangke Kaong village Tbaung Khumum district, Kampong Cham province of Southeastern Cambodia in January 1971 and were executed in that district in June 1971," the document read. "Upon their arrival it was disclosed that the Americans were journalists who had been picked up by KC authorities in Svay Rieng Province, to the South of Kampong Cham Province, during the previous year. One American, whose name sounded like LOVERY (Khmer phonetics), was approximately 1.90 meters tall. He was thin and had a long, thin face. He spoke English, French and Khmer and owned a platinum necklace which had a round medallion attached to it that looked like a coin. The other American, whose name was forgotten, appeared to be about 25 years old, 1.90 meters tall, had a large build and blond hair and blue eyes. He spoke French and English. Both Americans had cameras with them."

The report described how the Americans had been forced to travel from village to village as the Khmer Rouge fled invading ARVN (Army of the Republic of Vietnam) forces. "The Americans were forced to carry ammunition cases and other items for the KC." When ARVN ceased its operations in the area, the Khmer Rouge "set up its headquarters on the western fringe of the Tapao rubber plantation."

Once settled, the Americans apparently began creating problems for their captors. "The Americans were required to eat the same, or less than the KC soldiers because the ARVN troops had confiscated most of the KC food stocks. Subsequently, the Americans complained that they were undernourished and requested that they receive the same food as the KC cadre. Their requests were ignored so they went on a hunger strike for a day and a half, but the KC cadre were not moved by this action. Ultimately the Americans tried to leave their residence to find food and cigarettes in another village but were stopped by the KC security guards. When they persisted in leaving, Chan[g] Seng, the deputy chairman of Tbaung Khmum district, had them bound and incarcerated."

The Americans were sent to an unidentified prison camp and stayed there for two weeks. "During that time," read the report, "they were harshly interrogated by Uk Saren, the chief of security of Tbaung Khmum district, who accused them of being spies. When their interrogation was over, the journalists were summarily executed as spies by Saren and his security cadre in June 1971."

Besides Uk Saren, the name of another official slipped by the censor's pen: Bou Savorn, believed to be Khmer Rouge district security chief.

This report was first evaluated in Thailand by the Joint Casualty Resolution Center (JCRC), whose mission was to search for the remains of U.S. personnel. Those who first looked at the report in Thailand suggested that this account of an execution could refer to Sean Flynn and Dana Stone, who were also captured in Svay Rieng Province.

"When captured, Flynn was age 31 and his photos depict a thin person possessing a long thin face and the presence of a necklace," the JCRC report read. "His records stated that the necklace is composed of a gold chain with two Buddhas on it that are made of dark metal." Stone, the comment notes, "was age 29 when captured, has hazel eyes, brown hair, and his photos reflect a large build with a long thin face."

The evaluators, however were not very convinced of the match. "It is noted," read the JCRC comment, "that the source's height description of the two journalists does not reflect the fact that Flynn at 1.87 meters is approximately 20 centimeters taller than Stone. A fairly noticeable factor." The two Westerners were not described as short and tall, as they were in many other reports that were equated with Flynn and Stone. In fact, the Caucasians in this report were said to be of almost identical height, and very tall. At six feet, Humphrey was about an inch shorter than McKay.

Back at Arlington Hall, Van Beck weighed in with her own evaluation, insisting that the sighting related "in part" to the McKay and Humphrey Sangke Kaong sightings, which she described as "positive" identifications. She added a telling observation: "The name 'lovery' best equates with 'Larry' Humphrey."

Still, the question remained: Were the executed Dana Stone and Sean Flynn, or Clyde McKay and Larry Humphrey? Almost two decades later, Tim Page, the war photographer, would pick up where Van Beck left off.

A CLOSE FRIEND of Flynn's, Tim Page was recovering in a hospital with war wounds when his friend disappeared in April 1970. Haunted by Flynn's disappearance for years, Page finally traveled to Chi Pou in 1989, searching for traces of the missing photographers. He was accompanied by a film crew. In the documentary *Danger at the Edge of Town,* and in his subsequent book, *Derailed in Uncle Ho's Victory Garden* (1997), Page followed the trail of Flynn and Stone to Kampong Cham Province, where he believed the two men were held from 1970 through 1972. His search was triggered by declassified DIA documents he had received in 1989 from a researcher, the most important of which was the JCRC field report about the execution of two American journalists by Khmer Communists in Kampong Cham Province. Page and his team traveled deep into Kampong Cham, to Ta Pao and Sangke Kaong and other villages, and interviewed witnesses who claimed to have seen the two Americans mentioned in these reports.

These witnesses were all survivors of the Khmer Rouge regime, and despite the common assumption that the Khmer Rouge had wiped out everyone in the countryside, or at the very least displaced them, these people were still very much around and willing to talk. Page's search then led him back to Phnom Penh were he found Ta Sabun, a Khmer Rouge functionary who had become an official in the subsequent Hun Sen government.

Page's crew interviewed Ta Sabun on camera and Sabun slyly sidestepped all questions about the execution of two Americans. Finally, Page was taken by witnesses to a site that was said to be where the two Americans were buried in a village named Bei Met (Three Meters). The grave had already been dug up by the time Page got there, and he was only able to find a pair of teeth and some pieces of bone.

"I took the teeth to a dental forensic scientist at Cardiff University," Page said. "And they had done an analysis that said the teeth came from a tall man and a short man, they both died violent deaths and both had malaria. One of them was tall and the other short."*

Page's dogged search for his friends inspired Richard Arant, who picked up the thread in the early 1990s. Arant began his career in 1972 as an enlisted army man with the JCRC in Thailand. While in the service he studied Thai, Laotian, and Khmer, and he worked in military intelligence, gathering information about American POWs in Vietnam, Laos, and Cambodia by interviewing refugees from those countries that had entered Thailand. In 1987 he was recruited by the DIA to work in Stony Beach—the DIA's POW/MIA office in Thailand—which was established in 1988. (The name Stony Beach had no meaning, according to Arant, but was arbitrarily chosen, perhaps out of a book.)

In searching through POW/MIA reports from the early 1970s, Arant stumbled on the sightings of Humphrey and McKay, and Flynn and Stone. He had also seen Tim Page's documentary, and it made a deep impression. "It seemed rather pathetic to me," said Arant, "that the U.S. administration had always claimed that the MIA issue was of the highest national priority, that was the terminology that had been used since the Reagan era, but they did little about it. And here was a guy going in on his own, looking for his

*A document from the American Dental Association states that "the size of teeth [is] genetically determined. Teeth are highly independent in their development [and] tend to develop in a genetically predetermined course. Tooth development and general physical development are rather independent of one another."

own buddies. And the American government had never taken the opportunity to do that. Yet this guy was going in and interviewing people and making a film and he had no problems."

Arant also read Page's book. "It was plain to see, that there were plenty of Cambodians out there still who knew about this stuff," said Arant. "The argument that had always been used over the years, when the opportunity first came to work in Cambodia, there were a lot of people who said, 'It's no use working there, all the people were killed by Pol Pot.' That's ridiculous. Not once did we ever leave Phnom Penh and go out into Cambodia that we didn't come back with reports. Of course we were looking in areas where we had good reason to believe that people were being held, following up on old reports. Most of the Americans that disappeared were in the eastern part of the country. The same people are still living there. Yes, lots of folks died, but the idea that Pol Pot massacred the whole country is just ridiculous."

Surprisingly, however, there was no mention in Page's book, or his movie, of McKay and Humphrey, who were frequently confused with Flynn and Stone in the sightings. "The reports were all coming back with these references to McKay and Humphrey," said Arant. His curiosity piqued, Arant pushed for an investigation into the disappearance of the mutineer and the deserter.

"People in the military were upset that anyone would bother to look for Humphrey and McKay," said Arant. "I didn't care if they were collaborators. They were young. Maybe they did something stupid. Made a bad decision. Who cares why they were there? They were missing Americans."

Arant's superiors apparently cared. They were disturbed by his request. The missing Americans were defectors. McKay was not even a soldier, he was a civilian; Humphrey was a deserter. There was some offense taken by bureaucrats outside the Stony Beach office to spending time and resources searching for defectors and nonmilitary personnel.

"One Joint Task Force colonel asked me, 'Why would you want to look for a deserter?'" Arant recalled. "During late 1991, I wrote a paper proposing how we [DIA's Stony Beach team] could help resolve the MIA issue in Cambodia. An admiral from the CINCPAC joint staff said, 'At first glance this looked good, but won't this interfere with what we want to do in Vietnam?' One young guy said to me that our job was not to really find anyone, it was just to tie up loose ends. That's what the intelligence service meant to him."

Arant was disgusted with this thinking. "Who cares who or what the prisoner is? He was missing, held against his will," Arant said of Humphrey. "He was probably a naïve kid, he was a spec 4. Did he know what the Khmer Rouge was? Do you think he was living freely? Bullshit. You want to know all you can about all of these people. We went in and asked hard questions."

Although Stony Beach had conducted many POW/MIA searches in Vietnam and Laos at the end of the war, Cambodia had been off-limits for years. The United States did not recognize the Vietnamese-installed Hun Sen government, instead siding with the Cambodia coalition government in exile led by Sihanouk and including the Khmer Rouge.

The Paris Peace Accords in 1991 between Hun Sen and several Cambodian nationalist groups led by Sihanouk and Pol Pot ushered in the United Nations Transitional Authority in Cambodia (UNTAC), a peacekeeping army of twenty-five thousand whose mission was to disarm factions, resettle refugees, and prepare the country for national elections. During late 1991, after a highly publicized investigation of a POW photo scam, the Stony Beach investigators were invited to open up an office in Phnom Penh.

Arant first began investigating the McKay and Humphrey case in 1992. For background and leads, Arant searched through documents in Tuol Sleng, the interrogation center in Phnom Penh (now a museum), where the Khmer Rouge tortured and killed thousands of Cambodians, including members of their own party. The Khmer Rouge extracted confessions from the victims, and although the veracity of these documents is questionable—people confessed to imaginary crimes just to stop the torture—they do provide some reliable data. For example, Arant was able to establish who the top cadre were in the Tbaung Khmum district. He discovered that someone named Mat Ly was the number three security chief under Chang Seng, who was number two, and Mam Sabun—otherwise known as Ta Sabun—was number one. (Ta is a form of address, similar to Mr.) Ta Sabun was a former Khmer Rouge official who had been interviewed earlier by Tim Page.

In 1992, in Phnom Penh, Arant found the number three man, Mat Ly, who was then a member of the Cambodian National Assembly. Arant interviewed him, and Mat Ly admitted that back in 1971 on his rounds in his district he had come across two American collaborators named McKay and Humphrey who were living with Khmer Rouge forces. "Mat Ly claimed that he was involved in military matters," said Arant, "and was out in the field a lot. He was distancing himself from the case. But he did admit that he had met them on a number of occasions. He remembered their names." Arant said that Mat Ly called one by the nickname of "Khlei" which was short for "Mak Khei." The other American was known as "Ham," short for "Ham Free."

In 1992 Arant wrote up a report on this meeting. "A Cambodian government official reported having firsthand contact with two American collaborators in Kampong Cham Province during 1971 and 1972. The two were known to him as Humphrey and McKay," read the report. "The source revealed during an interview that he had had numerous firsthand contacts with two American collaborators in 1971 and 1972. The contacts occurred in a number of villages located in Kampong Cham Province. According to the source, the two Americans, whose names were Humphrey and McKay, were alive in late 1972. Upon returning to the area from a mission in the field, the source was told by local villagers that the two Americans had been executed." The report goes on to say that, according to the source, Humphrey and McKay had lived in Sangke Kaong. "Although viewed as collaborators, their activities were closely monitored by the Khmer Rouge."

But no sooner had Arant nailed this startling lead, then it slipped away from him. Stony Beach went through a management shake-up. The administration of the division was transferred to the army's joint task force, directly under the command of Brig. Gen. Thomas Needham who reshuffled the staff, starting with Arant. "So here was this little Air Force Captain doing what he saw as his business and they didn't like it," said Arant. "Their feeling was, 'You can't trust intelligence officers.' Needham came down and proceeded to give me the works. I remember him, this hard-nosed guy, staring at me from across a table. He decided that my attitude was not respectful. I was ready to go out and do the investigation, and a message from CINCPAC in Hawaii finally arrives and it says I'm not going to Cambodia. They were saying that the POW/MIA issue was not an intelligence issue, it was a human interest issue. Therefore I was not needed."

Arant quit. He went back to the States, became a civilian, and bought a home. Almost immediately, he was called back. The DIA needed someone who spoke Khmer, so Arant was hired as a civilian investigator. "Needham tried to stop the DIA from hiring me," said Arant. But it was too late, he was back in Thailand. In 1993 the Defense Department transferred him to

Phnom Penh to fill a position as a temporary substitute for a military attaché to the U.S. embassy, where he was not allowed to pursue POW/MIA issues. "This was bureaucratic turf stuff," said Arant. "They would have been totally enraged if I was in-country asking about missing Americans because that was *their* turf." When he finished his military duty in February 1994, Arant went back to Thailand, "and drank coffee until late '95."

In Cambodia, meanwhile, Sihanouk's royalist party won the UNTAC-supervised election and then eventually reached a compromise with the opposition Cambodian People's Party, led by Hun Sen, whereby they both shared power. The coalition government created a more open climate in the country, and suddenly the U.S. embassy was being approached by scores of Cambodians who had seen Caucasians in the countryside in the 1970s. Arant was sent back to Cambodia to follow up on these reports.

As soon as Arant overcame one hurdle, however, another stood in his way. Although the UNTAC presence had opened up the country to foreigners and had helped forge connections with some U.S. organizations—including Stony Beach—the Cambodian government was uneasy with efforts to search for missing Americans. They realized that it was in their interest to assist investigators from the States, because cooperation could bring American investment in the country. However, they also felt that digging up the Khmer Rouge past might damage the relationship more than build it, especially when most of these sightings involved the alleged execution of American POWs by Khmer Rouge officials, many of whom were now integrated in the new government.

The Cambodians assigned a guide, Gen. Nuon Sareth, to accompany Arant on his investigations. According to Arant, the two-star general had joined the Khmer Rouge revolution when he was a teenager. He had defected to Hun Sen's Vietnamese-backed army, worked his way up to general, and following the overthrow of the Khmer Rouge was given the post of deputy minister of agriculture and minister of the interior. He was working with Arant in his additional capacity as the chairman of the Royal Cambodian Government POW/MIA Committee, which had just been formed.

"Initially, I asked permission to talk to a lot of potential sources, almost all of them former Khmer Rouge cadre. They wondered why I wanted to talk to all these people," said Arant. "They were worried that if I sat down to interview the old revolutionary cadre, they'd be offended and there would be an international problem." But to the complete surprise of both Arant and General Sareth, the Cambodians were happy to talk. "They enjoyed talking about their revolutionary background. They were not embarrassed or defensive."

Sareth sat in on the interviews with sources. Arant was not sure if Sareth was there to monitor the conversation or to guarantee his safety. Eventually, Sareth began to notice that the sources were stiff in his presence, but they would loosen up and talk more freely when he left the room, according to what Arant told him. After realizing that Arant was not looking to establish guilt or assign blame for the alleged executions, Sareth began to drop out of the interviews, allowing Arant to conduct them with absolute freedom.

"The purpose of the investigation was to attempt to clarify details surrounding the Flynn/Stone case and the Humphrey/McKay cases," Arant wrote in his Stony Beach report. Although Arant and General Sareth interviewed sources in Phnom Penh, most of the work was done out in the countryside. The team was accompanied by a small militia of guards, which provided security against the scattered remnants of the Khmer Rouge that were still roaming Kampong Cham.

Piece by piece, Arant put together a complex puzzle. "It all began with the original wartime reports from '70 and '71," said Arant. "We'd go out there and start finding more witnesses, we would get all they know, find out about the people who were in charge back then. We were just trying to collect the facts and let the facts speak for themselves." Arant's method was not to ask questions about missing Americans. He came equipped with names of Cambodians, people who had served in the Khmer Rouge in the district in which the missing Americans were sighted. So he would start his questioning by asking about these cadres. The testimony sometimes would wind its way to the subject of Humphrey and McKay and sometimes not. Even when it did not, Arant still believed that the interviews were constructive because they created a sociological and historical map, and eventually that map would lead him to these two men. Although in his report Arant cautioned that it "provides limited first-hand and hearsay information concerning foreigners detained in Kampong Cham province during 1971–1972," by the end of his mission, he was confident that he had established several important facts.

Based on the interviews, Arant determined that two Americans, who closely fit the description of Humphrey and McKay, crossed the Mekong River at the village of Chi Hae, which is approximately ten miles south of the city of Kampong Cham. The location of the village suggested, by Arant's analysis, that the two men had come to Chi Hae by way of highway 7, the road from Phnom Penh. This, according to Arant, ruled out Flynn and Stone who, having been captured in Svay Rieng Province, would have arrived in Kampong Cham Province from a position much further east. This information came from Long Sokha Bun Ny, a woman whom Arant identified as a source who had been interviewed by Tim Page in his documentary.

The two Americans had been captured by either the Viet Cong or the Khmer Rouge somewhere near Chi Hae. They were kept in the village for several weeks and then brought to the Tbaung Khmum district headquarters, which was located near Sangke Kaong and Ta Pao. A nurse, who worked at a Khmer Rouge training school in the area, was interviewed by Arant and told him that she saw the Americans in late 1970 to late 1971. "One of the two was slightly taller than the other," read the report. "The taller one appeared to be younger and was of thinner build and had longer hair. Both had brown hair. Neither wore eyeglasses. The taller one wore a necklace with a large round pendant. The younger one wore a necklace with a small crucifix."

Also corroborating Arant's Chi Hae theory was Mat Ly, whom Arant re-interviewed in Phnom Penh. By that time, Mat Ly was old and in ill health. In his report Arant mentioned that the old man had trouble standing, but he was eager to help. He told Arant that the two Americans were brought to the Tbaung Khmum district commander, whose name was Mam —or Ta—Sabun. Mat Ly recalled that the two Americans were brought there from Chi Hae.

In October 1995, Arant interviewed Mrs. Bun Ny, the woman who had been interviewed by Tim Page. By 1995 she was a Cambodian government official in the Ministry of the Environment. In the early 1970s, during the war, Mrs. Bun Ny had been one of four secretaries working for Mam Sabun in Kampong Cham. "Ta Sabun charged his four secretaries with the care and feeding of the two Americans who resided next to Ta Sabun's headquarters in Phum Ta Pao near the Sangke Kaong market," read Arant's report. In Page's documentary, Mrs. Bun Ny apparently had identified one of the men as "Seen Fleen."

In her interview with Arant, however, Bun Ny retracted her statement. She said that when she was interviewed for the film, officials of the Cambodian government influenced her answers. The government had asked her "to provide only that information which it was absolutely necessary to provide," read Arant's report. Mrs. Bun Ny also said that she was prompted to say the name "Seen Fleen" by one of her interviewers who, by her description, appeared to have been Tim Page. Also, in the film she appears to identify positively a photo of Flynn as one of the Americans. Arant showed her the same photo, but the second time around she changed her mind. "Bun Ny ruled out the same photo she apparently identifies as 'Seen Fleen' in the December 1990 interview," read Arant's report. The investigators also showed her other photos. "She studied the photo book with great care, but was unable to recognize photos of Flynn, Stone, Humphrey or McKay."

Bun Ny recalled that the two Americans were brought to district headquarters at night sometime in 1971, escorted by Khmer Rouge forces. "The Americans were then dressed in khaki camouflage military uniforms," read the report, "but they soon requested the standard black uniforms worn by the cadre/locals, and those uniforms were sewn for them." Bun Ny told Arant that she saw a document that indicated that the pair had been captured at Chi Hae. They were supposed to be brought to the zone headquarters but were dropped off with Mam Sabun instead.

"Bun Ny became emotionally attached to one of the Americans nicknamed 'Khloy' since he was so gregarious and fun-loving," the report said. "The other, known only as 'Thom' (large, big) was sullen, detached and seldom spoke to anyone. Khloy spoke some French, Spanish and English. Khloy told Bun Ny that he was a reporter. Khloy told the girls that he and 'Thom' had been captured at Chi Hae, and that 'Thom' was a soldier. Khloy claimed that his mother was an actress and his father was a politician or civil servant (Bun Ny can't remember which). Khloy's mother wanted him to become an actor, but Khloy wanted to 'play' for a few years first, and being a reporter was his way to 'play.' Khloy wore a small crucifix on a necklace. He gave the crucifix to Bun Ny, who later lost it. Thom wore a larger necklace with a coin-shaped platinum pendant approximately 40 centimeters in diameter."

According to Bun Ny, the Americans were marched off to different locations in the countryside to avoid a U.S. bombing campaign of the area around district headquarters. "The Americans lost what had been considerable freedom of movement and other rights," when they finally returned to Ta Pao. Eventually the Americans were transferred to a "security site," probably a prison camp, which was located in a banana plantation. Bun Ny went out and visited a friend who worked as a secretary to the chief of the security site and saw the Americans there. "They were not bound or shackled when she saw them." Bun Ny then testified that several months later, her friend told her that the Americans had stopped eating, had become sick, and finally died. The friend escorted Bun Ny to a gravesite within a banana garden near the camp. "Bun Ny saw the two separate adjacent grave mounds. She can remember no trees other than banana trees nearby, and remembers no markings near the graves."

Bun Ny's testimony muddied the waters. There was a little bit of Flynn and Stone and some McKay and Humphrey in her recollections. The reference to Thom as a soldier would point to Humphrey. The very use of the word Thom, meaning "big," would definitely rule out Stone, who was small, but not Humphrey who was six feet tall. The name Khloy is obviously close to Clyde; Clyde spoke French and Spanish, languages that Flynn supposedly spoke as well. Khloy's story about his mother being an actress would relate obviously to Flynn's mother, Lili Damita, and putting off his own acting ambitions to "play" at being a reporter is certainly a Flynn story. But Flynn's father, Errol Flynn, was not a politician nor a civil servant; neither was McKay's stepfather, who was a retired Marine colonel. The strongest piece of evidence in Bun Ny's testimony that would point to Khloy as being Flynn is the fact that she told Arant she was "fixated"—in Arant's words—to his "blue eyes, his long and sharp nose and his overall very handsome look." McKay was very handsome as well. His nose, by Western standards, was not especially long and sharp; it was rather normal. However, by Cambodian standards it might be considered long and sharp. As for the eyes, however, McKay's were brown. Flynn's eyes were blue.

Arant's reports read like a Khmer Rouge family tree, with names and titles and relations and connections among hundreds of people whose lives may have touched upon, in some small way, the lives of these missing Americans. Many of these Cambodians, as Arant dryly notes, were purged, executed by Angka—the Khmer Rouge central command—for various reasons. Some were accused of being traitors. One purged Khmer Rouge official was described as "a notorious woman-chaser whose immoral activities eventually resulted in his death." Others simply died of natural causes, like Mam Sabun and Chang Seng. And then there were those who were said to be alive, but Arant was unable to find them, including one more of Mam Sabun's four secretaries, a girl who worked with Bun Ny and whose name was Khema.

Khema had defected to the Lon Nol government in 1974 after she was caught stealing valuables from the Khmer Rouge unit. Arant knew about Khema because other people had spoken about her. He knew, for example, that she had been interviewed back in 1974 by a Lon Nol official about the two missing Americans. Khema was, in fact, the source of the DIA report that talked about the execution of two American journalists. She had been interviewed while held at a rallier center in Kampong Cham. She had told her interrogator about two missing Americans who were executed by Ta Sabol or Ta Sabun. They had to be the same pair that Mrs. Bun Ny spoke of. However, unlike Bun Ny, Khema said the two men were executed; they did not die by starving to death. And one of the Americans, again which Bun Ny failed to mention, was named "Lovery."

Arant decided it would be important to travel to Chi Hae, the place on the Mekong River where he suspected Humphrey and McKay were captured. He and his Cambodian squad reached the village by boat. Just up the river from the village they found a man named Chhung Eng, a member of the local Cambodian People's Party militia, who said that two Americans lived in the village Phum Prek Rumdeng sometime during the rainy season of 1970 or 1971. They were in the custody of the Khmer Rouge who placed them in a house owned by a villager. Chhung Eng said the two Americans were very young, in their twenties, and wore civilian clothes. The fact they were still wearing civilian clothes was significant. It meant that they were recently captured. In Cambodia, as well as in Vietnam, Western prisoners who were in captivity for more than a few months were issued "black pajamas."

Eng said the prisoners were "American correspondents" who lived in town "for quite some time" before being taken away to a district office. Eng led the investigators to the homes of the wife and the niece of the villager who had sheltered the Americans, as the man himself had recently died. The wife remembered the Americans as young, and that one was about six to eight inches taller than the other. They stayed at her house for about two months and then they were taken to "upper echelon" so that they could be sent back home. The niece, who had also lived in the house when the Americans were there (she was twelve years old at the time), recalled that the two Americans wore civilian clothes and that one was clearly taller than the other, but by how much, she was not sure.

Arant and his team traced the movement of the two men north from Chi Hae to Suong, twenty kilometers south of Sangke Kaong. Suong is the largest town in the area. They visited local police headquarters, hoping to make contact with a source who had worked in the Khmer Rouge hospital there during the war. They never did make contact. However, a police officer told Arant that his wife had worked at a Khmer Rouge prison site in Ta Pao. She was summoned to the station.

This chance encounter produced one of the strongest pieces of evidence of McKay and Humphrey's presence in the region. At the time of the interview, Mrs. Sedtha was fifty-one years old. She had joined the Khmer Rouge in March 1970, at the prompting of friends. She was assigned to the district office of Mam Sabun and Chang Seng. Mrs. Sedtha also said that she was the first cousin of Ta Savorn, the chief of security of Tbaung Khmum district, and the same man as Bou Savorn (since "Ta" is an honorific) who was identified in the earlier report on the "capture, containment and execution of two American journalists." Mrs. Sedtha told Arant that she saw the two Americans at Mam Sabun's district office. The villagers said that they were journalists. "Mam Sabun told her," the report read, "that while the two claimed to be correspondents, Angka knew that in fact they were 'marines' who had served on an ammunition transport ship."

Why would these two "marines" call themselves correspondents? Arant theorized that they did it to save their skin. "They had to have a good cover story," said Arant. "They realized that working on a ship carrying arms for the government would draw suspicion. And if this was McKay and Humphrey, which it probably was, these guys were accused of being CIA spies by Sihanouk, of bringing in arms for Lon Nol. The Khmer Rouge would have known about this and would have little sympathy for them." Also, if Louise Stone did indeed persuade Humphrey and McKay to join or seek out the Khmer Rouge, and perhaps even asked them to search for her husband and Flynn, they may have assumed the identity of journalists perhaps as a way to gain access to the captive photographers.

Glatkowski, in a recent interview, said that before McKay and

Humphrey escaped they talked about posing as journalists. Glatkowski said it was his idea and that he had given McKay a camera to carry as a prop. This was the baker's camera that he had "liberated" from the *Eagle*. Apparently, the Cambodians held Glatkowski's belongings in safe keeping, and then returned them when he was released from Takh Hmau. According to Glatkowski, McKay and Humphrey understood that if they posed as journalists, their chances of surviving in a war zone were better. As noncombatants, reporters were generally treated more humanely when captured by the other side, and were almost always released alive. In any case, as Arant wryly noted, "Ta Sabun didn't believe their story. He knew who they were."

Mrs. Sedtha had personal contact with this pair of Americans, having spoken to one of them while they were in Mam Sabun's office. The man she met spoke Khmer and was only slightly shorter than his companion, which was the case with Humphrey, who was shorter by an inch than McKay and could speak Khmer. She also said that the taller one had a necklace with a large coin-shaped pendant. One side of the pendant bore the image of a bald man. According to records, McKay wore a necklace with a Buddha pendant.

"The two Americans first requested that they be issued the standard black KC-style clothing," Arant's report read. "Later they requested weapons and ammunition, saying that they were revolutionaries. Angka did not give them weapons. After quite some time at the district office, the Americans demanded to meet the leaders of Angka. They said that if they did not get to see the Angka leadership, they would go on a hunger strike." (This tactic echoes McKay and Humphrey's hunger strike while they were held on the prisoner ship in Phnom Penh, as well as McKay's hunger strike when he was in the Barcelona jail.) Angka refused their request. After the start of the hunger strike they were placed under arrest by the chief of security, Ta Savorn.

The Americans put up a fight, according to Mrs. Sedtha. They were then tied up and sent to the security site. Several days later, they were bound and taken away by Savorn and members of the district headquarters defense unit. "They were in good health and were able to walk out of the prison to the execution site which was approximately 500 meters north of the prison site," Arant's report read. "They were shot at the execution site. Mrs. Sedtha saw the two unmarked graves. The graves were located approximately two meters apart among the rubber trees. After the execution, the execution team took the tall man's necklace and pendant to turn in to Mam Sabun, the district chief. Mrs. Sedtha recalls the member of the team saying that one of the bullets had struck and damaged the pendant."

A Cambodian military attaché, Col. Khieu Samorn, who was part of Arant's investigation team, told him that Mrs. Sedtha's testimony was very convincing. "He remarked that she had a good explanation of why she was assigned to the prison site: She was the first cousin of the security chief," the report read. "And she answered questions without hesitation. She did not try to make any excuses about the execution or about the health of the two Americans at the time of the execution. The reason for the execution was clear to her: the foreigners had challenged the authority of Angka and the results of such a challenge were inevitable."

Arant also interviewed a source named Sao Sam San, a Cambodian who served in a North Vietnamese unit operating in Tbaung Khum district near the Chupp Rubber Plantation. San's testimony corroborates Mrs. Sedtha's. He told Arant in a 1997 interview that in late 1971 or 1972 he saw two Americans in a banana grove at Ta Pao, near a place called the Vietnamese Well. San described the Americans as collaborators; one of them spoke Khmer and told San that they were "journalists who had escaped from the Lon Nol regime detention at the Royal Hotel north of Wat Phnom, Phnom Penh, by slipping their guards while on a short trip to the nearby 'Phsar Thmei' market. These two Caucasians were both of approximately the same height." The American who spoke Khmer told San that they wanted to join the revolution. They never got a chance, according to San, because they were executed by Tbaung Khmum district secretary Mam Sabun. "San heard that both of the Caucasians had been executed as a result of an argument with Ta Sabun," the report read. "They had noticed that Ta Sabun's food was better than that of Sabun's revolutionary subordinates, and openly criticized Ta Sabun on the matter."

The evidence here again points to Humphrey and McKay, rather than Flynn and Stone. Humphrey spoke Khmer, and both fled from the custody of the Lon Nol government. The "Royal Hotel" may refer to the Hotel Royal, which is near the Wat Phnom. Louise Stone had been staying there and had invited Humphrey and McKay to swim in the pool. The "Royal Hotel" also might be a reference to the Royal Government of Cambodia's official guest house where McKay and Humphrey were held, under guard by the Cambodian military.

"It is unfortunate that Mam Sabun and Chan[g] Seng passed away before they could be given the opportunity to assist in efforts to learn the fate of, and locate the remains of, those foreigners who went missing or were held in detention in their areas," Arant wrote in his report. "But no doubt the information is still available from surviving relatives and lower-level personnel associated with them during 1970–75."

Mrs. Sedtha told Arant that McKay and Humphrey's grave site was in Bei Met, the alleged location of the graves of Stone and Flynn. In 1989 Tim Page had been there, digging in the hard earth with a few hoes. Several years earlier the Cambodian government—following a tip from a former Khmer Rouge soldier who said the site was a burial ground for American soldiers—had dug up the location with heavy equipment. Hun Sen's government, hoping to please the United States, found some fragmentary skeletal remains, and—according to Arant—offered them to the U.S. government, which refused to accept them, pleading lack of diplomatic relations between the two governments, suggesting instead that the Red Cross be used as intermediary. Finally, in 1991, the DIA accepted the remains and shipped them out to CILHI, the army's central identification lab in Honolulu, Hawaii. Arant could never determine what the lab's final analysis showed. Col. Chea Socheat, the Cambodian intelligence officer who personally supervised collecting those remains, told Arant that he and other experts directly involved were convinced the remains from Bei Met were Caucasian. Colonel Socheat was called to CILHI several years after the handover to inspect the remains and help sort out some confusion as to which remains came from where. Arant does not know whether the Humphrey and McKay families were provided with all information collected on the case or whether mitochondrial DNA samples were taken. If the two families were not contacted, said Arant, "I would not consider this as having been a serious attempt to [determine whether] such remains may have been those of Humphrey and/or McKay."

Those old bones, most likely, hold the key to the mystery. Modern DNA sampling may yet unlock the door, and the final destination of McKay and Humphrey may yet be revealed.

"Humphrey and McKay were up there," said Arant, referring to Kampong Cham Province. "I'd put my life on it. I'd put my life on it."

21 FOUND

The road is newly paved. Except for that, the trip up highway 6 out of Phnom Penh has changed little from thirty years ago, according to Sok Sin, an interpreter and guide who has traveled this road many times. He was born in Kampong Cham, and his uncles, aunts, and cousins still live in the region, spread out through the Cambodian countryside. Sok Sin is at the wheel of his four-wheel-drive 1991 Mitsubishi, a big car for Cambodia. On 13 March 2000, one day before the thirtieth anniversary of the *Columbia Eagle* mutiny, he is driving Richard Linnett and Roberto Loiederman, the authors of this book, up to Sangke Kaong. "You have to be careful for the smooth tongues," said Sok Sin, by way of a bit of traveler's advice, paraphrasing a Cambodian saying about hustlers and fast talkers. His own tongue is a bit guttural and choppy, but we have grown used to it, and understand him quite well. We pass a funeral on its way to a colorful Wat, where a burial—within a stupa, above ground, the Buddhist way—is to take place. A cart carrying ashes is followed by a procession of people on foot. Then we pass cornfields and houses on stilts, some with palm thatch roofs and others made of wood, for those who can afford it.

The road is filled with motos and Sok Sin toots his horn as he passes them, often forcing them onto the shoulder. He passes cars the same way, tooting and then squeezing them, even as cross traffic comes straight at the Mitsubishi. This is the way most drivers get around the country. No one ever stops, the idea is to keep moving. Cambodians are in a constant state of motion, all day, from one destination to the next, hardly stopping long enough to rest, or even to work. Indeed, it is hard to tell if anybody does work, everyone just seems to be moving.

We pass through green fields of early rice and then cashew trees and mangoes. The air is heavy with smoke and exhaust fumes. Five motos are in front of us now, in a group. The drivers look like harmless teenagers having fun. "They are a gang," says Sok Sin, very seriously. "They rape girls and rob people. See, they have no license plates." He's right, they don't have plates. And we notice that people walking on the side of the road seem to stiffen as they pass. We overtake the boys; they are wearing sunglasses and bandannas and exchange looks with us. Sok Sin explains that most of these kids are the children of wealthy families. They don't work, they just terrorize people. He tells us that his son is a member of a gang. He tries to talk to him about getting a job, about making money, but his son does not pay attention. Sok Sin admits that it is hard to get a job in Cambodia, there are few openings. The government employees make the real money, he tells us. And the Thais cut down Cambodian forests for lumber while the Vietnamese take the rice harvest. There is very little left for Cambodians, Sok Sin tells us. Despite this, however, new houses are being built, Wats and stupas and mosques for the Muslim Cambodians are going up. There is much activity in the countryside.

And there are lots of weddings. This is marriage season. As we pass through villages, traditional Khmer music screams out of loudspeakers while processions of people, like the funerals, also on foot, gather under colorful canopies. The men are sinewy and hard. The women, especially the girls, are dressed up in bright skirts and dresses, clogs on their feet, which dangle from the motos as they sit side-saddle, balancing themselves perfectly, fearlessly, as the bikes bounce and swerve to avoid smoke-spewing cars and trucks. Even in the unpaved backroads, deep in the countryside, where the dust rises thick and congestive, the girls hold onto their hats and shield their eyes, sometimes hugging little brothers or sisters who are squeezed between them and the driver.

Monks walk in line in bright orange saffron robes, carrying umbrellas made of the same cloth. They stop, open their umbrellas, and stand in front of shops waiting for the shopkeeper to come out with a donation, for good luck. Sok Sin shakes his head. He does not like the monks. "They are lazy," says Sok Sin. "They don't want to work." And then he says something that seems absolutely preposterous. "They like pornography. They beg for money and then they buy pornography."

Sok Sin is not your ordinary guide. His specialty is handling trips for journalists, both print and broadcast. All along the road to Kampong Cham, he rattles off names of writers he has worked with: Henry Kamm, William Shawcross, Philip Gourevitch, Sydney Schanberg, Tim Page, David Chandler, Nate Thayer, and Elizabeth Becker, to name a few. He is not really boasting, nor is he trying to make his latest clients feel small and insignificant. No, he just wants to let his customers know that he has experience, and that his competitors, of which there are a few in Phnom Penh, do not hold a candle to him. In other words, he is selling himself, even after he has been hired. This is the Cambodian way. They are always willing to please, whether they are interpreters, moto drivers, or merchants; they always show gratitude and pleasure in serving you. And they are kind as well. However, if you cross the smiling Cambodian, if you break a promise, he gets angry and holds a smoldering grudge. A Westerner can recognize in this incendiary temper the passion that fueled the holocaust of the Khmer Rouge, in which Cambodians slaughtered not just those they considered foreigners, but also themselves.

In the town of Kampong Cham, we take a ferry across the Mekong River. A new bridge is being built across the river; it is tall, modern, and near completion. It leads from the town to the countryside of Kampong Cham, where there are still only dirt roads and tiny, backward villages. This is red earth country, clouds of dust fill the air. We pass through villages celebrating weddings, one after another, music blaring through bullhorns. Red ripe watermelons are for sale in roadside stands, as is jackfruit and cashew fruit. We pass through the town of Suong, which has a large market bustling with activity. Turning off the main road, we take narrow lanes up through the rubber plantations. In some places, trees are being cut. There are stretches of overgrown hevea groves; long idle, they resemble locations for war movies. One expects to see a troop of VC or Khmer Rouge emerge from the woods.

Our maps are U.S. Joint Operations Graphics (Air), circa 1970. They are extremely detailed, every tiny village is meticulously marked. The maps were made so that B-52 bombers flying overhead knew where to drop their ordnance. Ignoring our map, Sok Sin has been stopping and asking for directions. He figures that we are very close to Sangke Kaong. Finally, we reach another dusty little village. This is it. We have arrived. Sok Sin jumps out of the car. He asks a woman if there are any old-timers in town. The woman points to a house. We take off our shoes and climb up wooden steps, at least ten feet above the ground. Inside the house, the slat floor is smooth and polished; the place is cool and pleasant. An old man and woman greet us, then family members, including children, appear. We all sit on the floor and Sok Sin does the talking. He asks the old folks if they lived here during the war. Yes, they did. Do they remember two Americans who lived here as captives of the Khmer Rouge, during the war? Yes, they remember them.

"The journalists," says the old man, who is shirtless and wears only a cloth tied round his waist. He is lean but in very good shape for his age. He must be seventy years old. "The two Americans were very tall," Sok Sin says, interpreting the old man's words. "And they were almost the same size." One was not shorter than the other, he tells us. "They already had Khmer Rouge uniforms," he says. We show him pictures of McKay, and he nods; yes that is one of them, he says. "When the planes came over, they were very interested," says the old man. "But they could not look. It was prohibited." The villagers, meanwhile, were not allowed to look at the Americans. That too was prohibited.

The Americans were kept in the house of Ha Lang and her husband, they tell us. The house no longer exists, but Ha Lang is still in town, and they point in the direction of her current home. She took care of the two men, always giving them fruit to eat, says the old man. Has anyone else been through town looking for traces of these two Americans? Yes, they reply, before the first election, in 1993, many Americans came in helicopters looking for people who knew of the Americans, but no one since then. The old couple tells us that the two Americans were taken to a place five kilometers away, a place called Three Meters, or Bei Met. They never heard from them again.

We walk through the village. It's hot, about 90 degrees and humid. We pass small yards with penned-in chickens and pigs, past coffee bushes and mango trees. Sok Sin points to a house filled with men. He tells us they are Vietnamese carpenters—the best kind of woodworkers. Much better than Cambodian carpenters who are too lazy, he says. We are led to the home of

Ha Lang by her son-in-law, a tall, lean, bronzed man in his early twenties. He seems much too tall for a Cambodian, at least six feet. He is very pleasant and wears an orange saffron robe wrapped around his muscular waist. We walk down very narrow lanes, too narrow for cars, and a train of children follows behind us. They do not beg, they are simply curious. They probably have never seen a foreigner face-to-face before. Although not the jungle, Sangke Kaong is still remote.

Finally, we arrive at the correct house, also on stilts, this one with a solid wood roof instead of palm thatch, and the stilts are covered in a wood sheathing. It is the house of someone of means, but not wealthy, just comfortable. We take off our shoes, climb the steps, and enter. Immediately we are greeted by Ha Lang and her husband Sem Lan; they are at least ten years younger than the first couple we saw.

The husband is shirtless, with a shift wrapped around his waist. Ha Lang wears a white sleeveless shirt with loose pants, an orange and yellow diamond pattern. They cross their legs and sit down with us. She remembers the Americans. They were journalists and they came to live with her in July 1970 through 1971, she says, for six months. She says that the tallest one was 1.90 meters tall, and the shorter one was 1.80, a difference of 10 centimeters. The shorter man knew how to read and write in Khmer, says Ha Lang. Both men used to buy incense and pray that they would be able to see their families, their parents again. Ha Lang used to make wine out of sticky rice and she would give them two liters.

"They were very, very good drinkers," Sok Sin translated. The men also carried with them a bit of money, about twenty thousand riels each. "She says they spent their own money to buy Cambodian Pol Pot uniforms," says Sok Sin. "Nobody ordered them to do it. They [the Americans] said everybody dress like that so they do it too." Ha Lang also says that they told her they used to live in Thailand.

Humphrey lived in Thailand. He was based in Thailand.

Could there have been any other Americans in the area at that time, besides the two men who lived with her? "No, only two," says Sok Sin, translating for Ha Lang. She says that the villages in the area are small and there has always been communication among them. Ha Lang shares an anecdote with us. "She says when they were here, in her house, and all the people came to look, the smaller one who spoke Khmer yelled at them: 'Why do you come to see me? Do you think I am a monkey in a cage?'"

Ha Lang recalls that the men arrived under guard, but after they settled in, they were free to walk around and go anywhere in the village. They spent most of their time sitting around the house. Occasionally they helped her make noodles.

"The district chief from Khmer Rouge, his name was Ta Sabun," says Sok Sin, translating. "He took them to Three Meter, Bei Met." According to Ha Lang, this happened after the South Vietnamese bombed her village to root out the VC and the Khmer Rouge. She and her husband fled the village. When she returned, she went to see the Americans, to visit them, but the Khmer Rouge would not let her in. "Entry prohibited," says Sok Sin, translating. Ha Lang says that the Khmer Rouge eventually killed the Americans at Bei Met, during the rainy season, around May of the year 1971.

We run a series of names past her. Sean, Dana, Larry, Clyde . . .

At the name Clyde, Ha Lang smiles and says "Khly" several times, nodding. She speaks to Sok Sin, repeating the sound "Khly." Sok Sin translates: "Yes, one of them was Khly. She says the small one called the big one Khly, like that. Khly."

Her husband, Sem Len, pointed to a photo of McKay that we showed him. "Khly," he repeated. "That one," Sok Sin translates. "That one is Khly."

Were Ha Lang and her husband telling the truth? There did not seem to be any reason for them to lie. We did not offer them money, and only when we returned later did we give them some small gifts: a few loaves of bread and some cigarettes. We did find out later that Tim Page had interviewed Ha Lang in 1989. In his book Page called her Lek Lang. He was certain that she was talking about Flynn and Stone.

Were we really certain that Khly was Clyde McKay?

The events occurred thirty years ago. The memories of Ha Lang and the other villagers of Sangke Kaong are obviously far from perfect. We mentioned to Sok Sin that Tim Page came here looking for Flynn and Stone and suggested that he interpreted Ha Lang's words so that they fit his theory. Sok Sin looked at us from behind the towel wrapped around his perspiring head.

"Yes," Sok Sin said, "and you find what you want to find, too."

It was impossible to be absolutely certain. We did have some solid testimony, however, and we had the feeling, verging on certainty, that we were in the place where Clyde McKay had lived.

And where he had died. Nearby, among the rubber trees.

EPILOGUE

As this book was being written, Alvin Glatkowski turned fifty years old. He resides in the United States and wishes to live anonymously. Since the *Columbia Eagle* mutiny, he has never been on a merchant ship and he has no interest in going to sea again. He is not ashamed of what he did in March 1970, nor is he repentant. His only regret, he still maintains, is that he and McKay did not destroy the *Columbia Eagle* and sink its cargo of munitions. The destruction of the vessel would have saved lives, he believes, which was his goal.

Glatkowski is still suspicious. He cannot shake the feeling that the mutiny may have been a conspiracy that delivered weapons rather than stopped them, and that he was used as a pawn. Can we tell Alvin Glatkowski, definitively, that Clyde McKay and Larry Humphrey were not spies, agent provocateurs, CIA agents?

McKay's friends and family never had any indication that the young, adventurous seaman was connected to clandestine activities. Humphrey's brother and sister, however, were not so certain about Larry. His sister was suspicious of the Khmer and Thai books that he carried around with him, the books they called "Larry's bibles." Moreover, when Humphrey was in Cambodia, his brother—also in the army at the time—asked a general about contacting his brother and the general allegedly "indicated that Larry was on some type of intelligence mission for the United States Army and that his presence in Cambodia was a part of that mission."

Corporal Humphrey's record shows that although he once was assigned to the 203d Military Intelligence Detachment in Fort Hood, Texas, he had no sensitive security clearance and worked there solely as a cook. The only red flag in his dossier dates from his early enlistment at Fort Hood, when investigators found out that he frequented a place called the Oleo Strut Café, in nearby Killeen, where antiwar activists gathered.

Otherwise, inquiries by the FBI and journalists revealed no proof that either Clyde McKay or Larry Humphrey worked for any agency of the U.S. government, or for any other government or group. Our own investigations, carried out over a number of years, yielded the same result.

The overwhelming likelihood is that in this case, there was no conspiracy. Indeed, there was no need for an elaborate covert operation to deliver weapons by sea to Lon Nol. The coup leader was in control of the Cambodian army, which was already sufficiently armed to handle what became, essentially, a bloodless putsch.

It would have been informative, certainly, to have been able to talk directly to Clyde McKay. In a sense, however, the pieces of his biography that he left behind speak volumes, including an undated story that he wrote. It is about a man he identifies only as "X," who is searching for a philosophy of universal love. "Christendom asks me to love my neighbor as myself, but who should I consider my neighbors?" X concludes that like the Good Samaritan, he should have compassion for all and help the needy, especially those who are different from himself.

It appears that McKay, like his character X, carried this conviction with him when he signed on the *Columbia Eagle* and decided that he would stop a ship's cargo of bombs from reaching its destination.

McKay's family has had to live with the painful burden of mourning someone whose death was never verified. McKay's mother—Jean Bair—told us, "For several years I felt that he was alive, but that he wasn't communicating with us because he knew he'd be wanted and he didn't want us to have any information about him. So I used to dream about him, that he would contact us, that he was aboard some ship, and we'd go down and see him. I had all these dreams that the phone would ring and he would talk to us on the phone."

After many years of living with that hope, Mrs. Bair went on a religious retreat. "When I was at this retreat, I just went out in the woods and I sat down on this boulder, I had my Bible and I was overwhelmed, I was crying and I was missing Billy so much. I asked God to please tell me something so that I could be at peace finally about this, and I turned to a page at random and read: it was Jeremiah 38, and I read this: 'Then they took Jeremiah and cast him into the dungeon.'"

In her mind, Mrs. Bair associated Jeremiah's dungeon with the cage in which her son had been kept, for a time, in Cambodia. "And that gave me comfort, because Jeremiah had his trust in the Lord. And I think that Billy also had his trust in the Lord. I think he did. He thought he was doing the right thing. So when I read that, I thought, well, I guess that's my answer."

THE SS *Columbia Eagle* discharged its cargo of munitions and napalm at Subic Bay Naval Base and returned to the west coast. Soon thereafter, the Columbia Steamship Company sold it to Taiwanese businessmen. In June 1971, in the port city of Kaoh Siung, Taiwan, the *Eagle* was dismantled and sold piece by piece for parts and scrap metal. As seamen say when a ship is scrapped, "They turned her into razor blades."

APPENDIX

Columbia Eagle Crew List

Note: Crew members are listed by job rating. AB, able seaman; BR, bedroom steward; FWT, fireman; OS, ordinary seaman; * castaway; ** mutineer.

Captain: Donald Swann
Chief Mate: Herrick Morgan
Second Mate 4–8: Robert Stevenson*
Third Mate 12–4: Herbert Gunn
Third Mate 8–12: George Roush*
Chief Engineer: Walter Drabina
First Assistant: Leopold Tober
Second Assistant 4–8: Jeffrey Wright
Third Assistant 12–4: Curtis Ridge*
Third Assistant Day: Maurice Ellis*
Third Assistant 8–12: Clifton Johnson*
Radio Operator: Orville Mills
Bosun: James Northcutt
Day-Man: Norman Pettersen*
AB 4–8: Jack Kingsley*
AB 4–8: George Fletcher*
OS 4–8: Jose Casugay*
AB 8–12: Robert Sheldon*
AB 8–12: Fred Morishige*
OS 8–12: Alfredo Zulueta*
AB 12–4: Marco Smigliani*
AB 12–4: Roger Hammett
OS 12–4: Billy Campbell
FWT 4–8: Gerhardt Ratter*
Oiler 4–8: Luke Ciamboli*

FWT 8–12: Clyde McKay**
Oiler 8–12: Jose Caceres*
FWT 12–4: Roy McCarthy*
Oiler 12–4: Paul Aubain*
Electrician: Donald Sather
Wiper: Dan Mornin
Steward: Parker Holt*
Chief Cook: Jose Fernandez*
Baker: Philip Livingston*
Third Cook: John Browder*
Saloon Mess: Carl Woodard*
Crew Mess: James Johnson*
Pantryman: Bruce Gray
BR: Alvin Glatkowski**

BIBLIOGRAPHY

Primary Sources

Official U.S. Government Documents

Defense Intelligence Agency. Clyde McKay file (including Defense and State cables and DIA reports), FOIA request 935-85, 43 pages.

Harris, George L., et al. *U.S. Army Area Handbook for Vietnam.* Washington, D.C.: U.S. Government Printing Office, 1964.

Joint Casualty Resolution Center, NAS Barbers Point, Hawaii. Columbia Eagle Mutiny file (including State Department cables and MSTS memoranda), 35 pages.

Naval Intelligence Service. Documents regarding the Columbia Eagle Mutiny, FOIA request 5262F85-303, serial 00-00890, approximately 100 pages.

———. Report of Investigation ("sitreps"). Lt. Commander Norman Idleberg and Don Webb reporting, 1 April 1970, 57 pages.

Tulich, Eugene N., Lieutenant USCG. "The United States Coast Guard in South East Asia During the Vietnam Conflict." U.S. Coast Guard Historical Monograph Program, 1975.

United States Army Intelligence Command. Report on Larry Humphrey and military personnel file, file 1025-6006, 108 pages.

United States Coast Guard. Merchant Marine Detail, Saigon, R.V.N, O.N. 247080 Case P-60-70/PRS. "Incident Report: Revolt and Mutiny on Board the SS Columbia Eagle," 20 July 1970, approximately 500 pages. Includes statements and interrogations of the men left on board as well as the castaways, a certified copy of the vessel's Deck Bell Book, Shipping Articles for McKay and Glatkowski, consular reports concerning Gray, Sather, and Mornin, and photographs taken aboard the vessel by investigators, April 1970.

United States Department of the Army. United States Army Intelligence and Security Command file on Clyde McKay (including Department of Defense cables and Defense Intelligence reports), 47 pages.

United States Department of Defense. Briefing Notes to the Press on the Columbia Eagle Mutiny by Jerry Friedheim, 16 March 1970 to 8 April 1970, 50 pages.

United States Department of Justice. Federal Bureau of Investigation report and documentation of the mutiny, SS Columbia Eagle file 45-11002, sections 1–6, 446 pages.

United States Department of the Navy. "Security Measures Regarding U.S. Merchant Seamen," memorandum, 20 March 1970.

———. Telegrams re: Columbia Eagle, FOIA Case 0041/12573, 7 December 1987, 175 pages.

United States Department of State. Telegrams regarding Clyde McKay, FOIA case 8600743, 16 January 1987, 60 pages.

———. Telegrams regarding the Columbia Eagle Mutiny, FOIA case 8503103, approximately 250 pages.

Wedertz, Ralph, Chief Yeoman, USCG. "The Columbia Eagle Incident," 8 page report.

Young, J. M., Lieutenant Commander. "SS Columbia Eagle Incident Highlights," CINCPACFLT report, 17 March 1970.

Legal Documents

Billy E. Campbell v. Columbia Steamship Co. U.S. District Court Central District of Calif. Civil Action No. 70-495. Answer of Billy E. Campbell to Interrogatories Propounded to Claimant, 13 October 1970, 60 pages.

Billy E. Campbell v. Columbia Steamship Co. U.S. District Court Central District of Calif. No. 70-1356-CC. Deposition of Billy E. Campbell, 24 February 1971, 95 pages.

———. Larsen, O. K., Jr., investigator. Billy E. Campbell statement, Long Beach, Calif., 12 May 1970, 36 pages.

———. McGinnis, James E., M.D. Psychiatric examination report of Billy E. Campbell, Los Angeles, 23 December 1970, 30 pages.

———. Roberts, Lewis A., M.D. Psychiatric examination of Billy E. Campbell, San Francisco, 7 March 1972, 10 pages.

Columbia Eagle v. U.S. Government. Armed Services Board of Contract Appeals #1681. 22 August 1972. "An appeal from a decision of the contracting officer under a time charter party between appellant and Military Sea Transportation Service. Of the Department of the Navy," approximately 100 pages. Contains testimony of Capt. Donald Swann, Lt. Norman Idleberg, and Donald Webb.

United States v. Alvin Leonard Glatkowski. Case 6245, U.S. District Court, Central District of California, 1971: Mutiny on the High Seas, Assault with a Dangerous Weapon on High Seas, Transportation of Kidnapped Person in Foreign Commerce, Neglect of Duty by Seamen. Stipulation re Testimony of Witnesses; Psychiatric Evaluations by Drs. John Paul Walters, Eric Marcus, George

Abe, and L. D. Ciaramelli; Pre-Trial Rulings, Depositions, Motions for Discovery, Trial Memoranda and Judgment. Also, subsequent Appeals, Arguments, and Judgments. Approximately 100 pages.

———. Case 10759, Attempted Escape from Confinement, 1972–1973: Trial Abstract, Appeal Arguments and Judgments. 30 pages.

Shipping Documents

Bruce Engineering Co. "Victory Ship Stowage and Capacity Booklet." New York, 1946.

Logbook, SS Columbia Eagle. 16 February–4 May 1970, pp. 1902–2062. United Sates Coast Guard, San Francisco, Calif.

Lloyd's Register of Shipping. *List of Shipowners.* London, 1970–1971.

Naval Weapons Station. "Safe Ocean Transport of Military Explosives and Hazardous Munitions." Concord, Calif., November 1966.

Ocean Cargo Manifest, SS Columbia Eagle. Military Traffic Management and Terminal Service, 19 January 1971, Oakland Army Base, Oakland, Calif.

Interviews and Correspondence

Allman, T. D. Audio tape interview, 18 July 1986.

Antippas, Andrew. Telephone interview and email correspondence, February–May 2000.

Arant, Richard. Telephone interview and email correspondence, April–June 2000.

Bair, Jean. Audio tape interviews, May and August 1998, 25 transcribed pages.

Basiger, Lois. Interview, September 1998.

Berbrich, John. Telephone interview, May 2000.

Blackburn, Robert. Interview, May 2000.

Brown, Jerry. Audio tape interview, August 1998.

Burrell, Kerry. Interview, September 1998.

Ciamboli, Luke. Audio tape interview, 6 August 1985; letter to Richard Linnett, 19 December 1985, 20 pages.

Dok Sokhay. Audio tape interview, March 2000.

Glatkowski, Alvin. Audio tape interviews, 25 May 1981, 4 February 1984, 28 July 1985, 20 October 1985, 20–21 August 1987, and August 2000.

Gunn, Herbert. Notes from interview conducted by Martha Honey, July 1970.

Hammett, Roger Enoch, Jr. Audio tape interviews, February and August 1999; written account provided to the authors, 13 pages.

Hannon, Michael. Interview, May 2000.

Hardy, Ann (pseudonym). Audio tape interview at Otis Air Force Base, Mass., 6 July 1985, 20 transcribed pages.

Honey, Martha. Audio tape interviews, 26 August 1985, December 1998, and April 2000.

Idleberg, Norman, Lt. Cdr. Audio tape interview, March 1998.

Johnson, Clint. Audio tape interview aboard the *Lane Victory,* November 1998.

Longenecker, Flo. Interview, March 2000.

McKay, Clyde. Personal letters, papers, and notes written by Clyde McKay, as well as letters and wires from members of McKay's family to him; McKay's correspondence with U.S. and Spanish government officials and agencies; letters and wires between the McKay family and various U.S. government agencies and officials. More than 200 pages. Courtesy of Jean Bair.

McKay, Clyde, Jean Bair, and Franklin Cave. Audio tape interview with Joyce Smith and Tim Wright, December 1967, 45 transcribed pages. Courtesy of Jean Bair.

Mills, Orville. Notes from interview conducted by Martha Honey, July 1970.

Moss, Scott, mental health coordinator, FCI Lompoc. Audio tape interview, 26 May 1985.

Morgan, Herrick. Interview, June 1998 and August 1999.

Page, Tim. Telephone interview, 3 April 2000.

Pestana, Frank. Interview, May 2000.

Safford, John. Audio tape interview and correspondence, October 1998.

Sheldon, Robert. Notes from interview conducted by Marcy Kates, July 1970.

Sihanouk, Prince Norodom. Interview (with T. D. Allman), New York City, July 1986.

Smigliani, Marco. Audio tape interview and correspondence, February 1999.

Swann, Donald O'Bannon. Audio tape interviews, April and May 1998.

Van Beck, Margaret. Telephone interview, May 2000.

Webb, Donald. Audio tape interview, April 1998.

Young, Perry Deane. Telephone interviews and email correspondence, May–June 2000.

Secondary Sources

Articles and Unpublished Works

Aarons, Leroy F. "Hijackers Reputation Back Home Belies Hippie Life, Sea Escapade." *Washington Post,* 19 March 1970.

"Accused Hijackers of Munitions Ship Described as Neat, Homeloving Workers." *Oregonian,* 20 March 1970.

Allman, T. D. "Anatomy of a Coup." *Far Eastern Economic Review,* 9 April 1970.

———. "A Loner and a Follower Hijacked 'Eagle.'" *Washington Post,* 9 April 1970.

Beech, Keyes. "Crew of Mutiny Ship Tell Story for the First Time." *Los Angeles Times,* 18 March 1970.

———. "First Interview—Mate Tells Ship Hijack." *San Francisco Examiner,* 18 March 1970.

Blake, Gene. "Ship Hijacking Suspect Enters Innocent Plea." *Los Angeles Times,* 29 December 1970.

Braestrup, Peter. "Two Crewmen in Hijacking Get Asylum in Cambodia." *Washington Post,* 17 March 1970.

Braestrup, Peter, and William Chapman. "U.S. Ship Diverted in Reported Mutiny." *Washington Post,* 16 March 1970.

"Cambodia Shelters Hijackers." *Oregonian,* 17 March 1970.

Day, James V. "Military Cargo and the Civilian Carrier: The Problem of Procurement." *U.S. Naval Institute Proceedings,* March 1974.

Emery, Fred. "Cambodians to Return Hijacked Ship Today." *London Times,* 8 April 1970.

———. "Columbia Eagle's Napalm on Show." *London Times,* 9 April 1970.

———. "Two Who Say They Support S.D.S. Tell How They Hijacked Ship." *London Times* dispatch, in *New York Times,* 25 March 1970.

Fineberg, Richard A. "Cambodian Premier Links CIA to Sihanouk Ouster." Dispatch News Service, 6 April 1970.

Glatkowski, Alvin. "Letter to Friends." Written in Lompoc Prison and addressed to the Columbia Liberation Defense Committee, The Santa Barbara Legal Collective; intended for publication, 31 December 1973, 25 pages, unpublished.

Glatkowski, Alvin, and Jan Kirby. "Columbia Eagle." 1987, unfinished screenplay.

Hoffman, Fred S. "U.S. Ammunition Ship Seized by 5 in Crew." Associated Press, 16 March 1970.

Honey (nee Westover), Martha. "Interview Article." September 1970, unpublished.

———. Letter to Charles Peters at the *Washington Monthly.* 8 January 1971.

———. Letter to James Boyd at the Fund for Investigative Journalism. 8 January 1971.

———. "The Mysterious Hijacking of the Columbia Eagle." Not dated, unpublished.

———. Notes of Interviews with SS *Columbia Eagle* Crew Members. 28 May–11 July 1970.

Horne, A. D. "Eagle Skipper Says 2 Hijackers Got $992 from Him at Gunpoint." *Washington Post,* 19 March 1970.

Hubbard, Clifford. "From Good Scout to Alleged Pirate." *Virginian Pilot,* 20 March 1970.

Kamm, Henry. "Arms Ship's Cast-Offs Said to Blame Two 'Hippies' for Seizure." *New York Times,* 16 March 1970.

Keatley, Robert. "Ship Mutiny May Foil Cambodia's Attempt to Oust Red Troops." *Wall Street Journal,* 17 March 1970.

Kendall, John. "Grand Jury Indicts 5 Manson Followers." *Los Angeles Times,* 19 December 1970.

———. "Manson 'Girl' Still in 'Psychotic State,' Psychiatrist Claims." *Los Angeles Times,* 2 March 1971.

Mankin, Erick. "Mutineer Awaits Victory in Private War." *Santa Barbara News and Review,* 26 March 1975.

"Mate Says Crew of Columbia Eagle Puzzled by Order to Abandon Ship." *Oregonian,* 17 March 1970.

"Mutiny by Ruse." *Time Magazine,* 30 March 1970.

"Mutiny on the Eagle." *Newsweek,* 30 March 1970.

"Mutiny Ship Perplexes Cambodian Officials." *London Times,* 18 March 1970.

"Mutiny Suspect 'Didn't Know Where He Was At.'" *Los Angeles Times,* 17 March 1970.

"Nine Bay Men Aboard Mutiny Bomb Ship." *San Francisco Examiner,* 16 March 1970.

Richards, Leverett. "Ammo Ship's Master Tells Scuttling Threat." *Oregonian,* 19 March 1970.

Sell, Ted. "Order to Rescue Mutiny Ship Issued and Quickly Revoked." *Los Angeles Times,* 19 March 1970.

"Skipper of Hijacked Ammo Ship Seeks Release from Cambodia." *Oregonian,* 18 March 1970.

Soper, Will. "The Columbia Eagle Mutiny." *Boston Phoenix,* 31 July 1973.

Stone, Louise. "Ship Hijackers Meet Heavy Fate." Dispatch News Service International, 11 January 1971.

Szulc, Tad. "Cambodia To Give Haven to Two Linked to Ship's Seizure." *New York Times,* 17 March 1970.

———. "Ship Pirates Warn of More Mutinies." *New York Times,* 18 March 1970.

———. "Ship's Captain Said Hijackers Extracted Money." *New York Times,* 19 March 1970.

———. "U.S. Arms Ship to Thailand Seized by Men with Guns." *New York Times,* 15 March 1970.

Tedrick, Dan. "Billy." A biography of Clyde McKay, 1984, unpublished manuscript.

"Their Son Not a Mutineer, Parents Insist." *Los Angeles Times,* 17 March 1970.

"Trial of 13 Black Panthers Is Started in Los Angeles." United Press International dispatch, in *New York Times,* 2 June 1971.

"Two American Ship Hijackers Want to Quit Cambodia." Associated Press dispatch, in *New York Times,* 3 July 1970.

"U.S. Hijacker in Cambodia Surrenders." *Los Angeles Times,* 15 December 1970, 14.

Vietnam Veterans Against the War/Winter Soldier Organization, Columbia Eagle Liberation Defense Committee, Santa Barbara/Lompoc Chapter. "Columbia Eagle Liberation," pamphlet, 1974.

Walsh, Jack. "Doped Hippies Hijack Ammo Ship." *(Long Beach, Calif.) Press Telegraph,* 16 March 1970.

Williams, Jeff. "Columbia Eagle Forlorn in Cambodia Port." *Oregonian,* 21 March 1970.

———. "Yank Pirates Seek Help From Russia." *San Francisco Examiner,* 3 July 1970.

Wright, Robert A. "Relatives Discuss Two Who Seized U.S. Munitions Ship in the Gulf of Siam." *New York Times,* 18 March 1970.

Books

Anson, Robert Sam. *War News.* New York: Simon & Schuster, 1989.

Becker, Elizabeth. *When The War Was Over.* New York: Public Affairs, 1998.

Caldwell, Malcolm, and Lek Hor Tan. *Cambodia in the Southeast Asian War.* New York: Monthly Review Press, 1973.

Chandler, David P. *Brother Number One.* Boulder, Colo.: Westview Press, 1999.

Deac, Wilfred P. *Road to the Killing Fields.* College Station, Tex.: Texas A&M University Press, 1997.

Kamm, Henry. *Cambodia: Report from a Stricken Land.* New York: Arcade Publishing, 1998.

Karnow, Stanley. *Vietnam: A History.* New York: Viking Press, 1983.

Kirk, Donald. *Wider War.* London: Praeger, 1971.

McClench, Donald. *Primer on Navigation.* New York: Van Nostrand Reinhold Company, 1967.

Nolan, Keith. *Into Cambodia.* New York: Dell Publishing, 1990.

Page, Tim. *Derailed in Uncle Ho's Victory Garden.* London: Simon & Schuster, 1997.

Shawcross, William. *Sideshow.* New York: Simon & Schuster, 1979.

Sihanouk, Norodom, and Wilfred Burchett. *My War with the CIA.* New York: Pantheon Press, 1973.

Webb, Kate. *On the Other Side: 23 Days with the Vietcong.* New York: Quadrangle Books, 1972.

Young, Perry Deane. *Two of the Missing.* New York: Coward, McCann and Geoghegan, 1972.

ABOUT THE AUTHORS

Richard Linnett was born in Newark, New Jersey, and is a graduate of George Washington University in Washington, D.C., and the writing program at the Columbia University Graduate School of the Arts in New York. He is a reporter whose investigative stories have appeared in many publications. He is currently a business reporter on a weekly magazine in New York City. He met surviving *Columbia Eagle* mutineer Alvin Glatkowski in Washington, D.C., in 1978.

Roberto Loiederman was born in Buenos Aires, Argentina, and grew up in Baltimore. A veteran television writer with a B.A. from The Johns Hopkins University and an M.A. in English Literature from San Francisco State College, he shipped out on fourteen different merchant vessels from 1966 to 1974, first as ordinary seaman, then as able seaman. His first three ships went to Vietnam during the height of the war. He has lived in Asia, Latin America, and Israel and since the early 1980s has been a Los Angeles resident.

The Naval Institute Press is the book-publishing arm of the U.S. Naval Institute, a private, nonprofit, membership society for sea service professionals and others who share an interest in naval and maritime affairs. Established in 1873 at the U.S. Naval Academy in Annapolis, Maryland, where its offices remain today, the Naval Institute has members worldwide.

Members of the Naval Institute support the education programs of the society and receive the influential monthly magazine *Proceedings* and discounts on fine nautical prints and on ship and aircraft photos. They also have access to the transcripts of the Institute's Oral History Program and get discounted admission to any of the Institute-sponsored seminars offered around the country.

The Naval Institute also publishes *Naval History* magazine. This colorful bimonthly is filled with entertaining and thought-provoking articles, first-person reminiscences, and dramatic art and photography. Members receive a discount on *Naval History* subscriptions.

The Naval Institute's book-publishing program, begun in 1898 with basic guides to naval practices, has broadened its scope in recent years to include books of more general interest. Now the Naval Institute Press publishes about one hundred titles each year, ranging from how-to books on boating and navigation to battle histories, biographies, ship and aircraft guides, and novels. Institute members receive discounts of 20 to 50 percent on the Press's more than eight hundred books in print.

Full-time students are eligible for special half-price membership rates. Life memberships are also available.

For a free catalog describing Naval Institute Press books currently available, and for further information about subscribing to *Naval History* magazine or about joining the U.S. Naval Institute, please write to:

Membership Department
U.S. Naval Institute
291 Wood Road
Annapolis, MD 21402-5034
Telephone: (800) 233-8764
Fax: (410) 269-7940
Web address: www.usni.org